The Yosemite Grant, 1864–1906

A PICTORIAL HISTORY

The Yosemite Grant, 1864–1906

A PICTORIAL HISTORY

Hank Johnston

YOSEMITE ASSOCIATION

YOSEMITE NATIONAL PARK, CALIFORNIA

This book is dedicated, with love,
to my long-time dear friend

Leroy Jess Rust

who lived his whole life in Yosemite Valley.
He was a champion skier and ice skater, a respected ski coach,
an ardent hiker and backpacker, a tireless civic supporter,
the Yosemite postmaster for many years,
and an all-round good fellow.
Before he died in 1992, he asked me
to send him a book, "wherever I am."
Well, Rusty, here's the book—wherever you are.

COVER: Tourists in Yosemite Valley, 1890.

FRONTISPIECE: The Hutchings House in Yosemite
Valley, pictured here circa 1864–65, was constructed by
Gus Hite in 1859. Note the original bridge spanning the
Merced River at right (described in Chapter 11).

Yosemite Association
P.O. Box 545
Yosemite National Park, CA 95389

The Yosemite Association is a non-profit, membership organization
dedicated to the support of Yosemite National Park. Our publishing
program is designed to provide an educational service and to increase
the public's understanding of Yosemite's special qualities and needs. To
learn more about our activities and other publications, or for information about membership, please write to the address on this page, or call
(209) 379-2646.

Book design by Robin Weiss Graphic Design, San Francisco.

Library of Congress Cataloging-in-Publication Data

Johnston, Hank,
    The Yosemite Grant, 1864–1906 : a pictorial history / Hank Johnston.
    p. cm.
    Includes bibliographical references (p.) and index.
    ISBN 0-939666-79-0
    1. Yosemite Valley (Calif.)—History. 2. Yosemite Valley (Calif.)—
History—Pictorial works. 3. Giant sequoia—California—Yosemite
Valley. 4. Giant sequoia—California—Yosemite Valley—pictorial works.
I. Title.
F868.Y6J54 1995
979.4'47—dc20   95-4780
                                                        CIP

Unless otherwise noted, the photographs in this book are from the
Yosemite Research Library collection, maintained by the U.S. National
Park Service in Yosemite National Park.

Table of Contents

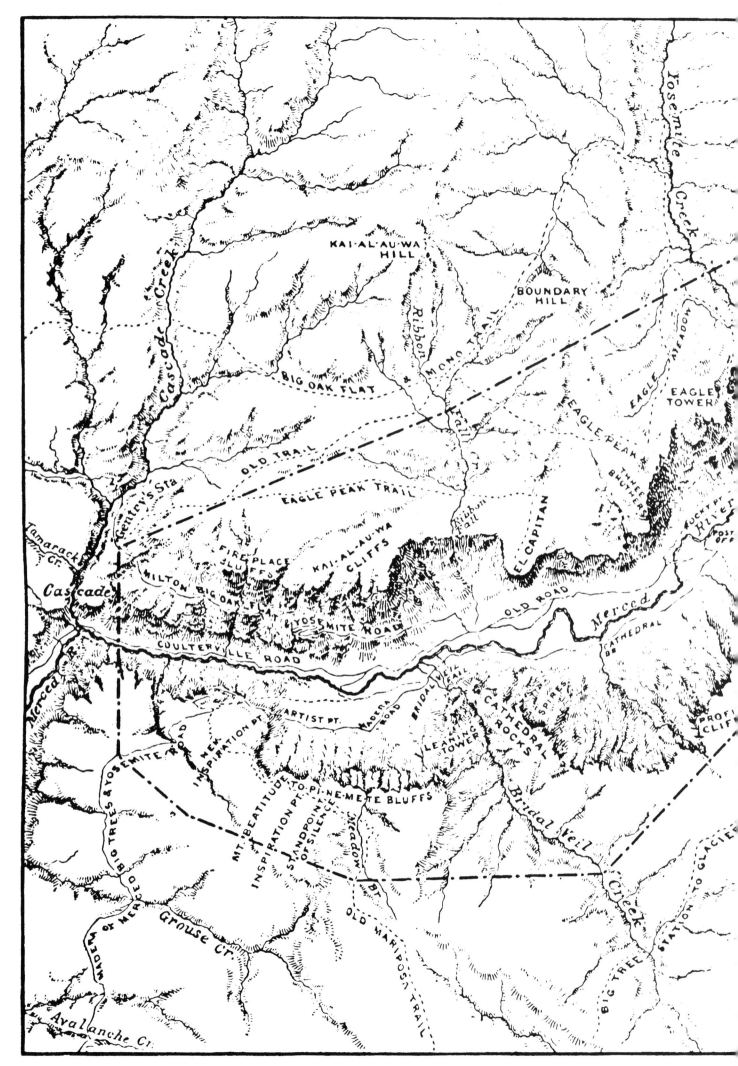

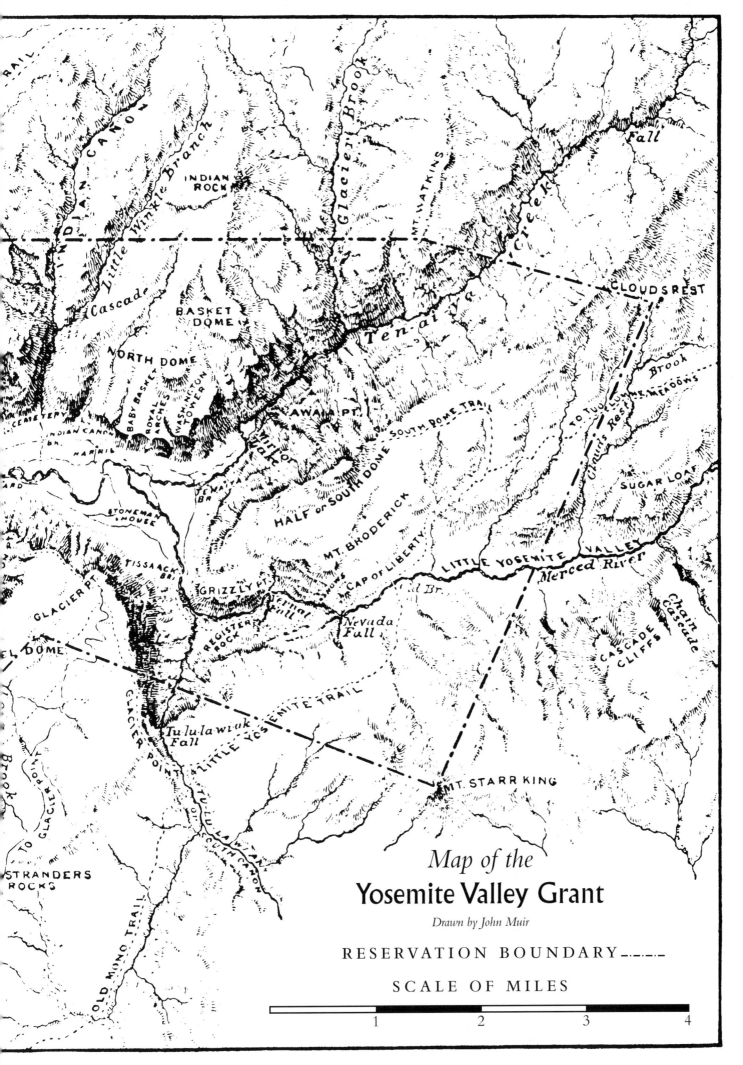

Map of the
Yosemite Valley Grant
Drawn by John Muir

RESERVATION BOUNDARY —·—·—

SCALE OF MILES

1   2   3   4

Introduction

Set like a jewel in the center of California's Sierra Nevada, Yosemite Valley is a seven-mile-long, glacier-carved canyon encircled by some of the most spectacular domes, cliffs, and waterfalls in the world. Emerson said it was the only place he ever found that came up to the brag about it, and exceeded it.

So surpassing is Yosemite's beauty that Congress ceded the Valley, along with the Mariposa Grove of Big Trees, to the state of California as America's first scenic preserve—"inalienable for all time"—only thirteen years after it was effectively discovered by non-Indians in 1851. This historic legislation, enacted at the height of a bloody Civil War, marked the real beginning of the national park idea, a concept long since embraced by countries around the world.

In 1890 the federal government created a much larger protected area surrounding the original 36,111-acre Yosemite Valley Grant, but not including it or the Mariposa Grove twelve and one-half miles to the south. Soon to become known as Yosemite National Park, the 1,457-square-mile rectangular territory (932,600 acres) took in the Minarets, Devils Postpile, and the high-country headwaters of the Merced and Tuolumne Rivers. Over the years numerous boundary changes gradually restructured the park to its present irregular configuration of nearly 1,170 square miles, more than 94 percent of which is classified as wilderness.

This book is an attempt to create a comprehensive record of Yosemite's pioneer human history, starting with the first written accounts in 1833 and continuing through the re-cession of the Yosemite Grant by California to the federal government in 1906. So far as I know, no previous publication has been devoted solely to this early period, although other writings about Yosemite have explored various aspects of the subject over the years. Wherever possible, I have endeavored to present new or expanded information rather than simply rehashing the same familiar—and often erroneous—reports that have long been extant. Similarly, I have tried to illuminate the text with illustrations not ordinarily seen. If some of the financial figures appearing throughout the book seem trivial by modern standards, remember that they represent a sum worth many times the amount in today's inflated economy.

For easier reading, the story is told chronologically in narrative fashion rather than topically. Sources and additional data can be found in the lengthy notes at the end of each chapter. Appendices include the two legislative acts that established the grant, along with other pertinent information, and a detailed index makes specific subjects, which often extend over several chapters, easier to find.

A history of any kind is naturally dependent on its source material. In this regard, I am greatly obliged to Linda Eade, Yosemite research librarian, and Jim Snyder, Yosemite park historian, for their expert assistance. During my several years of research on the project, Linda and Jim unfailingly answered my countless requests for information, volunteered important leads and suggestions, and did it all with the best of spirit. In addition, Jim, whose knowledge of Sierra history is near encyclopedic, read every word of the initial draft and saved me from several misstatements and omissions along the way.

I am grateful as well to Steven P. Medley, president of the Yosemite Association, for his many discerning suggestions during prepublication. Steve is a first-rate editor and an even better friend. My thanks go also to Fresno cartographer Don DeVere, who drew the three excellent illustrative maps that bear his name. Others who provided valuable material include Shirley Sargent, my publishing partner and fellow Yosemite author; Barbara Beroza, associate curator of the Yosemite Museum; Stan Hutchinson, expert on the California Big Trees; Ken Renshaw, Ira B. Folsom's great-grandson; N. King Huber, who recently retired from the United States Geological Survey; Virginia Best (Mrs. Ansel) Adams, who was born in the Valley in 1904; and the staffs of the Bancroft Library, the California State Library, the California State Archives, and various county historical societies.

The Yosemite Grant encompassed a unique piece of unforgettable real estate set aside for the public good by almost miraculous foresight. Researching and writing about its forty-two-year existence was an informative and rewarding experience. I hope this book will bring the reader the same satisfaction.

HANK JOHNSTON
Yosemite, California

These frolicsome early tourists may have been the first mountain bikers in Yosemite Valley.

The Discovery of Yosemite
(1833–1853)

THE FIRST INHABITANTS

Archaeologists estimate that human habitation began in Yosemite Valley between three thousand and four thousand years ago, give or take a millennium, when Paiutes crossed over the Sierra from the east to hunt and gather food. Some centuries later, ancestors of the Sierra Miwok slowly spread into the Yosemite region from the west, most likely to escape the summer heat and exploit the natural resources. As time went on, a sub-tribe of the Miwok established permanent villages along the Merced River in and below Yosemite Valley, a place they called "Ah-wah-nee," probably from the Miwok word meaning "place of a gaping mouth."[1]

The members of this tribe were known as the Ahwahneechees (people in Ahwahnee) and the group may have numbered several hundred members at its peak. As they were neither herdsmen nor farmers, their lives revolved largely around the gathering of food. For meat the Ahwahneechees killed grizzly and black bears, deer, small animals and birds, and caught fish. They also seasonally gathered seeds, berries, clover, mushrooms, and especially the acorns of the black oak, their most important foodstuff, from which the women made acorn mush and bread. In the summer, the tribe traveled across the Sierra to trade with the Mono Lake Paiutes along the east side of the range. There they obtained chunks of obsidian for arrowheads and other implements, as well as salt, rabbit skins, and pine nuts.

Sometime near 1780, after untold generations of relative tranquility, a "fatal black sickness" (probably smallpox or cholera acquired by contact with coastal Indians who had been infected by whites) virtually exterminated the Ahwahneechees. The few disheartened survivors fled from their Yosemite villages to affiliate with neighboring tribes. The Valley was thereafter avoided by Indians from a "superstitious fear" and remained uninhabited for a number of years.

About 1820 an Indian named Tenieya, the son of an Ahwahneechee chief and a Mono Paiute mother, who had been raised among the Monos along the eastern base of the Sierra, was induced by a very old medicine man of the former tribe to return to the deep, grassy valley that had once been his father's home. Gathering the few remaining descendants of the Ahwahneechees, along with outlaws, refugees, and the disaffected from various tribes on both sides of the Sierra as far south as the Kings River, Tenieya reoccupied Yosemite Valley as chief of a very mixed group that eventually may have totaled about two hundred Indians.[2]

The new band became known to other area tribes as the *u-zu'-mai-ti* or *oo-soo'-ma-tee,* which means grizzly bear in most Miwok dialects. Tenieya said his followers selected the name because they were expert at killing the grizzlies that inhabited their mountain home, and the name

struck fear in their enemies.[3] Early historical accounts, beginning about 1850, usually refer to Tenieya's tribe in some approximation of the term "Yosemite." This was apparently as close as writers could come to the oral rendition of the name.[4]

Tenieya and his people prospered in Ahwahnee for more than three decades. His children reached maturity and had families of their own. The group evidently lived well. But in the middle of the nineteenth century, sudden and irreversible changes began taking place in California. In the long run, the effect of these changes would wipe out the Yosemites as a tribal entity as surely as the "fatal black sickness" had done away with the Ahwahneechees many years before.[5]

EARLY EXPLORATIONS

The recorded history of Yosemite began in October, 1833, when Joseph R. Walker (1798-1876) led a party of some sixty hunters and trappers in the first east-to-west crossing of the lofty Sierra Nevada. Walker's orders from his superior, Captain B. L. E. Bonneville, U. S. A., were to "steer through an unknown country, towards the Pacific" in quest of beaver furs and geographical information. The expedition's exact route has long been an enigma to historians, except that the course followed a portion of the old Mono Indian Trail running along the crest between the Merced and Tuolumne Rivers directly through the heart of what is now Yosemite National Park. After weeks of grueling effort in freezing weather without sufficient food, the men growing more rebellious by the day, Walker and his company finally crossed over the snow-covered heights and "arrived at the brink of the mountain" from where they could see the welcome expanse of the sunny San Joaquin Valley in the distance.

Two years after the arduous trek, Zenas Leonard (1809-1857), clerk of the expedition, wrote a lengthy article about the party's experiences for

These remarkable peaks on the north rim of Yosemite Valley were called the "Three Brothers" by Lafayette Bunnell because their "number coincided with the three brothers, sons of Tenieya, who were captured by us while hidden among the rocks of the peaks." (Forrest Jackson)

his local newspaper in Clearfield County, Pennsylvania. First published serially by the paper in five installments during 1835 and 1836, and afterward (1839) reprinted with minor changes in book form, Leonard's narrative proves that the party traveled extensively in the Sierra north of Yosemite Valley, but whether or not scouts along the flanks actually looked down into the spectacular gorge itself remains a matter of conjecture. The conclusion of some historians that members of Walker's expedition saw the Valley is based on a single paragraph from Leonard's journal:

"We traveled a few miles every day, still on the top of the mountain, and our course continually obstructed with snow hills and rocks. Here we began to encounter in our path many small streams which would shoot out from under these high snow-banks, and after running a short distance in deep chasms which they have through the ages cut in rocks, precipitate themselves from one lofty precipice to another, until they are exhausted in rain below. Some of these precipices appeared to us to be more than a mile high. . ."[6]

Other historical writers, however, including this one, do not think that anyone viewing the breathtaking panorama of Yosemite Valley for the first time would have given so perfunctory a description of the scenery. Irene Paden, writing in *The Big Oak Flat Road to Yosemite,* argues quite persuasively that Leonard was really talking about the Cascade Creek area farther to the west, and that the Walker party, while it unquestionably crossed what later became Yosemite National Park, never saw the Valley itself.[7]

But Leonard and his companions were surely the first non-Indians to see the Big Trees of the Sierra Nevada. After leaving the region of snow and reaching timbered country, Leonard wrote: "In the last two days traveling, we have found some trees of the Redwood species, incredibly large—some of which would measure from 16 to 18 fathom round the trunk at the height of a man's head from the ground." The trees were undoubtedly the *Sequoia gigantea* of the Merced Grove or the Tuolumne Grove, possibly both.

A less controversial sighting of Yosemite Valley occurred in October, 1849, although the discovery did not become general knowledge for nearly a century. In 1947 the diary of William Penn Abrams, unquestionably contemporary and authentic, was brought to the attention of historians.[8] Abrams was a carpenter and millwright who had been commissioned to investigate potential mill sites on the Merced River to supply lumber for nearby mining camps. In the fall of 1849, he and a long-time friend named U. N. Reamer left from James Savage's trading post at the junction of the Merced River and the South Fork tracking a grizzly bear. Abrams' diary entry for October 18, 1849, contains the following (punctuation added):

"Returned to S.F. after visit to Savage property on Merced River. Prospects none too good for a mill. Savage is a blaspheming fellow who has five squaws for wives for which he takes his authority from the Scriptures. While at Savage's Reamer and I saw grizzly bear tracks and went out to hunt him down, getting lost in the mountains and not returning until the following evening. Found our way to camp over an Indian trail that led past a valley enclosed by stupendous cliffs rising perhaps 3,000 feet from their base and which gave us cause for wonder. Not far off a waterfall dropped from a cliff below three jagged peaks into the valley, while farther beyond, a rounded mountain stood, the valley side of which looked as though it had been sliced with a knife as one would slice a loaf of bread, and which Reamer and I called the Rock of Ages."

Unlike Zenas Leonard's lackluster description, Abrams' vivid word picture leaves little doubt that he and Reamer saw Cathedral Rocks, Bridalveil Fall, and Half Dome, probably from near Old Inspiration Point, but the men did not descend into the Valley itself. Abrams made no mention of Indians, even though Tenieya and his people were residing in the Yosemite region at the time.

GOLD AND THE ONSET OF THE MARIPOSA INDIAN WAR

Before the coming of the white man, Indians of various tribes had roamed the foothills of the Sierra Nevada for centuries. Nature supplied everything needed for their culture: berries, fish, game, nuts, acorns, and insects, along with a generally salubrious climate. The discovery of gold on the American River in January, 1848, however, quickly brought dramatic changes to California's rural landscape and ended the Indians' nomadic way of life forever. In the years immediately following the gold strike, tens of thousands of eager prospectors swarmed over the countryside, probing every river bank and gravel bar in a frenzied search for riches. Tent camps sprang up, soon to be replaced by crude wooden structures, which in short order became towns. California's population soared from two thousand Caucasians at the beginning of 1848 to more than fifty-three thousand by the close of 1849.

The largely Anglo-American newcomers, many imbued with two centuries of prejudice, considered the Indian a nuisance to be pushed aside or killed without remorse. They took over his land, burned his villages, hunted his game, overran his sacred burial grounds, destroyed his environment, and seized his young women, willing or not, for "wives" and servants. In 1851 Commissioner of Indian Affairs Oliver M. Wozencraft decried the situation in "An Open Letter to the People Living and Trading Among the Indians in the State of California." Wozencraft wrote:

"Since the discovery of gold in this region, the section of the country that was and is peculiarly the home of the Indians has been found rich in the precious metal, and consequently filled with a population foreign to them; and this has been done in most instances without attempting to conciliate or appease them in the grief and anger at the loss of their homes. I am sorry to say that in many instances they have been treated in a manner that, were it recorded, would blot the darkest page of history that has yet been penned... Indians have been shot down without evidence of their having committed an offense, and without even an explanation to them of the nature of our laws... They have been rudely driven from their homes, and expatriated from their sacred grounds where the ashes of their parents, ancestors, and beloved chiefs repose. This is not only inhuman and unlawful, it is bad policy."

Granted no legal or civil rights, and suffering from loss of food and territory, Indians began stealing the settlers' horses and cattle, which they butchered and ate. Hostility between the two groups reached a climax late in 1850 in the southern mining district of Mariposa when the Indians made a last, desperate effort to win back their traditional domain. War parties from several area tribes began raiding the white man's trading posts and corrals, stealing goods and livestock, and even murdering a dozen or more of the hated intruders before fleeing back to the mountains. Thus began the so-called Mariposa Indian War— really only a series of skirmishes—during which Yosemite Valley was effectively discovered and first entered by the new Californians.

The central figure in the conflict was a trader named James D. Savage. A California pioneer of 1846, Savage began prospecting at Woods Creek near present Sonora in the summer of 1848. He soon discovered that trading trinkets and overpriced merchandise to the local Indians for gold was easier and more profitable than doing the hard labor himself. During the next two years, Savage set up a series of transitory trading posts, periodically moving his Indian employees to new locations to avoid trouble with encroaching white miners. He was first at Big Oak Flat (originally known as "Savage's Diggins"), then at Piney Creek near Horseshoe Bend on the Merced River a few miles southwest of present Coulterville, and in late 1849 at the junction of the Merced River and the South Fork, fourteen miles southwest of Yosemite Valley.

Savage took Indian wives (some say five, others more than thirty), learned the dialects of the various tribes, and became the most influential man in the area, even though many Indians resented his exploitive methods.[9]

In the spring of 1850, a war party of Yosemite Indians raided Savage's South Fork post in an attempt to drive the trader out of their territory. Savage repulsed the attack with the help of his Indian miners and subsequently followed the Yosemites east up the Merced River Canyon until reaching a narrow, rocky gorge that made further pursuit too dangerous. Fearing a second attack from the Yosemites, Savage again moved his operation. Sometime in the summer of 1850 he opened two new trading posts: one near the confluence of Agua Fria and Mariposa Creeks, the other about twenty miles farther south on the Fresno River near Coarse Gold Gulch.

On December 17, 1850, Indians attacked Savage's Fresno River store, destroying everything they could not use or carry, and killing three of the four white attendants. The fourth clerk, a man named Brown, managed a daring escape under a shower of arrows. One account says he was aided by an Indian to whom he had previously given favors. A second version has Brown, "a large man of great strength and activity," holding his pistol to the head of one of the attackers while making his way across the river, then outrunning his pursuers during a vigorous chase. About the same time, another raiding party stole sixteen mules and forty head of cattle from Savage's Mariposa corral.[10]

These assaults were followed by a widespread outbreak of violence in the region south of Mariposa, with the Indians sometimes dealing telling blows. The sheriff quickly formed a posse to put down the marauders, and two small battles were fought with mixed results. Fearing a general uprising, local authorities appealed to the governor of the newly formed state for help.

THE MARIPOSA BATTALION

Governor John McDougal, who once told the state legislature that the "extermination of the Indians was inevitable," authorized the formation of a volunteer militia known as the Mariposa Battalion to put down the insurrection. According to the published roster, the force that was mustered into service at Agua Fria, then the county seat, on February 12, 1851, consisted of 204 officers and men, most of whom were miners from the surrounding area. James Savage was elected commanding officer with the rank of major.

Before any formal action could be taken, three United States Indian Commissioners arrived, escorted by more than a hundred U.S. Army troops, and halted proceedings while they attempted to persuade the Indians to accept treaties and move to reservations being set up along the base of the foothills. Many of the tribes accepted the offer, but several of the wilder bands, including the Yosemites, refused to consider leaving their mountain homelands.[11] The state legislature, confident that Congress would later reimburse California for the cost of the campaign, then authorized the governor to send the Mariposa Battalion against the holdouts. One company proceeded to the areas of the Kings and Kaweah Rivers. On March 19, 1851, the other two companies, with Savage in personal command, departed camp heading for a mysterious valley said to be the stronghold of the Grizzly Bears or Yosemites. After forging through deep snow over Chowchilla Mountain, the volunteers surprised and, without resistance, captured a large band of Nutchu Indians along the Merced River South Fork near present Wawona.

Savage thereupon established a headquarters camp, probably somewhere along Eleven Mile Creek, and sent a messenger ahead demanding the surrender of the Yosemites and their relocation to a reservation. Chief Tenieya himself soon appeared at the soldiers' camp, and after pleading unsuccessfully that his people would die on the plains, agreed to lead Savage to his *rancheria* in the Valley.

As it was necessary to divide the force of 106 men into two groups (one remaining in camp to secure the Nutchus), foot races were held to determine those in the best physical condition. The next morning, March 27, 1851, Major Savage and fifty-seven mounted soldiers started for Yosemite Valley, traveling along an Indian trail that approximated the stage road later constructed between Wawona and Yosemite. On the way, they met a straggling group of seventy-two Indians, mostly old women, mothers, and children, slogging slowly through the snow on their way to surrender. Tenieya was sent back to the battalion camp with this group, while Savage and his soldiers—suspicious because no young men from Tenieya's band were present—continued northward led by a young Indian guide. Late that afternoon, after successfully negotiating the challenging south side cliffs, the party became the first white men known to have entered Yosemite Valley.[12]

By favorable chance, among the battalion volunteers was an observant, twenty-seven-year-old private named Lafayette Houghton Bunnell who—alone among those present—wrote an eyewitness account of what took place: a book called *Discovery of the Yosemite and the Indian War of 1851 Which Led to That Event*. Although not published until nearly three decades later, Bunnell's book nonetheless remains the only first-hand record of this notable moment in Yosemite's human history.[13]

That evening around the soldiers' campfire, set up in view of Bridalveil Fall, a discussion took place about an appropriate name by which to designate the Valley. After various choices were rejected, Bunnell proposed calling it "Yo-sem-i-ty," the name of Tenieya's tribe as he understood it, saying that it was "suggestive, euphonious, and certainly American" and would perpetuate the memory of the Indians who were being forced from their home. The name, according to Bunnell, was almost unanimously adopted.[14]

The following day Savage and his men searched the Valley floor from end to end, but found no Indians except an ancient woman who had been left behind by her fleeing tribe members. With supplies running low, the soldiers remained only long enough to burn the Indians' dwellings and food caches, hoping in this way to starve the Yosemites into moving to the reservation. On the morning of March 29, Savage and his troops departed the Valley and returned to their temporary base near Wawona. The entire force then set out for the battalion headquarters camp on the Fresno River. They arrived empty-handed, however, for nearly all the Indians captured by the battalion, including Chief

Dr. Lafayette Houghton Bunnell named Yosemite Valley in March, 1851.
(Author's collection)

Tenieya and his followers, escaped in the night and scattered back into the mountains. Thus ended the initial Yosemite campaign.

Were the members of the Mariposa Battalion really the first non-Indians to enter Yosemite Valley? All evidence indicates that they were, even though several others later claimed to have made prior visits. These assertions were advanced long after Yosemite had become famous, and offered no substantiation. Moreover, Chief Tenieya told Bunnell that his party was the first to enter the Valley, and that it could not have been entered by any outsider without his knowledge.[15]

THE SECOND INVASION OF YOSEMITE

On May 5, 1851, a new expedition of thirty-five men under Captain John Boling left for Yosemite Valley with instructions to "surprise the Indians and whip them well, or induce them to surrender." Following the same route that Savage had used, Boling reached the Valley on May 9 and established his camp near the present Sentinel Bridge. The next day five young Indian men were captured, including three sons and a son-in-law of Chief Tenieya. One son and the son-in-law

Stephen Frealon Grover, a member of the unfortunate party of miners ambushed by the Yosemites in 1852, later became a prominent citizen in Santa Cruz. (Edward G. Chandler collection)

were subsequently released upon their promise to persuade the old chief and his followers to surrender. Soon after, one of the three remaining hostages was wantonly shot by an overzealous soldier; the other two managed to escape under heavy fire. Later, after a brief skirmish, Tenieya himself was captured and brought to the soldiers' camp. He became grief-stricken when he recognized the murdered Indian as his youngest son.[16]

On May 22, after a lengthy march on foot up Tenaya Canyon and Snow Creek to an "elevation almost entirely covered with snow," Boling's troops surprised and captured the remaining Yosemites in a village on the shore of present Tenaya Lake. Hungry and exhausted, the weary band of thirty-five Indians surrendered without incident. With the delivery of the Yosemites a week later to Fort Miller, the newly established post of the regular army on the San Joaquin River, the campaign of 1851 was over. On July 1, 1851, Companies "B" and "C" of the Mariposa Battalion were mustered out (Company "A" had been disbanded on May 15).

In the weeks that followed, Tenieya, unhappy with the lowland climate and the forced association with traditional enemies, repeatedly begged the agent-in-charge for permission to leave the reservation and return to his beloved Yosemite. Near the end of June his request was apparently granted upon his promise to remain peaceful. In due time, some of the chief's followers quietly slipped away from the reservation

This blue-and-white metal plaque was affixed to an upright rock near the southeast corner of Bridalveil Meadow from 1921 until it disappeared sometime in the late 1950s.

A view of Bridalveil Fall taken from Bridalveil Meadow near the site of the killing of Rose and Shurborn in 1852. (Jeff Nixon)

and joined him in their old mountain home. No attempt was made to go after the runaways.[17]

LIEUTENANT TREDWELL MOORE'S EXPEDITION

Nothing more was heard from Tenieya and his people until the spring of 1852 when a party of eight miners from Coarse Gold Gulch was ambushed by Yosemites on or about May 28, shortly after entering the Valley on a prospecting trip. Two of the miners named Rose and Shurborn were killed; a third man named Joseph Tudor was seriously wounded, but managed to join the other survivors in making a desperate escape.

Upon the group's arrival back at Coarse Gold Gulch on June 2, a party of twenty-five or thirty of their fellow miners immediately set out for Yosemite for the purpose of "chastising those Indians." They found the bodies of the two murdered men and buried them on the edge of the little meadow below Bridalveil Fall, but failed to capture any Indians.[18]

The episode took a bizarre twist in 1926 when the contents of a curious "Reminiscence"[19] written by Stephen Grover, a member of the unfortunate prospecting party, came to public attention in an article by Carl Russell, Chief Naturalist at Yosemite National Park, that appeared in the *California Historical Society Quarterly*.[20] According to Grover, it was Tudor and Shurborn who were killed, not Rose. Grover implied that Rose had somehow set up the attack with Chief Tenieya to kill Tudor and Shurborn, Rose's partners in a mining venture, and that Rose had faked his own death at the time, only to show up a week later and take sole possession of the mine, which he later sold.

Some writers have accepted Grover's romanticized account as fact, but his claims are not realistic. For one thing, Grover tells a wild tale of being besieged by more than 150 whooping and yelling warriors, "constantly firing arrows at us." Tenieya's diminished band, however, probably numbered only a few dozen members at the time, including old people, women, and children. Furthermore, Rose, Tudor, and Shurborn were well known to the miners who buried the two bodies in Bridalveil Meadow, and misidentification seems very unlikely. And even if we assume the doubtful premise that Rose could somehow have managed to secretly negotiate the lengthy round trip through strange and hostile country from Coarse Gold Gulch to Yosemite

Fort Miller was established along the San Joaquin River in May, 1851, as one of a series of California forts built by the War Department to secure its new territory militarily.

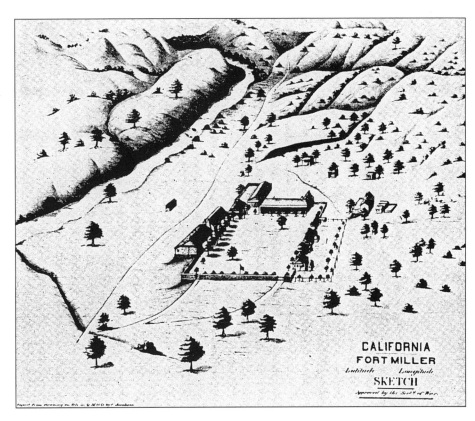

CALIFORNIA
FORT MILLER
SKETCH

Lake Tenaya, named for the old chief of the Yosemites, was probably the location of Lieutenant Moore's capture of twenty-one Indians on July 4, 1852. The lake was a favorite summer camping spot of the Yosemites. (F. B. Watson)

Valley and back to set up the subsequent ambush with Tenieya, there would have been no reason for the old chief to conspire with a white man in such a complicated intrigue. Since there is no report other than Grover's of Rose's miraculous survival—an event that would certainly have been a major news story at the time—it seems doubtful that Grover's story is true.[21]

On June 15, 1852, a company of federal soldiers departed Fort Miller in search of the Yosemites responsible for the attack on the miners. The force consisted of First Lieutenant Tredwell Moore, Second Lieutenant Nathaniel H. McLean, Assistant Surgeon William Edgar, another unnamed assistant surgeon, two sergeants, three corporals, one musician, twenty-seven privates, and "one non-commissioned officer on extra duty," a total of four officers and thirty-four rank-and-file.[22] Accompanying the troop was Major James Savage of Mariposa Battalion fame, along with some volunteer scouts and friendly Indian guides who knew the topography. The circumstances of the punitive campaign are described by Lieutenant Moore in two dispatches sent within a day of each other on July 8 and 9 to his military superiors at Pacific Division Headquarters in San Francisco.[23]

On June 20, Moore and his party set up a base camp, which he called "Camp Steele," somewhere "between the Middle and South Forks of the Mercede."[24] From the description, the camp was probably situated along the southern branch of the old Mono Trail, perhaps near present Westfall Meadows. Scouting parties were immediately sent out in all directions to search the surrounding country. Many deserted *rancherias* were found, but no Indians. Major Savage and some of the friendly Indians struck a fresh trail heading toward the east. They were forced to abandon the hunt after running low on provisions. (Savage must have returned to the San Joaquin Valley very soon after this incident because he arrived at Fort Miller on July 29 after spending time at the Four Creeks area on the Kaweah River, about sixty miles southeast of the fort.)[25]

On July 1 Moore dispatched Lieutenant McLean and ten men to

TO COMMEMORATE
DR·LAFAYETTE HOUGHTON BUNNELL
ONE OF THE FIRST PARTY OF WHITE MEN
TO ENTER THE YOSEMITE VALLEY
IN MARCH 1851·
HE PROPOSED THE NAME
YOSEMITE
AND WAS THE FIRST
TO PROCLAIM ITS
BEAUTY AND WONDERS
TO THE WORLD·

DEDICATED
BY THE CALIFORNIA
MEDICAL
ASSOCIATION
·1925 A·D·

The California Medical Association attached this metal plate to a large boulder near the northeast corner of Bridalveil Meadow in 1925 to honor Dr. Lafayette Bunnell's contribution to Yosemite history. (Hank Johnston)

Yosemite Valley with orders to destroy the Indian villages and supplies that evidently had been discovered on an earlier scouting trip. The same day, Moore and twelve soldiers left Camp Steele to pursue Major Savage's route of the previous week. Along the way they came across a well-traveled trail and followed it over the "main ridge of the Sierra" on the morning of July 4, making camp at noon. Scouts soon located an Indian *rancheria* only four miles away. Moore divided his party into two groups, took the Indians by surprise, and captured six men and fifteen women and children in broad daylight without resistance.[26]

One of the men admitted seeing the attack on the miners, but said he had not been a participant. Trinkets and clothing belonging to the murdered men were found, however, which implicated the captives in the division of the spoils, if not in the murder itself. The following morning, July 5, the six Indian men were executed by a volley of musketry.[27]

Meanwhile, Lieutenant McLean's party found and destroyed a large quantity of acorn stores in Yosemite Valley. During the week-long foray, one of McLean's men received two arrows in his neck while on sentry duty. The wounded soldier, a man named Riley, died of his injuries on July 7, the day before McLean arrived back at Camp Steele.

After learning from the captured women that nearly all the Yosemites had been present at the ambush of the prospectors, Lieutenant Moore determined to pursue Tenieya and the remnants of his tribe across the

Lieutenant Tredwell Moore's soldiers were the first white men known to have entered the Mono Basin. They discovered the unusual Mono Lake, shown here, and made the outside world aware of its existence. (F. B. Watson)

Sierra to Mono country. He returned first to Camp Steele and dispatched a letter to his superiors informing them of his actions and asking for reinforcements to escort the pack train. He also requisitioned ten six-shooters, which, he said, would be of more use to his scouts than their cumbersome muskets. At this point, Moore's reports end, but his ensuing actions can be reasonably well followed using information from other sources.

Army records show that Major George W. Patten arrived at Fort Miller on July 17 with a company of infantry from the Benicia barracks. A small troop of nine or ten soldiers was soon sent to join Moore at Camp Steele as he had requested. According to an account given to Lafayette Bunnell by Gus Gray, a scout for the party, Moore's forces then set out along the Mono Trail and crossed the Sierra by way of Soda Springs and Mono Pass. After descending to the plains along the east side of the range, they explored the region north and south of Mono Lake for some distance, finding a number of Mono Paiutes, but no trace of Tenieya and the Yosemites. They also discovered some gold-bearing quartz, obsidian, and other minerals, the report of which later induced Mariposa miner Leroy Vining and a few chosen companions to establish themselves on what became known as Leevining Creek. Moore then retraced his route back across the Sierra via the southern branch of the old Mono Trail. After sixty-four days in the field, he returned to Fort Miller with forty-two men on August 17, 1852.

A secondhand account of Moore's expedition into Mono Basin, obtained from the Army Quartermaster for Fort Miller, appeared in the

Stockton Journal on August 24, 1852. The story gives the first public description of Mono Lake:

The original caption on this J. J. Reilly stereo view reads "The Old Indian Chief of Early Days in Yosemite Valley, Cal." The identity of the man is unknown.

"After descending into the plains and marching a short distance in search of Indians, they discovered, about fifteen miles from the base of the hills, a large lake some twenty-five or thirty miles long, by the same measurement in width, which they named Lake Mono, after the tribe of Indians that inhabit that section. This lake does not appear to have any outlet, and is of a very brackish taste. There are several streams of pure water—two of considerable magnitude—emptying into it, on the borders of which is the only wood to be found. Sea gulls, geese, and ducks abound on its water, and its banks are covered with *tache le mere* and sand."

Although they failed in their principal mission of capturing Chief Tenieya, Moore and his soldiers succeeded in opening a new route across the Sierra for white men. They also became the first non-Indians definitely known to have entered the Mono Basin. As a result of information brought back by the party, Mono Lake appeared on a published map for the first time in 1853 (John Trask's *Map of the State of California*).

Tenieya remained with the Monos until the summer of 1853 when he apparently decided it was safe to return to Yosemite Valley. Soon after, some of the young Yosemites made a raid on the Mono Lake camp of their former hosts, stealing horses that the Monos had taken from white settlers to the south. They drove them to Yosemite Valley over a roundabout route, hoping in this way to avoid detection. A short time later, while the Yosemites were feasting on the stolen horses, the Monos set upon them and stoned Tenieya and many of his followers to death. Eight young men escaped by fleeing down the Merced River Canyon. The women and children who survived the attack were made captives and taken back to Mono Lake. This was the last event in Yosemite Indian hostilities.[28]

NOTES AND REFERENCES

1. Although the translation of Ahwahnee as "deep, grassy valley" was accepted for many years, more recent linguistic studies indicate that the interpretation "place of a gaping mouth" is probably nearer the mark. The Miwok stem-word "AWA" means "mouth," and it was the Miwok practice to name places after their fancied resemblance to a part of the human body. Elizabeth Godfrey, *Yosemite Indians,* rev. ed. (Yosemite: Yosemite Association, 1977). The previous translation of "deep, grassy valley" originated with Lafayette H. Bunnell in his classic book, *Discovery of the Yosemite and the Indian War of 1851 Which Led to That Event,* 4th ed. (1911; reprint, with a preface by Hank Johnston, Yosemite: Yosemite Association, 1990). Bunnell inferred the meaning from Chief Tenieya, who communicated it by signs, not spoken words. Bunnell admitted he was not certain of the translation (see note 13).

2. Bunnell, *Discovery of Yosemite,* is the only source of information about the demise of the Ahwahneechees and Tenieya's subsequent claiming of the Valley with a new tribe. He describes how Tenieya himself told him the history of the Ahwahneechees and Yosemites. In a letter to the Yosemite Board of Commissioners in 1890, Bunnell said that he obtained "most of the legendary lore" from the old chief while they rested in the shade of the big incense cedar tree that was enclosed inside the famous "Big Tree Room" by James Hutchings about 1867. The tree still stands across the road from the south end of Sentinel Bridge. The dates given are estimates based on Tenieya's statements and known facts. An excellent description of Indian life in Yosemite is contained in Godfrey, *Yosemite Indians.*

3. Although the precise derivation of the word "Yosemite" is not absolutely certain, there are a number of references to the Yosemites as the "Grizzlies" in early reports, and several prominent anthropologists have confirmed the "grizzly bear" definition given to Bunnell by Tenieya. Others have defined "Yosemite" to mean "they are killers," which carries a similar suggestion of the fierce character of the tribe. For a discussion of various theories about the origination of the name, see Craig Bates, "Names and Meanings for Yosemite Valley," *Yosemite Nature Notes* 47, no. 3 (1978): 42-44; Linda Wedel Greene, *Historic Resource Study: Yosemite,* 3 vols., (Washington, D.C.: U.S. Department of the Interior, National Park Service, 1987), 22-23; and Godfrey, *Yosemite Indians,* 3-4, 35 (and see note 14).

4. The name "Yosemite" was written in various ways in early reports. These included such spellings as Yoosemite, Yosemeto, Yosemita, Yo-Semitee, Yo-Hamite, Yohemity, Yo Semite, Yeosemoty, Yosemitz, and Yosemity.

5. Some writers refer to the "Ahwahneechees" and "Yosemites" interchangeably, but this is incorrect if we are to believe Chief Tenieya's own statement to Bunnell. He said he became chief only after the mixed band known as the Yosemites moved into Yosemite Valley in the early 1800s, long after the demise of the original Ahwahneechees.

6. Zenas Leonard, *Narrative of the Adventures of Zenas Leonard* (1839; reprinted as *Adventures of a Mountain Man,* ed. Milo Milton Quaife, Lincoln and London: University of Nebraska Press, 1978). Copies of the scarce first edition are now valued in the many thousands of dollars. Fortunately, the text has been reprinted by various other publishers over the years.

7. Lafayette Bunnell, who knew Walker quite well in the mid-1850s, said: "Capt. Joe, with his Mexican woman, were camped near Coulterville for about a month . . . and I was frequently at his camp and obtained much useful information from him. . . Walker told me that he kept his course near the divide over which the Mono Trail ran until reaching Bull Creek, when he descended into camp, not seeing the Valley proper." Quoted in Hank Johnston, *Yosemite's Yesterdays,* Volume II (Yosemite: Flying Spur Press, 1991), 9. There are a number of theories about Walker's route. Divergent opinions are given by Francis Farquhar in "Walker's Discovery of Yosemite," *Sierra Club Bulletin* 27, no. 4 (August 1942): 35-49; and by Irene Paden and Margaret Schlichtmann in *The Big Oak Flat Road to Yosemite* (1959; reprint, Fredericksburg, TX: Awani Press, 1986), 259-64.

8. The Yosemite entry in the Abrams diary was first uncovered by William C. Barry of Glendale, California, early in 1947 while tracing the genealogy of the Abrams family. The diary had previously been examined in 1910 for the Oregon Historical Society, but the reviewer failed to connect Abrams' scenic description with Yosemite Valley. The passage quoted here originally appeared in Weldon F. Heald, "The Abrams Diary," *Sierra Club Bulletin* 32, no. 5 (May 1947). For information about Abrams himself, see Dennis Kruska, "William Penn Abrams, Forgotten Yosemite Adventurer," *Yosemite* 52, no. 3 (summer 1990): 5-8.

9. James Savage's singular place in Yosemite history is rather remarkable considering that he spent only two nights in the Valley, never saw many of the prominent features such as Vernal and Nevada Falls, and was killed the year following his only visit. Descriptions of Savage and his life appear, among other places, in Carl Russell, *One Hundred Years in Yosemite* (1922; reprint, with an introduction by Hank Johnston, Yosemite: Yosemite Association, 1992); Robert Eccleston, *The Mariposa Indian War 1850-51. The Diaries of Robert Eccleston: The California Gold Rush, Yosemite, and the High Sierra,* ed. C. Gregory Crampton (Salt Lake City: University of Utah Press, 1957), 106; Bunnell, *Discovery of Yosemite;* and especially, Annie Mitchell, "James Savage," *Los Tulares* no. 82 (September 1969).

10. The raid on Savage's Fresno River store is described in several accounts, notably, Bunnell, *Discovery of Yosemite;* James Hutchings, *In the Heart of the Sierras* (Oakland and Yosemite: Pacific Press Publishing House, 1886); Eccleston, *Mariposa Indian War;* Russell, *One Hundred Years;* and "Letter from Adam Johnston, United States Sub-Agent, to Luke Lea, Commissioner of Indian Affairs, March 7. 1851," in *Senate Executive Document No. 4,* Special Session, 1853, 231-33. Details of Savage's losses at his Fresno trading post are contained in "Claim of J. D. Savage for Remuneration of Losses Sustained Through Indian Depredation," also published in *Senate Executive Document No. 4,* Special Session, 1853.

Carl Russell and others have written that Savage's Mariposa Creek store was also sacked, with the resultant deaths of three clerks, but this is erroneous. Savage himself said in his claim:"At the same time [as the Fresno store raid] my tent on the Little Mariposa suffered the loss of sixteen mules and forty head of cattle." He makes no mention of any attack on the post itself, or its personnel.

11. On September 30, 1850, Congress passed a law authorizing the president to make treaties with the California Indians. A sum of twenty-five thousand dollars was appropriated (the cost eventually exceeded one million dollars!). Three commissioners were appointed: Redick McKee of Virginia, George W. Barbour of Kentucky, and Oliver M. Wozencraft of Louisiana. Accompanied by a force of regular army troops consisting of ten officers and 101 men, the commissioners moved slowly along the edge of the foothills, setting up temporary camps while establishing contact with various mountain tribes by couriers. The first treaty was signed in March, 1851, and in all, the commissioners, separately or together, made eighteen treaties with perhaps twenty-five thousand California Indians. (One of the treaties is reprinted as Appendix A, following the main text.)

Although the commissioners thought they were doing the right thing, the treaty-making turned out to be a farce. The commissioners knew nothing of the so-called "tribes" that signed the various agreements—many turned out to be merely local bands, villages, or even individual families—and it is doubtful that the Indians understood what they were signing. The treaties were criticized in California by both settlers and miners, who feared the loss of cheap labor and valuable lands. The state legislature likewise condemned the pacts. In May, 1852, the treaties were submitted to President Millard Fillmore, and he, in turn, sent them to the U.S. Senate on June 1. The treaties were subsequently rejected by the Senate, which meant that the California Indians never legally had any treaty relations with the federal government. (Congress later authorized seven reservations to be set aside for the California Indians. These were established between 1853 and 1887.)

The treaty signed by sixteen tribes—but not the Yosemites—in the San Joaquin Valley-Mariposa foothill area was consummated on April 29, 1851, at Camp Barbour, the commissioners' camp established April 14 on the upper San Joaquin River. This became Fort Miller a month later (see note 22). The treaty provided for a tremendous Indian reservation of approximately a thousand square miles paralleling the Sierra foothills from the Chowchilla River on the north to the Kaweah River on the south.

The impressive document with its many signatures had not yet reached the seat of government in San Francisco before whites began violating its terms. Prospectors continued to mine illegally on reservation lands without regard to tribal rights. Lawless elements made frequent unprovoked attacks on small parties of innocent and defenseless Indians. Within three years most Indian groups had become severely demoralized by white contact, and the population had suffered acute decline from disease and abuse. In 1855 it was estimated by one Indian agent that there were fewer than two thousand Indians left in the entire San Joaquin Valley. Moreover, many of these, men and women alike, were considered "diseased, drunken, and almost worthless." The treatment of California's Indians can never be considered one of America's prouder chapters in the so-called "winning of the West."

12. Bunnell, *Discovery of Yosemite,* gives the date of discovery as "about the 21st of March, 1851." Russell, *One Hundred Years,* concluded that it was actually March 25, 1851, a date he apparently took from a secondhand newspaper account, "The Indian Expedition," which appeared in the San Francisco *Daily Alta California* on April 23, 1851. The publication of Eccleston, *Mariposa Indian War,* in 1957 established the precise date as March 27, 1851. Eccleston's entry for that day begins: "Today about noon, Major Savage started for the Yoosemita Camp with 57 men & an Indian guide." Eccleston was the only member of the battalion known to have kept a diary. Historians today can only wish that he had been a swifter runner, for he was among those left in camp by the Yosemite discovery party.

13. Lafayette Houghton Bunnell was born in Rochester, New York, in 1824; spent his boyhood in Michigan and Wisconsin, where he grew up among the Indians and learned their ways; studied medicine for three years with his physician father and another doctor; served as a hospital steward in the Mexican War, then came to California in 1849. In February, 1851, Bunnell joined his fellow miners in the Mariposa Battalion and remained for the five months that the group was active. Although he performed some small medical duties, he was not the "surgeon with the Mariposa Battalion" as various writers have mistakenly described him (Bunnell himself lists the battalion doctors in his text). Characterized as "one of the most energetic, go-ahead businessmen in the County" by the *Mariposa Chronicle* in 1854, Bunnell occupied himself with various projects in the Mariposa area until the fall of 1857, when he returned to Wisconsin. His experiences in the Yosemite region, which are recounted in his book, represent some of the best information available for the period.

Bunnell enlisted in the Union Army at the start of the Civil War as a hospital steward with the Second Wisconsin Volunteers. His practical experience and training, along with an honorary Doctor of Medicine degree from a non-functioning LaCrosse, Wisconsin, medical school, enabled him to be appointed an assistant surgeon with the rank of major in 1864. After the war, Bunnell settled in Homer, Minnesota, practiced medicine to a limited extent, wrote about local history, and in 1880, "to correct existing errors relative to Yosemite Valley," brought out his masterwork, *Discovery of the Yosemite,* which went through four editions, the last published posthumously in 1911. It is currently available in a new printing issued in 1990 by the Yosemite Association.

Bunnell died in 1903 at the age of seventy-nine. His memory is perpetuated in Yosemite by the place names Bunnell Cascade and Bunnell Point along the upper Merced River. In 1925 the California Medical Association affixed a round metal plaque honoring Dr. Bunnell to a large boulder near the eastern edge of Bridalveil Meadow, where it can still be found. Additional biographical information about Bunnell is contained in Johnston, *Yosemite's Yesterdays II,* 6-13.

14. "At the time I proposed this name," Bunnell wrote in *Discovery of Yosemite,* "the signification of it (a grizzly bear) was not generally known to our battalion, although 'the grizzlies' was frequently used to designate this tribe. Neither was it pronounced with uniformity. . .Major Savage . . . told us that the name was Yo-sem-i-ty, as pronounced by Tenieya . . . and that it signified a full-grown grizzly bear" (see note 27).

15. Typical of these claims is an account from the Modesto *Stanislaus News,* January 22, 1875, in which the writer says that James Savage had accurately described the waterfalls of Yosemite to him in August, 1849. In response to this, Lafayette Bunnell stated in a letter to the *Mariposa Gazette* on March 13, 1875, that Savage told him he had never been in the Valley before March, 1851. Bunnell surmised that Savage had visited the Cascade Falls area west of Yosemite while pursuing the Indians who attacked his trading post at the South Fork in 1850, as recounted in the text.

Another so-called "discovery" appears in an article called "Sherman Was There, the Recollections of Major Edwin A. Sherman with an Introduction by Allen B. Sherman," *California Historical Society Quarterly* 23, no. 4 (December 1944). Sherman (1829-1914) wrote his memoirs in 1904 from notes made many years earlier. In his account he tells of prospecting on the "upper bar of the Merced River" in May, 1850, when Indians stole a number of horses from other prospectors just below his camp. Sherman and a companion volunteered to help recapture the animals. "We followed the trail for about 2½ days to the edge of a stupendous deep gorge," Sherman wrote, "which we descended; and then, continuing along the edge of a stream, which was the Merced River, we suddenly came upon the Indians' camp and opened fire. They immediately fled higher up the valley, abandoning the horses (one had been killed). We then retraced our route with the recovered animals. By the time we reached our camp, we had been absent six days. That deep chasm we called 'The Devil's Cellar.' It now goes by another name and a second discoverer, Captain Savage. The year afterward, he gave it the name of the 'Yosemite Valley.'" From the description, we can infer that Sherman probably reached the deep gorge in the Merced River Canyon just east of present El Portal. His failure to mention any other scenic landmarks makes it almost certain that his party never made it into Yosemite Valley itself.

There are other, similar stories of visits to Yosemite prior to March, 1851, and the possibility always remains that some unknown wanderer may have actually accomplished the feat. But as James Hutchings, Yosemite's pioneer publicist-innkeeper, summed it up in 1886: "No responsible data to establish such a fact has yet come to my knowledge."

16. Captain John Boling (the name is sometimes spelled "Bowling" in early accounts, but a descendant says the correct form has always been "Boling") wrote two reports of the second expedition—one from Yosemite Valley on May 15, 1851, and the other from his base camp on the Fresno River on May 29. They were published in the *Daily Alta California* on June 12 and June 14, 1851. Boling's first account, which provides useful dates, differs from Bunnell's version in *Discovery of Yosemite* in certain details, notably in the story of the death of Chief Tenieya's youngest son. Since Bunnell was there and—unlike Boling—had no personal reason not to be objective, his description, which is summarized in this text, most likely comes closer to the truth.

17. Tenieya stayed at the Fresno reservation for only a month before returning to Yosemite Valley. Eccleston, *Mariposa Indian War,* contains the following entry under the dates June 22 through June 26, 1851: "The old Yosemity Chief & some of other Indians have left the Rancheria."

18. Contemporary accounts of the attack on the miners can be found in the *Daily Alta California* for June 10 and June 18, 1852. Bunnell, *Discovery of Yosemite,* gives a similar report. From 1921 until the late 1950s, a plaque erected by the Society of California Pioneers marked the approximate site of the graves of the murdered miners. Its present whereabouts are unknown.

19. Stephen Frealon Grover (1830-1907) came to the California gold fields in December, 1850, from his native Maine where he had been engaged in the lumber business. After several years of prospecting in the Sierra foothills, he joined with his brother Whitney in a lumbering operation in the Santa Cruz mountains near Soquel. Grover achieved considerable financial success, eventually building a fine house called the Grover Mansion on Walnut Street in Santa Cruz. He also had a street named after him in the same city. Sometime in his later years, Grover wrote out his story of the Indian attack, entitled "A Reminiscence," which he gave to his daughter, Mrs. A. E. Chandler, likewise a Santa Cruz resident. She sent the manuscript to Galen Clark in Yosemite in 1901. On Clark's death it passed to the Yosemite photographer George Fiske. On Fiske's death, the paper was acquired by the National Park Service.

20. "Early Years in Yosemite," *California Historical Society Quarterly* 5, no. 4 (1926). Russell later reprinted Grover's account in *One Hundred Years.*

21. For a comprehensive examination of the murder of the miners, see Hank Johnston, "The Mystery Buried in Bridalveil Meadow," parts 1 and 2, *Yosemite* 54, no. 2 (spring 1992): 1-6; no. 3 (summer 1992): 11-13.

22. Beginning in 1849, the U. S. War Department built a number of forts (Fort Ord, Fort Tejon, Fort Bragg, *et al.*) in various parts of California to secure its new territory militarily. One of these posts was Fort Miller, which was erected on the site of Camp Barbour, the temporary headquarters of the Indian commissioners during April, 1851, to protect the new reservations in the area and keep the peace between Indians and whites. On May 26, 1851, Lieutenant Tredwell Moore officially designated the new post as Fort Miller in honor of Major Albert S. Miller, Moore's commander at the Benicia barracks near San Francisco at the time.

Moore's forces consisted of Companies "B" and "K" of the Second Infantry, a total of two officers and fifty-one men. The troops had previously been part of the regular army escort of the Indian commissioners. In due time, the army built a number of permanent structures at Fort Miller, including a long blockhouse, stockade, barracks, hospital, blacksmith shop, mess, officers' quarters, and bakery, all surrounded by a connecting four-and-one-half-foot adobe wall with four gates. The fort was occupied continuously by the army until September, 1858, when the troops moved out and a caretaker was placed in charge.

In August, 1863, Union forces reoccupied Fort Miller as a precaution against suspected Southern sympathizers in the region. The post was closed permanently in November, 1865, and the buildings sold at public auction. Today the site lies under the waters of Lake Millerton behind Friant Dam. For more information on Fort Miller, see Bertina Richter, *Fort Miller, California, 1851-65* (New York: Peter Lang, 1988). The make-up of Lieutenant Moore's Yosemite party is taken from the Fort Miller monthly report for June, 1852, signed by Moore himself, copy in the Yosemite Museum.

23. For more than a century, the account given in Bunnell's *Discovery of Yosemite* was considered our principal source of knowledge about Lieutenant Moore's expedition. In 1987 three previously unknown letters from Moore to his superiors were found buried in the National Archives in Washington, D.C. The letters correct some inaccuracies in Bunnell's report and provide considerable additional information about Moore's activities. The first dispatch, dated June 12, 1852, was written before Moore left Fort Miller and adds little to our knowledge of events. The second two letters, dated July 8 and 9, furnish most of the facts stated in the text. Moore's letters are reproduced in their entirety in Thomas Fletcher, *Paiute, Prospector, Pioneer* (Lee Vining, CA: Artemisia Press, 1987). It was Fletcher who found the letters in the National Archives and first made them available to the public.

24. In the custom of the time, Lieutenant Moore named Camp Steele in honor of fellow officer Frederick Steele, adjutant, Second Infantry, stationed at Monterey. The location "between the Middle and South Forks of the Mercede" is taken from Moore's Fort Miller monthly report for June, 1852 (see note 22). This is probably a more precise description than the one contained in Moore's second letter to headquarters in which he depicts Camp Steele as being "on the Head Waters of the Merced."

25. Savage's return to Fort Miller from the Four Creeks on July 29, 1852, is mentioned in an inspection report of the post issued by George A. McCall of the Inspector General's Department on the same date. The report is reproduced in Richter, *Fort Miller.* Eighteen days later, on August 16, 1852, Savage was shot and killed by one Walter H. Harvey during a fight between the two men.

26. Moore's description of crossing the "main ridge of the Sierra" on July 4 most likely referred to his passing through the Cathedral Range between Little Yosemite Valley and Tuolumne Meadows. This would have brought his forces

within a few miles of Tenaya Lake, a favorite summer camping area of the Yosemites, where Moore probably found the Indian *rancheria.*

27. According to Bunnell, *Discovery of Yosemite,* Lieutenant Moore received some severe criticism for his "display of autocratic power in ordering the five Yosemites shot." (There were actually six. Bunnell was mistaken about both the number of victims and the location of the execution, which Bunnell said occurred in Yosemite Valley.) Bunnell also said that Moore later wrote a letter to the *Mariposa Chronicle* sometime after that newspaper began publication in January, 1854, in which he attempted to justify his actions. "In this letter," Bunnell said, "he dropped the terminal letter 'y' in the name 'Yosemite,' as it had been written previously by myself and other members of the battalion, and substituted 'e' as before stated. As Lieutenant Moore's article attracted a great deal of public attention at that time, the name, with its present orthography, was accepted... His position as an officer of the regular army established a reputation for his article that could not be expected by other correspondents."

It has long seemed odd to me, however, that Lieutenant Moore, who left the area in May, 1853, would find it necessary to publicly defend his execution of the six Yosemites two years after the incident. It also has seemed unlikely that one letter in a remote foothill newspaper, no matter who the author, could permanently alter the spelling of Yosemite. In this regard, I recently had the opportunity to examine a virtually complete file of the *Mariposa Chronicle*— January 20, 1854, to March, 1855, when succeeded by the *Mariposa Gazette*— and I found no letter from Moore as Bunnell describes. It therefore appears quite possible that Bunnell, writing more than a quarter of a century later, was mistaken about the matter, and that the present spelling of Yosemite derived naturally over a period of time. Certainly there are a number of written references to Yosemite using a terminal "e" prior to 1854.

Lieutenant Tredwell Moore (1825-1876), a native of Ohio, graduated from West Point in 1847. He was assigned to the Benicia barracks in the Bay Area before 1851. In 1851-52 he was in charge of Fort Miller at various times; he also served as second officer on occasion. He later saw duty in the Civil War and was brevetted a brigadier general in 1865 for "faithful and meritorious services."

28. The long-accepted version of the death of Chief Tenieya given here is from Bunnell (*Discovery of Yosemite*), who was living and working in the lower Merced River Canyon near present Briceburg at the time and based his account on reports from the Yosemite Indians fleeing the massacre. Although there seems to be no reason to suppose that either Bunnell or the Yosemites would invent such a shameful end for Tenieya, some writers have seized on an interview with Maria Lebrado, the so-called "last survivor" of the Yosemites, to offer a different version of Tenieya's death. (Maria, a granddaughter of Chief Tenieya, was one of the seventy-two Indians captured along the trail by the Mariposa Battalion on March 27, 1851, during the volunteers' first invasion of Yosemite Valley.)

The interview was given to Carl Russell in 1928 when Maria was almost ninety, with her daughter acting as interpreter. Maria said that Tenieya and four other Yosemites were killed at Mono Lake by Paiutes as a result of a quarrel during a gambling game. Some Paiutes were also killed. "The Indian, Tom Hutchings, was present during the fight," Maria told Russell. "He burned the bodies of the Yosemite Indians and brought some of the burned bones back to Yosemite Valley. He told the other Yosemites about what had happened. Tom was half Paiute... Hite's Cove mine had just been opened. My half-sister Lucy lived with Mr. Hite and was always known as Lucy Hite. Tom Hutchings took Tenieya's bones to Hite's Cove for burial. On the way, Tom stopped with

Yosemite Indians and other Indians who were friendly to the Yosemites at the South Fork, where a big cry was held. The cry lasted two weeks. After the cry, the bones were taken down the South Fork to Hite's Cove. In the month that followed, some white prospectors killed an Indian boy. In retaliation, some Yosemite Indians killed two white men in Yosemite Valley. They killed them with arrows. Very few Yosemite Indians had guns."

There are too many problems with Maria's story to accept any part of it as fact. For one thing, she says that Tenieya was killed some months before the attack on the miners in May, 1852. All other reports agree that the chief was not murdered until the late summer or fall of 1853. In addition, she says that Indian Tom Hutchings carried the remains of the five dead Yosemites back to the South Fork where a great two-week "cry" was held. This would have meant that Indian Tom crossed the Sierra on foot near the dead of winter—a practical impossibility. Moreover, one cannot help wondering why Indian Tom, who later became an employee and devoted member of the James Hutchings family (he even took the family name), never mentioned this important event to his close friend Hutchings. (Hutchings gave Bunnell's version of Tenieya's death in his book, *In the Heart of the Sierras*.)

The most obvious incongruity is Maria's description of Tom Hutchings' burial of Tenieya's bones at Hite's Cove. Lucy Hite, who was a child about Maria's age of ten at the time, didn't take up with John Hite until at least a decade later. And it is a matter of record that Hite found his gold mine in 1862, long after the events Maria is describing occurred. More information about Maria's life and her interview with Russell can be found in Johnston, "The Mystery Buried in Bridalveil Meadow." A further description of Indian Tom is contained in Hutchings, *In the Heart*, 416-21. For a contemporary account of Indian life in Yosemite Valley after the demise of the Yosemites, see Hutchings, *In the Heart*, 421-37.

CHAPTER II

Pioneer Days in Yosemite Valley
(1853-1864)

THE BEGINNING OF TOURISM

After the massacre of Chief Tenieya and his followers by the Monos in the fall of 1853, the surviving Yosemites never regrouped. Instead, just as the Ahwahneechees had done several generations earlier, the few remaining members of Tenieya's band dispersed among their neighbors—some with the Mono Lake Paiutes, others with various Miwok tribes along the Tuolumne River. The last Yosemite Indian died in 1931.

Tenieya's demise encouraged two parties of miners from the North Fork of the Merced River to visit Yosemite Valley late in 1853, according to Lafayette Bunnell. The first group of three Michigan men reported finding some promising ore along the lower Merced River Canyon. "Their glowing descriptions on their return," Bunnell said, "induced five others from the North Fork to visit it also. . . These two parties were the first white men that visited Yosemite Valley after the visit of Lieutenant Moore the year before."[1]

An undocumented account of another 1853 journey to the Valley appears in a brief history accompanying several issues of the *Biennial Report of the Commissioners to Manage the Yosemite Valley and the Mariposa Big Tree Grove*, 1867-1904, as follows: "In 1853 Mr. Robert B. Stinson, then a resident of Mariposa, started out on a hunting expedition with a party of ten others, and in their wanderings in search of game, as well as out of curiosity, penetrated as far as Yosemite, where they spent some time."[2]

Another unsubstantiated report asserts that Robert Lamon, a brother of James Lamon, Yosemite's first full-time white resident, made an 1854 sightseeing trip from Mariposa to the Valley accompanied by five friends and an Indian guide.[3]

A better-validated claim is that of James Capen "Grizzly" Adams, who with two companions passed through Yosemite in the spring of 1854 while on a lengthy hunting trip to the headwaters of the Merced River. The Yosemite Valley scenery, Adams said, "produced impressions on my mind that are ineffaceable."[4]

JAMES HUTCHINGS EXPLORES YOSEMITE VALLEY

Despite these occasional visits, general knowledge about Yosemite's wonders did not spread quickly. The few reports that appeared in San Francisco newspapers focused far more on the difficulties involved in subduing hostile Indians than on the scenery.[5] Nonetheless, the mention in one account of a "waterfall nearly a thousand feet high" caught the attention of a young Englishman named James Mason Hutchings. Hutchings, a gold seeker turned journalist, was in quest of material for a proposed illustrated magazine about California. Needing information and background, he began a twenty-eight-month tour that took him

Indian Squalls, Yo Semite Valley, Cal.

through most of the wild parts of the new state in search of material. When he heard about a waterfall more than six times the height of the famed Niagara, he had to see it.[6]

On July 5, 1855, Hutchings and two companions named Walter Millard and Thomas Ayres (1816–1858) left San Francisco on their way to visit the Calaveras Big Trees, the gold country of Mariposa, and Yosemite Valley. Millard was an old friend from England, Ayres an emerging young scenic artist who had been engaged by Hutchings to make sketches for several contemplated magazine articles about remote places where the clumsy photographic apparatus of the day could not be easily transported. The party reached Mariposa, the end of the stage line, on July 22. The following day they were joined by Alexander Stair of Coulterville, who had been recommended to Hutchings as a reliable companion by George Coulter, founder of the town. (Stair and a partner named James H. Baldrige purchased Coulter's store in January, 1854.)

At Mariposa, Hutchings could find no one who knew how to get to Yosemite Valley, but at length two former members of Tenieya's tribe were hired as guides. On July 25 the group set out on an "enigmatical course" over Chowchilla Mountain, and the following night made camp in the vicinity of present Wawona. The next afternoon, July 27, they reached their destination.[7]

"Descending toward the Yo-Semite Valley, we came upon a high point clear of trees," Hutchings later wrote, "from whence we had our first view of the singular and romantic valley; and as the scene opened in full view before us, we were almost speechless with wondering admiration at its wild and subtle grandeur." The place was Old Inspiration Point on the original Meadows Trail from Wawona.

During the next two days the adventurers explored the Valley "for ten miles, head to head," seeing Mirror Lake, Happy Isles, and Illilouette Fall in the process. Enchanted by the surroundings, Hutchings filled his

Beginning in the 1860s, a small, mixed group of Indians lived seasonally in Yosemite Valley in a rustic camp on the north side of the Merced west of Leidig's Meadow. The men worked as fishermen, woodcutters, and laborers. The women made baskets for sale to tourists and were employed as maids or laundry help at the hotels. J. J. Reilly took this stereo in Yosemite in the early 1870s.

The earliest known photograph of James Mason Hutchings, the publisher-innkeeper who was closely associated with Yosemite for nearly fifty years.

notebook with descriptions of the scenery. Ayres, meanwhile, occupied himself drawing six pencil sketches, four of which Hutchings later used in the first issue of his *California Magazine,* July, 1856, to illustrate an eight-page lead story about Yosemite.[8]

On Monday, July 30, the party reluctantly left the Valley and headed back to civilization. Upon arriving in Mariposa on August 1, Hutchings wrote an enthusiastic account of Yosemite's wonders that appeared in the *Mariposa Gazette* of Friday, August 3. The *San Francisco Chronicle* reprinted the *Gazette* article on August 18, and it was subsequently copied by newspapers around the country.[9]

"The enthusiastic descriptions given by the Hutchings party, on its return, aroused the curiosity of the people, staggered the skeptics, and silenced the croakers," said Lafayette Bunnell in *Discovery of the Yosemite.* "From this period may be dated the commencement of the visits of tourists."

Inspired by Hutchings' glowing report, two other expeditions set out for Yosemite later that August: one, a party of seventeen from Mariposa, included Galen Clark, who would be closely identified with Yosemite for the rest of his long life; the other, a group of adventuresome miners from nearby Sherlock Creek comprising "ten as fearless spirits and noble-hearted fellows as ever shouldered a rifle or gathered around a campfire."[10] Two members of the Sherlock contingent, brothers

Houston and Milton Mann, became so confident of an immediate boom in tourist travel that they began construction of a toll trail from Mariposa to the Valley in the fall of 1855.

The fourth party of that beginning year of Yosemite tourism was led by the Reverend W. A. Scott of San Francisco, who had learned about the Valley first-hand from his friend Hutchings. Among Scott's group of eleven was L. A. Holmes, editor of the *Mariposa Gazette,* who wanted to see for himself what all the excitement was about. After returning to San Francisco, Reverend Scott gave lectures and wrote articles about Yosemite that created considerable attention. "His magnetic enthusiasm," Hutchings said, "largely contributed to the development of an interest in the minds of the public to witness such sublime scenes as those he had so graphically portrayed."[11]

In October, 1855, Hutchings began selling a large lithograph of the "Yo-Hamite Waterfalls" taken from one of Thomas Ayres' sketches. The poster, sixteen by thirty-two inches, was the first artistic representation of any Yosemite scene to reach the public and generated even more curiosity. By the close of 1855, Valley tourism for the year totaled forty-two.[12]

EARLY TRAILS TO YOSEMITE

Although the publicity given the Valley by James Hutchings and others made the outside world aware of Yosemite's wonders in the late 1850s, it failed to spark any great rush of sightseers. Visitation for the decade following the inaugural tourist year of 1855 averaged fewer than eighty-five persons annually.

The major obstacle was the grueling, time-consuming journey required to reach the Valley. From San Francisco, most Yosemite-bound travelers embarked on an all-night, mosquito-plagued ship ride up the San Joaquin River to Stockton. Arriving at 6 a. m., the groggy passengers immediately set out on a jostling, dust-filled one- or two-day stage ride over bumpy foothill roads to the end of the line at Mariposa, Coulterville, or Big Oak Flat, depending on one's itinerary. Then came two or three more days of rigorous horseback riding over steep, narrow trails to reach the rim of Yosemite Valley. The final descent down a chancy cliff-side route to the Valley floor itself gave even the most intrepid traveler cause for concern. One visitor said that he failed to truly appreciate Yosemite because he spent most of his time there worrying about getting back to civilization.[13]

The high cost of the involved journey also deterred many potential tourists. The expense of ship and stage transport, along with the rental of horses, packers, and guides, was considerable. The majority of California visitors felt unable to spend the additional time and money that a Yosemite visit demanded.

Three trails provided the principal access to the Valley until stage roads were completed in the mid-1870s. From the south, brothers

Galen Clark visited Yosemite Valley in August, 1855. He spent most of the next fifty-five years in and near Yosemite Valley, serving twenty-two years as guardian of the Yosemite Grant in two separate terms.

Andrew, Milton, and Houston Mann, operators of a Mariposa livery stable, finished a forty-mile toll horse trail from the end of the road at Mormon Bar on Mariposa Creek to Yosemite Valley early in August, 1856. Two of the brothers had been members of one of the four 1855 tourist parties.

Built at a cost of "between $700 and $1,000," according to Galen Clark, the steep, roughhewn route ran generally east across Chowchilla Mountain to present Wawona, where Clark began operating a way station in April, 1857. From Clark's, the trail turned north and followed Alder Creek to its headwaters. Here it crossed to the Bridalveil Creek drainage, passed through several pleasant meadows, reached its highest point on the south rim of the Valley above Old Inspiration Point, and finally descended sharply to the Valley floor near the foot of Bridalveil Fall.

Tolls set by the Mariposa County Board of Supervisors were one dollar for "man or woman mounted, going and returning," and two dollars for "footmen, going and returning." Walkers were apparently charged more than riders because the Mann brothers gained additional revenue by renting horses and guides. When early travel to Yosemite fell far short of expectations, the Manns sold the rights to their trail to Mariposa County for two hundred dollars in 1860.

On the north side of the Valley, Lafayette Bunnell, George Coulter, and others constructed a trail in 1856 from Black's Ranch on Bull Creek, to which a rough seventeen-mile wagon road had already been built from Coulterville, all the way to Yosemite Valley. The thirty-three-mile route ran northeast from Bull Creek along the Deer Creek drainage to Deer Flat, then turned east through Hazel Green, Crane Flat, and Tamarack Flat to a point later known as Gentry's, from where it twisted down a steep sidehill descent to the Valley floor. Bunnell also blazed an alternate lower trail for use in early spring when heavy snow prevented travel on the shorter but higher route through Tamarack Flat. This trail headed south from Crane Flat down Crane Creek, swung east along a path a full thousand feet lower than the regular trail, and eventually rejoined the upper trail at the Cascade Creek crossing below Tamarack Flat. The seventeen-mile wagon road to the Bull Creek trailhead actually provided no advantage to Yosemite-bound tourists, as horses and guides could be procured only at Coulterville.

The following year (1857) Tom McGee, a local pack train operator, cleared and blazed the

The "Yo-Hamite or Great Falls" drawing by Ayres was made into a lithographed poster by Hutchings in October, 1855, the first artistic representation of Yosemite to reach the public.

western part of the old Mono Trail from Big Oak Flat, ten miles north of Coulterville, to a junction with the Coulterville Trail at Crane Flat and beyond. The thirty-three-mile route headed east from Big Oak Flat through First Garrote (Groveland), Second Garrote, and Hardin's Ranch on the Tuolumne River South Fork, then turned southeast to Crane Flat. From here to Yosemite Valley, fifteen miles distant, the merged trails used a common route. One group called its entire forty-eight-mile length the "Big Oak Flat Trail," while the other contingent referred to its fifty-mile route as the "Coulterville Free Trail." Thus began a competition between the two rival mining communities for Yosemite tourist dollars that continued unabated into the next century.[14]

EARLY OCCUPATION OF YOSEMITE VALLEY

The first shelter constructed by white men in Yosemite Valley was a roofless plank shack erected in the fall of 1855 by a survey party that included Lafayette Bunnell. The survey had been ordered by Colonel John Charles Frémont to determine the feasibility of bringing water from the Merced River to the dry diggings of Frémont's Mariposa Estate.

The builders "supposed that a claim in the valley would doubly secure the water privileges," Bunnell said. "We made this building our headquarters, covering the roof with our tents." In November, the party returned to Mariposa to wait out the winter. Work resumed early the following spring, but it soon became apparent that the scheme was an impractical one. "The difficulties developed by our survey disheartened the claimants," Bunnell said. "The claim rights, as well as the claim shanty were alike abandoned."

There were others besides Bunnell's surveyors in Yosemite during the summer of 1856, and not all of them were men. In July, Madame Gautier, hostess at the Union Hotel in Mariposa, became the first white woman to enter the Valley. The madame and four male companions accomplished the long horseback journey over Chowchilla Mountain from Mariposa with Bunnell himself as their guide.[15] A few days later, Mr. and Mrs. John H. Neal,[16] who would later be employed as Yosemite hotelkeepers, rode in from Mariposa accompanied by a Mrs. Thompson

For twenty-three years following the discovery of Yosemite in 1851, tourists could reach the Valley only by a tiring journey on foot or by horseback. (Author's collection)

of Sherlock Creek. The next year, women made up half of an unusual Yosemite tourist party of eight that was led by James Denman, principal of the first public school in San Francisco. "After this," Bunnell said, "it ceased to be a novelty to see ladies in the Yosemite. . . The fact being published that ladies could safely enter the Valley lessened the dread of Indians and grizzlies, and after a few brave reports had been published, this fear seemed to die away completely."

PRE-EMPTION CLAIMS IN YOSEMITE VALLEY

When California became the thirty-first state in the Union on September 9, 1850, much of the land within its extensive borders belonged to the federal government, which had acquired vast Western tracts from Mexico following the Mexican War of 1846-48. As part of the public domain, these areas were open to claim under the Pre-emption Law of 1841 (not to be confused with the Homestead Act of 1862). The law specified that a person could file a land application on a maximum of 160 acres and immediately occupy the property. If he improved his claim and lived on it for six months, he could buy it from the federal government for $1.25 an acre. This meant that the squatter had a right to buy his land ahead of anyone else.

Technically, the right of pre-emption applied only to surveyed portions of the public domain. Because the government understandably gave priority to the most populous areas, it appeared unlikely that the Sierra Nevada and other remote regions of the state would be surveyed—and thus opened to pre-emption—for some years to come. In 1854, however, the Federal Register for California at Benicia, Colonel William W. Gift, placed a notice in various newspapers in which he explained how to file a pre-emption claim, even on unsurveyed public parcels. According to Colonel Gift, although no regular plat could be registered in the General Land Office, the pre-emptor could enter the metes and bounds of his claim on the records of the county. Such entries, Gift said, would be considered a legal guarantee of title when the land was eventually surveyed, assuming all other requirements had been fulfilled.

"Under this impression," James Hutchings said, "settlements were made, titles respected, and frequent transfers of such titles given from one to the other, without their validity being questioned."[17]

Between August 23, 1856, and May 28, 1862, nine pre-emption claims of a quarter-section each were filed with Mariposa County on acreage within Yosemite Valley. A number of other claims were also staked out, but never entered on the county records. By 1862, nearly all of the best areas on the floor of the Valley had been appropriated by pre-emptors.[18]

THE LOWER HOTEL

In May, 1856, "four gentlemen—Judge B. S. Walworth, of New York; John C. Anderson, of Illinois; W. C. Walling, of Pennsylvania; and I. A. Epperson, of Indiana; all single"—took up claims in Yosemite Valley and began living there.[19] The men were most likely miners from the surrounding area who saw an opportunity to capitalize on Yosemite's potential as a tourist attraction. They soon started construction of an eighteen-by-twenty-foot building made from riven pine boards to be used as a stopping place for Valley visitors.[20] (The following year, others undertook a second establishment about seven-tenths of a mile east, so the first became, quite naturally, the "Lower Hotel," and the second, the "Upper Hotel.")

A brief description of the Lower Hotel project appeared as part of a lengthy article in the San Francisco *Daily Alta California* of August 6, 1856, written by Thomas Ayres, the artist who had accompanied James Hutchings on his pioneering expedition to Yosemite the previous year. Ayres made a return visit to the Valley in July, 1856, via the newly opened Coulterville Trail ("good though very steep"), accompanied by George Coulter's son, a lad of about thirteen.

"We rode slowly and almost reverentially along the base of El Capitan," Ayres said, "and fording the river beyond, reached the camp of Judge Walworth, directly opposite the 'High Fall,' where we remained during our sojourn in the Yohemity. The Judge and his companions, Messrs. Anderson, Walling, and Epperson, have located lands and partially completed a frame house, which is to be enlarged and opened for the accommodation of visitors early next season. Looking from the edge of the grove in rear of the house, we obtain a full view of the High Falls, which are the great feature of the valley as far as waterfalls are concerned..."

J. C. Simmons, a Methodist preacher, provides another report of the hotel undertaking in an account reprinted by the *Mariposa Gazette* on October 15, 1856: "Entering the valley on the morning of September 24," Simmons said, "I and the Messrs. Mann here found four men engaged in sawing lumber with a whip-saw for a house they intend erecting next spring for the accommodation of visitors—a very good and wise arrangement. All who go there now have to sleep in the open air—ladies and all.

"We enjoyed the hospitality of Judge Wallworth [*sic*] and companions today at dinner. They treated us to a fine mess of turnips grown in the valley... We found the Yo Semite Indians all gone. As one belonging to another tribe told us, 'Yo Semite Indians fight too much. All dead.' I know of but one of the tribe still living."

On August 23, 1856, Ben S. Walworth, who seems to have been the leader of the foursome of Yosemite settlers, filed a 160-acre claim with Mariposa County on a location "nearly opposite the falls."[21] The tract surrounded the impending hotel structure, which was situated about seven hundred yards east of Sentinel Creek on the south side of the Merced River below Sentinel Rock. Construction ceased on the building late in 1856 when the onset of winter drove out all Valley occupants, save two latecomers: Stephen M. Cunningham, a Bull Creek miner of "good intelligence," and an unidentified white companion (Hutchings says it was Buck Beardsley, a fellow Bull Creek miner). Cunningham journeyed to Yosemite in November, 1856, seeking opportunity, after hearing stories about the Valley's unique wonders.[22] He described his experiences in a letter to his parents dated August 20, 1857, (punctuation added):

"I started for the valley last November. It is situate on the head waters of the Merced River near the summit of the Sierra Nevada mountains. I arrived here about 1st of Dec. last, when a heavey snow storm set in

Descending the steep trails into Yosemite Valley from the rim was a precarious, nerve-racking experience for visitors.

and I could not get out untill the March following. There was not so mutch snow here in the valley but on the high lands between here and the settlements. I fortunately brought plenty of flour with me, and as game & fish are plenty here, I passed the winter pleasantly. There was but one white man with me, but many Indians about, who were friendly and have been of great service to me. This place I had described to me by the Indians and some few white men who had been here, and I determined to take up a preemption claim, which I have done and have made some improvements—not for the purpose of liveing here but to sell as soon as I can find a customer, as it is my earnest wish and I know my duty to come home to you. . ."

If Cunningham staked out a claim as he reports in his letter, he failed to follow up by entering it on the county records.[23] Hutchings said that Cunningham's "improvements" consisted of a rustic shake cabin erected a short distance east of Walworth's building, which he planned to use as a store. The cabin was afterward occupied temporarily by various artists, including Thomas Hill and William Keith.

By the summer of 1857, Walworth's box-like structure was sufficiently completed to he opened for business, although who operated the primitive facility is uncertain. Galen Clark said the place functioned mainly as a saloon "for that class of visitors who loved whiskey and the sport of gambling." Sometime before the following season (1858), Cunningham apparently bought into the Walworth claim, perhaps in partnership with John Anderson, the only one of the original foursome who seems still to have been involved.[24] John and Jean Frances Neal of Mariposa were hired to manage the operation. John had recently lost his jewelry business to fire; Jean Frances was the second white woman to enter Yosemite.

One early visitor described his stop with the Neals as follows: "I secured a bed, such as it was, for my wife, in a rough board shanty occupied by a family that had arrived a few days before to keep a sort of tavern, the woman being the only one within fifty or sixty miles of the place. For myself, a bed of shavings and a blanket under the branches of some trees formed my resting place."

Another 1858 Yosemite tourist, using the initials "J.W.O.," told the *Tuolumne Courier* of Columbia that he arrived at "Neal's Hotel" at two o'clock in the afternoon of July 17 and was given a "bower tent" to sleep in, prepared by the hospitality of the "accommodating host, John Neal." That evening, J.W.O. said, Cunningham entertained the guests by telling the legend of Tissiack (Half Dome).

By the spring of 1859, Cunningham and Anderson had made some improvements to their enterprise (the Neals lasted only one season as managers). On June 25, 1859, the *Tuolumne Courier* reported:

"Yo-Semite House—This splendid establishment under the management of Messrs. Cunningham and Anderson is now a full tide of success. The visitors at the falls are larger in number than in any previous season, attracted by the scenery in the neighborhood. All of the fashion and all of the notabilities of the state, and of other states, are seen there from time to time. Col. Fremont and Jessie will be there next week. Every accommodation possible is given to visitors, and all the appoint-

Mrs. John Neal, one of the first three white women to enter the Valley, managed the Lower Hotel in 1858 with her husband.

In the early 1860s, Carleton Watkins photographed this crude shack built with a splendid view of Yosemite Falls.

The ferryman awaits the return of his scow (note the heavy rope) at the Valley ferry in the 1860s.

Stephen M. Cunningham spent the winter of 1856-57 in Yosemite Valley. He subsequently became actively involved in the settlement of the Valley.

The original Lower Hotel building had been enlarged and improved when this photograph was taken by Watkins about 1863.

ments of a first-rate hotel are found in Yo-Semite House."

The *Courier's* laudatory review of the "Yo-Semite House" facilities may have been a bit overstated, as witness this account from a visitor a year or two later:

"Our bedroom . . . consisted of a quarter of a shed screened off by split planks, which rose about eight or ten feet from the ground, and enabled us to hear everything that went on in the other 'rooms,' which were simply stalls in the same shed. Ours had no window, but we could see the stars through the roof. The door, opening out into the forest, was fastened with cow-hinges of skin with the hair on, and a little leather strap which hooked on to a nail. . ."

Charles Weed photographed Gus Hite's rustic Upper Hotel in June, 1859, soon after it opened for business. Note the absence of doors and window glass.

The enterprising Cunningham also operated a ferry across the Merced River near the foot of the Coulterville-Big Oak Flat Trail in Yosemite Valley during this period (his application for a ferry license appeared in the *Mariposa Gazette* of July 14, 1858). James S. Hutchinson, member of a prominent San Francisco-area family, described Cunningham's ferry in a letter to his father dated June 7, 1859:

"Entering the valley we found three men engaged in adjusting the last rope to a flat boat for the purposes of a ferry. In fifteen minutes they had earned the first fruits of their enterprise—one dollar from each of us ferriage. The party who had preceded us had been compelled to leave their animals and cross the river in a canoe.

"Half a mile brought us to the camp of an old mountaineer who has laid a pre-emption claim in the valley and built the ferry boat and the ladders in use at the falls. Here was our destination right in front of the Great Fall and amid its deafening thunders. We returned to camp just at dark and sat around the campfire to dry off and to listen to some of Cunningham's adventures as related by himself."[25]

Cunningham seems to have operated the barn-like Lower Hotel alone in 1860 (Hutchings names him as the proprietor in the March, 1860, issue of his *California Magazine*). Sometime in the summer of 1861, Cunningham sold his Yosemite interests to Alexander Gordon Black, a Coulterville-area entrepreneur who owned a store and stopping place known as Black's Ranch near the head of the Coulterville Trail at Bull Creek.[26]

During the ensuing five years, Black leased the hotel intermittently to Peter Longhurst, a weather-beaten ex-miner turned Yosemite pioneer, and perhaps others. The premises were reported "unoccupied" by a Valley visitor in July, 1861, and J. D. Whitney said the building stood vacant for "several seasons."[27] Longhurst was definitely the manager in 1864, however, when Clarence King arrived with the California Geological Survey. King's account in *Mountaineering in the Sierra Nevada*

Thomas Starr King wrote a series of newspaper articles describing Yosemite's beauty in 1861. They attracted national attention to the Valley.

James Lamon was Yosemite Valley's first permanent white settler. John Muir called him "a fine, erect, whole-souled man . . . with a broad, open face, bland and guileless as his pet oxen."

eloquently describes Longhurst's performance as a flapjack fryer at breakfast. In 1866, a Mariposa County miner named George Frederick Leidig, a short, thickset German, and his young wife Isabella, an excellent cook and housekeeper, took over the operation of the Lower Hotel and began a four-year stint as managers for Black.

THE UPPER HOTEL

The first Yosemite "hotel" to actually receive overnight guests opened for business in the spring of 1857. On June 8, 1857, Gustavus Adolphus Hite, a saloonkeeper at Whittier's Hotel in Agua Fria, filed a pre-emption claim on 160 acres of Yosemite Valley land with Mariposa County and immediately erected a large blue canvas tent near the present Sentinel Bridge about seven-tenths of a mile up-river from the Lower Hotel.[28] Hite was an older brother of John Hite, who became a millionaire after discovering gold in 1862 at what is now known as Hite's Cove on the Merced South Fork. On June 19, 1857, the *Mariposa Gazette* carried the following short notice: "Messrs. Weaver and Hite have established a house in the valley where they are prepared to entertain visitors with eatables, drinkables, lodging, and general accommodations." (The name "Weaver" is most likely a misnomer. Both Bunnell and Hutchings say that Buck Beardsley, Cunningham's companion from Bull Creek, was Hite's principal associate in the Upper Hotel enterprise.)

In the spring of 1858, Hite began construction of an imposing twenty-by-sixty-foot two-story building of which each plank, rafter, and joist was laboriously whipsawed by hand from local timber. Everything else needed for the project had to be carried fifty miles by pack mule from the nearest supply point. In May, 1859, the rectangular structure, which had cost Hite about three thousand dollars to build and equip (including a crude log bridge across the Merced River), was finally ready for guests, although the rustic hostelry was far from complete. The two floors contained no partitions (ladies up, gentlemen down), and the various door and window openings were covered with cotton cloth. Among the earliest customers were James Hutchings, making his second visit to the Valley, and Charles Weed, an enterprising photographer who packed his bulky camera equipment across the mountains to take the first photographs of Yosemite scenes. Hutchings wrote about the event in the December, 1859, issue of his *California Magazine.*

Unfortunately for Hite and his associates, patronage at the new hotel failed to come close to expectations, and they found themselves unable to meet the obligation of the construction debt after only a single season. Early in 1860 the property was acquired at public auction by the firm of Sullivan & Cashman of Mariposa, holders of the lien.[29] The new owners leased out the premises in 1860 and '61 to Charles Peck, and later to Peter Longhurst. While Peck was in charge, Thomas Starr King, the noted Unitarian minister and lecturer, visited Yosemite and subsequently wrote a series of eight expressive letters to the *Boston Evening Transcript* describing the Valley's beauty. This was the first comprehensive account of Yosemite's unique attributes to reach widespread national circulation. On January 26, 1861, the *Transcript* carried King's account of his stay at the Upper Hotel—the "Shanty Hotel," as he called it.

"The hall upstairs is not finished off into chambers," King wrote, "but has spaces of eight feet square divided by cotton screens, within which beds without sheets are laid upon the bare floor. There are two rooms below which have beds on posts, and furniture for ladies. But what care we for rooms and furniture, when the windows are open, and we look out upon that opposite wall and the marvelous cascade, whose glorious music floods the air?

"'Mr. Peck, can you give us a broiled chicken, some bread and butter, and a cup of tea with fresh milk and cream?' Clover grows six feet tall on the Yo-Semite meadows, but landlord Peck replies, 'Gentlemen, I have no milk, for I do not keep a cow. There is no butter in the house, and chickens were never seen here.' What, o *Transcript,* do you think our meal consisted of? Stewed oysters and lobster! I hold up my pen and make oath. Among those wilds of the Sierra we had on the table oysters and lobster from New York, with a bottle of Boston pickles. And the shellfish were cooked for us by a Chinaman! The crustaces finding their way from the Atlantic, and the cook from the Pacific, to that magnificent glen so lately the undisturbed camp of the grizzlies. Is it not a sign of the Union which California is destined yet to celebrate between the remote East and West?"

In the spring of 1864, three years after selling his *California Magazine,* James Hutchings entered into the Yosemite hotel business by purchasing the Upper Hotel from Sullivan and Cashman for twelve hundred dollars. The transaction included the rights to Gus Hite's 160-acre pre-emp-

J. J. Reilly photographed Lamon about 1870 in front of his first cabin near the present concessioner-operated stables. The remains of the structure were removed in 1907 after the army took over administration of the Valley.

tion claim, which straddled the Merced River. Besides the hotel structure itself, there were also on the premises a "horse, outhouses, and a fence enclosing about three acres." Hutchings subsequently obtained a quitclaim deed, dated February 8, 1865, from Peter Longhurst for four hundred dollars, which covered Longhurst's 160-acre claim and other interests. Hutchings apparently planned to consolidate the two claims into the most desirable 160-acre piece, as pre-emption was limited to a single quarter-section per person.

On or about May 29, 1864, Hutchings arrived in the Valley with his wife Elvira and mother-in-law Florantha Sproat to take possession of his new enterprise. In August, Elvira gave birth to the couple's first child, a girl named Florence, the first white child born in Yosemite Valley. During the ensuing eleven years, the "Hutchings House," as the Upper Hotel soon became known, was a principal Yosemite stopping place.[30]

THE FIRST PERMANENT WHITE SETTLER

The first white man to live year-round in Yosemite Valley was James Chenowith Lamon (pronounced "Lemon"). Born in Virginia in 1817, the fifth of fourteen children, Lamon emigrated to Illinois with his family in 1835, then moved on to Texas with a brother four years later. Arriving in California in 1850, Lamon worked for a time in the gold fields of Calaveras and Mariposa Counties. In 1852 he joined one David Clark in a steam sawmill and wholesale lumber business on Bear Creek, about five miles north of Mariposa. Although the operation achieved fair financial success, the partners parted acrimoniously after their uninsured mill burned to the ground in 1858.[31]

Lamon said he made his first journey to Yosemite on or about April 18, 1859.[32] He worked for Gus Hite for part of that summer on the construction of the Upper Hotel before buying several unregistered claims from Milton Mann and others in the upper end of the Valley. He also filed a 160-acre pre-emption claim with Mariposa County in his own name on May 17, 1861. In the fall of 1859, Lamon began work on a ten-by-twelve-foot cabin built of logs and shakes, finishing it the following spring. He subsequently set out two four-acre orchards with some five hundred assorted fruit trees in each (the first adjoined his cabin east of the present Valley stables, the second stood in what is now the Camp Curry parking area); planted berry bushes and a vegetable garden; sowed crops; dug irrigation ditches; and added outbuildings and fences. Between 1859 and 1862, he spent his summers in Yosemite and his winters in the foothills. When he was absent from the Valley, he hid his tools in a cave.

In 1862-63 Lamon passed the winter entirely alone in Yosemite Valley. During that season, he found to his dismay that his cabin received little direct sunlight because of the long shadows cast by the south side cliffs. Before the second winter, which he also passed by himself, Lamon built a second log cabin—his "winter cabin," eight feet by ten feet with a basement—on the sunny north side of the Valley under Royal Arches. Lamon supported himself by selling the products of his orchards and garden to hotelkeepers and tourists. He kept a fine pair of big red oxen, "Dave" and "Brownie," with which he did plowing and cultivating, and hauled logs.[33]

By the close of 1864, thirteen years after its effective discovery by non-Indians, Yosemite Valley had attained a permanent white population of five persons: the Hutchings family and James Lamon.

NOTES AND REFERENCES

1. Lafayette H. Bunnell, *Discovery of the Yosemite and the Indian War of 1851 Which Led to That Event,* 4th ed. (1911; reprint, with a preface by Hank Johnston, Yosemite: Yosemite Association, 1990), 266-67.

2. No information about the Stinson journey—which very well may be apocryphal—seems to exist except for the brief notice in the *Biennial Report.* The account appeared verbatim in the *Sacramento Daily Record-Union* on January 30, 1886, undoubtedly reprinted from the *Biennial Report.*

3. Robert Bruce Lamon was born in Virginia in 1829. He emigrated to California in 1850, and later represented the Mariposa district in the California state legislature. He left California about 1858, studied law in the Midwest, and served as a judge in both Illinois and Washington, D. C. He visited Yosemite in the early 1890s, and died in 1899 in Washington. His claim of seeing Yosemite Valley in 1854 remains unverified (see note 32).

4. Theodore H. Hittell, *The Adventures of James Capen Adams, Mountaineer and Grizzly Bear Hunter of California* (1860; reprint, New York: Charles Scribner's Sons, 1911), 190.

5. According to Bunnell, *Discovery of Yosemite,* the miners who made up the Mariposa Battalion paid little attention to the Valley's physical wonders. Their purpose was to subdue the Indians as quickly as possible and get back to prospecting before the gold played out. As one member of the battalion later remarked: "If I'd known the valley was going to be so famous, I'd have looked at it."

6. James Mason Hutchings (1824-1902) was born in England. He received a good education in literature, history, and the sciences; left England in 1848 seeking adventure in America; came to California upon news of the gold strike, arriving at Hangtown (now Placerville) in October, 1849. After enduring the "ups and downs of mining," Hutchings became an editor with the *Placerville Herald* in 1853. The popularity of a newspaper column parodying the Fourth Commandment induced Hutchings to publish a treatise called "The Miner's Ten Commandments," which sold nearly one hundred thousand copies in letter sheet form within the first year after publication. Believing that an illustrated magazine about California supplying the public with "solid information" would be well received, he began monthly publication of *Hutchings' California Magazine* in July, 1856, and continued for sixty issues through June, 1861.

Hutchings gathered extracts from his magazine and issued them in book form in 1860. Called *Scenes of Wonder and Curiosity in California,* the hardback volume was advertised as a guidebook to Yosemite Valley, the Big Trees of the Mariposa and Fresno Groves, and other natural wonders of California. The book found a steady market, and Hutchings put out a number of editions between 1860 and 1876. In 1886 he published the book that crowned his writing career—*In the Heart of the Sierras*—a 496-page volume devoted almost entirely to Yosemite. A biography of Hutchings appears in Hank Johnston, *Yosemite's Yesterdays Volume II* (Yosemite: Flying Spur Press, 1991), 14-29.

7. In his book *In the Heart of the Sierras* (Oakland and Yosemite: Pacific Press Publishing House, 1886), Hutchings inexplicably gives dates for his historic 1855 Yosemite Valley visit that are different from those entered in his diary for that year. The diary dates, which are unquestionably correct, are used in this volume. "Diary of James Hutchings," 1855, copy in the Yosemite Research Library.

8. Thomas A. Ayres (often misspelled "Ayers"), a native of New Jersey, arrived by ship at San Francisco on August 8, 1849. He turned to art after an unprofitable attempt at mining. Ayres visited Yosemite Valley again in the summer of 1856, as described later in this chapter, and made additional drawings on his own behalf. Ayres drowned on April 28, 1858, when a ship on which he had taken passage from San Pedro to San Francisco capsized off the Farallon Islands.

9. Apparently no copy of that *Mariposa Gazette* is still in existence. The August 18, 1855, *Chronicle* article has been reprinted in Peter Browning, *Yosemite Place Names* (Lafayette, CA: Great West Books, 1988), 213-15, and other publications.

10. For a description of this excursion by a member of the party, see James H. Lawrence, "Discovery of the Nevada Fall," *Overland Monthly,* 2d ser., 4 (October 1884): 360. The title is a misnomer. Bunnell, *Discovery of Yosemite,* 81, describes how members of the Mariposa Battalion saw Nevada Fall in 1851.

11. One of Scott's accounts appeared in the *Sacramento Daily Union,* December 18, 1855.

12. Bunnell, *Discovery of Yosemite,* 275-76, said that a party of at least six men, including himself, worked on a water-survey project in Yosemite Valley for the Frémont interests near Mariposa during late 1855, and erected a crude, roofless structure. Because they were not tourists in the strictest sense, and because their exact number is uncertain, Bunnell's group is not included in the forty-two-person total for 1855.

13. There are a number of contemporary descriptions of the tribulations involved in traveling to Yosemite during this period. A detailed account of the several routes is given in James Hutchings, *Scenes of Wonder and Curiosity in California* (San Francisco: Hutchings & Rosenfeld, 1860), and later editions.

14. Further information on early Yosemite trail building can be found in Johnston, *Yosemite Yesterdays II,* 30-35.

15. An account of Madame Gautier's journey was published in the *Mariposa Democrat* on August 5, 1856. It was probably written by Warren Baer, one of the editors of the *Democrat* and a member of the madame's party. The *Democrat* repeated the article on July 23, 1857 (see note 20).

16. The name is spelled both "Neal" and "Neil" in early accounts. It also appears as "Neale" in a series of advertisements for John's Mariposa jewelry store in the *Mariposa Chronicle* in 1854, which may have been a professional affectation. Neal signed Snow's Hotel register in 1874 as "John H. Neal."

17. Hutchings, *In the Heart,* 102.

18. Pre-emption claims listed in the Mariposa County Land Claims book for the period are as follows: Ben S. Walworth, August 23, 1856; I. A. Epperson, August 30, 1856; H. G. Coward, May 18, 1857; G. A. Hite, June 8, 1857; J. Louis MacCabe, November 17, 1860; S. M. Cunningham, December 18, 1860; James C. Lamon, May 17, 1861; A. G. Black, August 23, 1861; and Peter Longhurst, May 28, 1862. Because most of the landmarks used to describe the metes and bounds of the nine pre-emption claims have little relevance today, the precise location of the various properties is uncertain ("Commencing at a blazed pine tree marked with a notice, and continuing northeast to a crotched oak tree, etc.").

In their *Biennial Report* for 1874-75, the Yosemite commissioners said, "Numerous parties laid claim to various portions of the valley. Most of these so-called claims were of the most ridiculous and shadowy description. Persons had gone in during the summer months hunting, or in search of adventure, had been attracted by the beauties of the valley, thought vaguely money was to be made out of it by some means of another, and therefore affixed the usual notice, as is done so frequently in the case of 'mining claims,' that the undersigned 'claimed one hundred and sixty acres of land,' etc. Many of these claims were never followed up by any residence, and were completely abandoned; others were kept alive by a residence during the summer months, either by the parties who originally took up the ground or by others to whom they had transferred their 'claim' generally, for either a gambling or liquor debt; and on one occasion, in the year 1862, as the Commissioners understand, the whole valley was put up for a raffle, and raffled away at a dollar a chance." (The "raffle" proposition seems unlikely to have taken place. By 1862 the claimants who owned the Upper and Lower Hotels, as well as James Lamon with his cabins and orchards, would hardly have agreed to such a scheme.)

19. The quotation about the quartet of settlers appeared in *The Country Gentleman* (Albany, N.Y.), October 9, 1856.

20. The *Mariposa Democrat* article of August 5, 1856, describing Madame Gautier's visit to the Valley includes this statement about the construction of the Lower Hotel: "At the base of this huge monster [Sentinel Rock] stands a board house, of eighteen by twenty feet in length, without floor or chimney. Near this house we stopped for the night and prepared our supper, which we ate with a hearty good relish; and after tracing the dim white line of the Yosemite Falls, which front the house on the north . . . we closed our eyes for the night."

21. Information about "Judge" Ben S. Walworth is sparse. Both Bunnell and Hutchings mention his name in connection with the building of the Lower Hotel (Hutchings calls him "Walsworth"), but provide no further details. Walworth evidently departed the Valley sometime before 1858.

22. Stephen Mandeville Cunningham (1820-1899), a native of New York State, came to California around the Horn in 1849 after a brief hitch in the U. S. Army during the Mexican War. He mined intermittently in various parts of the Mother Lode between 1849 and 1856; served for a time as a justice of the peace in Mariposa County; occupied himself with his Yosemite projects until 1861 or '62; volunteered for duty with the Union Army during the Civil War (December, 1864, until July, 1865); then returned to California and resumed mining in the Coarse Gold Gulch-Wawona area. On April 12, 1870, Cunningham filed a homestead claim on 160 acres in Little Yosemite Valley, which he subsequently failed to prove up. In 1869-70, he and Albert Snow combined on a toll trail from the bottom of Vernal Fall to the foot of Nevada Fall. After another period at mining, he was appointed sub-guardian of the Mariposa Grove in August, 1881. About that time, Cunningham took up a homestead claim on 160 acres at the mouth of Rush Creek near the north end of the present Wawona Campground and eventually built a substantial eighteen-by-twenty-one-foot cabin of yellow pine logs that fronted on the South Fork. He acquired a deed to the property on July 12, 1894.

During the tourist season, Cunningham divided his time between his homestead and a small cabin constructed in 1864 by Galen Clark in the Mariposa Grove, which was enlarged and improved in 1885. As his position as sub-guardian paid only $150 annually, he augmented his meager income by making curios out of sequoia wood and selling them to visitors. He also received a small income from lodging laborers who opened and repaired the roads in the grove. Reportedly a heavy drinker, Cunningham shared his homestead with an Indian woman known as "Short and Dirty" for years. Beset by ill health in the fall of 1898, Cunningham entered Sawtelle Veterans Hospital in Los Angeles on October 5. He died on July 3, 1899, and was buried on the hospital grounds. His homestead, called "Cunningham Flat," passed to a relative. It was later acquired by Henry Washburn at a delinquent tax sale and became part of the Washburn holdings at Wawona. The remains of Cunningham's decaying cabin were obliterated when a new campground was constructed in the area in 1951.

23. Cunningham's pre-emption claim of December 18, 1860, was in the Bridalveil Meadow area at the extreme west end of the Valley. It had nothing to do with his interest in the Lower Hotel. A copy of his letter to his parents is in the Cunningham file in the Yosemite Research Library.

24. John C. Anderson (1822-1867), a native of Illinois, came west during the Gold Rush. He arrived in Yosemite Valley in 1856 and became active in the building of the Lower Hotel. He continued to live in the Yosemite area until his death on July 13, 1867, when he was kicked by a horse or mule and killed. First buried at the foot of the Four Mile Trail, his remains were later moved to the Yosemite cemetery after that location was established in the early 1870s. An ornate marble headstone marks his grave.

Tradition has it that Anderson's green locust-wood switch was stuck in the ground to mark his original grave, that it took root, and that the locust trees now common in the Valley are all descendants of Anderson's switch.

25. Letter from James S. Hutchinson to his father, June 7, 1859, copy in the Yosemite Research Library.

26. Besides buying out Cunningham's interest in the Lower Hotel, Black must have also taken over Cunningham's pre-emption claim at the west end of the Valley (see notes 18 and 23). Black filed a claim with Mariposa County on August 23, 1861, and the description he gives of the metes and bounds of the property is identical to Cunningham's claim.

27. Josiah Dwight Whitney, *The Yosemite Guide-Book* (Sacramento: Geological Survey of California, 1869).

28. The "blue canvas tent" is mentioned by both Bunnell, *Discovery of Yosemite,* 280, and Hutchings, *In the Heart,* 109.

29. "C. D. O'Sullivan is a member of one of our first and most enterprising business firms and a resident of the County since 1850," said the *Mariposa Chronicle* in June, 1854. "He and his partner Michael Cashman have erected a large and commodious warehouse on Main Street, and plan the establishment of a new commercial house in San Francisco, which will be one of the heaviest business houses of this state." The *Chronicle* carried a series of advertisements for Sullivan & Cashman during 1854 ("Goods come direct from New York and Boston to our store").

30. In his book *In the Heart of the Sierras* (1886), Hutchings states that he arrived in Yosemite to take up hotelkeeping on April 20, 1864. In a much earlier article in the *Mariposa Gazette* (January 18, 1868), Hutchings says he arrived on May 29, which is probably the correct date.

31. In 1858 Lamon published an "open letter" in which he called David Clark a "rogue, perjurer, and scoundrel" and accused him of doctoring the company books for his own benefit, copy in the Yosemite Research Library.

32. According to a letter written to Cosie Hutchings, James Hutchings' younger daughter, in 1932 by Judson A. Lamon, a son of Robert Lamon and nephew of James, James Lamon learned of the Valley from his brother Robert, who claimed to have visited Yosemite in 1854 (see note 3). A copy of the Lamon letter is in the Lamon file in the Yosemite Research Library.

33. Lamon's winter cabin is described in Hutchings, *In the Heart,* 136-37, and John Muir, *The Yosemite* (New York: The Century Co., 1912), 238-239.

Establishment of the Yosemite Grant
(1864)

DISCOVERY OF THE GIANT SEQUOIAS

California's famous Big Trees occur naturally only in a series of more than seventy groves that stretch along the Sierra Nevada from the American River on the north to Tulare County on the south. (It is true that sequoias have been growing in other parts of the world for more than a century, but all originally derived from California seeds or seedlings.)

The first public mention of the Big Trees appeared in Zenas Leonard's report of the Walker party's 1833 trek across a portion of what is now Yosemite National Park, as related in Chapter I. Leonard wrote that the group encountered some trees "of the Redwood species, incredibly large"—undoubtedly the *Sequoia gigantea* of either the Tuolumne Grove or the Merced Grove, possibly both. Leonard's account received only limited distribution, and the discovery went virtually unnoticed at the time.

According to Lafayette Bunnell, James Burney, who became the first sheriff of Mariposa County in 1850, and three companions passed by a "few scattering" Big Trees on the "Fresno and South Fork divide" in October, 1849, while pursuing animals stolen by Indians. Burney thought the trees were a new variety of cedar and did not consider them especially remarkable, for he had seen accounts of even taller trees growing in Oregon.[1]

Robert Eccleston, the Mariposa Battalion's singular diarist, recorded the following entry under the date of April 19, 1851: "We saw a noble Redwood tree on the mountain which would measure all of 60 ft close to the ground & 4 ft from the ground about 50 ft. It tapered slowly til over half way up & it was of majestic height."[2]

The trees seen by Burney and Eccleston were probably outliers of the Fresno Grove, situated a few miles south of present Yosemite National Park. Unfortunately, the region was so heavily logged by the Madera Flume and Trading Company during the late nineteenth century that there is little likelihood that anything more than the stumps of these early discoveries survived.[3]

The first public awareness of the existence of the Big Trees came in the spring of 1852 when Augustus T. Dowd, a hunter employed by a canal company working on a water project near Murphy's Camp, Calaveras County, stumbled on the *Sequoia gigantea* of the Calaveras Grove. Word quickly spread that a modern miracle had been uncovered.[4]

"But a short time was allowed to elapse after the discovery of this remarkable grove," said James Hutchings, "before the trumpet-tongued press proclaimed the wonder to all sections of the state, and to all parts of the world, and the lovers of the marvelous began first to doubt, then

to believe, and afterwards to flock to see with their own eyes the objects of which they had heard so much."[5]

THE MARIPOSA GROVE

Stephen Grover, one of the Coarse Gold Gulch miners attacked by Yosemite Indians in May, 1852, wrote in his "Reminiscence" that his party passed through the Mariposa Grove both going and coming on their Yosemite trip. In retrospect, it seems doubtful that Grover's claim can be true. The Mariposa Grove would have been considerably out of the way for the group, especially on the return trip. Moreover, none of Grover's contemporaries ever mentioned seeing the Big Trees, an event that would have been important news at the time. Perhaps Grover saw some very large cedars near Miami Mills and later assumed that he had traveled through the Mariposa Grove on his ill-fated journey.[6]

In the summer of 1855, Richard H. Ogg (1824–1857), a hunter for the Mariposa Ditch Company, discovered three monstrous trees deep in the mountains near the Merced South Fork.[7] Ogg subsequently reported his sighting to Galen Clark, Milton Mann, and others. Clark kept a sharp watch for Ogg's three giants during his explorations of the area in 1856–57. Finally, in late May or early June, 1857, Clark and Mann

The Big Trees of the Mariposa Grove were discovered by Galen Clark and Milton Mann in 1857. (Author's collection)

suddenly came upon a whole grove of Big Trees while on a hunting trip southeast of Clark's claim. The two men gazed in astonishment at the hundreds of huge sequoias, many of which had already been living for thousands of years.

Mann immediately began, and shortly completed, a trail to the grove, hoping thus to attract additional Yosemite tourists to his Mariposa toll trail. Within weeks, Clark located two distinct groves and counted the trees in each. He reported that the Upper Grove held 265 large sequoias, the Lower Grove, 241. Several months later, Clark also found the three trees described by hunter Ogg in a gulch some distance from their fellows. "As all the giants were in Mariposa County," Clark later recalled, "I named them the Mariposa Grove of Big Trees."[8]

THE TUOLUMNE GROVE

On May 10, 1858, Dr. J. L. Cogswell and eight companions apparently became the first non-Indians—with the probable exception of the Walker party—to view the Tuolumne Grove of Big Trees. Cogswell's group had departed Garrote (Groveland) two days earlier on a sightseeing excursion to Yosemite Valley. While making camp in the vicinity of Crane Flat the second evening, one of the company shot a deer, but the wounded animal managed to escape in the gathering darkness. After breakfast the next morning, the party set out on the trail of the deer. The track led them north up the hill from Crane Flat, then topping the rise, took them down the opposite slope. Still intent upon the chase, the men came abruptly upon a small group of about ten magnificent Big Trees. Their discovery so impressed them that they forgot about the deer and spent the rest of the day exploring the area, eventually finding more than twenty sequoias.

One immense dead specimen drew particular attention. Although entirely denuded of bark, the huge bole still measured nearly thirty feet in diameter (experts estimate that the tree exceeded 120 feet in circumference in its prime). The base of the trunk contained a great hollowed-out cavity that had been blackened to charcoal.[9] Some distance above, the trunk split into two tall spire-like sections—the scorched and shattered remains of untold centuries of lightning strikes and forest fires. Dr. Cogswell's party named the tree "King Solomon's Temple," but in 1878 it became generally known as the "Dead Giant." The discovery was quickly reported to the newspapers, and the Tuolumne Grove, as it eventually was called, soon turned into a favored side trip for Yosemite-bound travelers.[10]

The "Dead Giant" in the Tuolumne Grove in 1928. The tunnel was cut through the bole in 1878 (described in Chapter VI).

THE MERCED GROVE

The identity of the first non-Indians to see this small group of about twenty-five large sequoias is uncertain. The Walker party may have viewed the trees in 1833. The earliest documented visit occurred in the summer of 1872 when surveyors for the Coulterville Road came across the grove while charting a new route to Yosemite Valley. Dr. John Taylor McLean, builder of the road, said he chose the name "Merced Grove" because of the proximity of the Merced River.[11]

YOSEMITE GAINS INCREASED RECOGNITION

By the early 1860s, the descriptive writings of James Hutchings, Thomas Starr King, and noted *New York Tribune* editor Horace Greeley had generated national interest in Yosemite. Greeley, who made a hurried trip West in 1859, was so impressed with the scenery that he called the Valley the "greatest marvel of the continent" and urged that the state of California provide immediately for the safety of the Mariposa Grove of Big Trees.

During this pioneering period, two adventurous photographers named Charles Weed and Carleton Watkins laboriously packed their bulky equipment across the mountains to Yosemite at separate times and provided the public with the first photographic evidence of the Valley's unique grandeur. Making a photograph in those days was a complicated procedure. A portable developing tent had to be set up near the proposed picture site. There in semi-darkness the photographer sensitized a

The Merced Grove, a small group of about twenty-five large sequoias, is situated two air miles southwest of Crane Flat. (Hank Johnston)

polished glass plate by coating it with a syrupy "collodion" emulsion. When the collodion reached the proper point of tackiness, the plate was transported in a light-proof holder to the waiting camera, and exposed for a few minutes to an hour or more, depending on the light. The plate was then hastily returned to the darkroom to be developed into a glass negative before the emulsion dried. For obvious reasons, the involved operation was known as the "wet-plate process."

In June, 1859, Weed accompanied James Hutchings' party to the grand opening of the Upper Hotel. Hutchings was seeking source material for his *California Magazine*. Weed's assignment was to take a "Yosemite Panorama" of ten-by-thirteen-inch photographs, which he and associate Robert H. Vance exhibited to great acclaim a few weeks later at Vance's San Francisco gallery. During his five-day visit, Weed made about twenty large glass negatives and forty stereographs of such diverse subjects as the Upper Hotel, Nevada Fall, and the Grizzly Giant in the Mariposa Grove. Weed's photographs also provided a basis for the illustrative engravings that later accompanied five Yosemite articles in *Hutchings' California Magazine*.[12]

Weed's historic first pictures have never received the attention they probably deserve because their quality was so quickly exceeded by the work of Watkins, another San Francisco photographer. Watkins, who made his first photographs of Yosemite in 1861, used a twelve-mule pack train to transport his supplies and equipment, which included a giant eighteen-by-twenty-two-inch camera capable of producing "mammoth-plate" pictures. The large-size prints were a real innovation in that early period of photography when the technique of making enlargements from small negatives had not yet been perfected. Watkins' mammoth-plate views captured the scale and majesty of the impressive Sierra scenery far better than Weed's and established a new standard in nineteenth-century landscape photography. By 1863, they were constantly on exhibition in leading New York art galleries.[13]

ENACTMENT OF THE YOSEMITE GRANT

Public parks have existed in this country almost since the beginning of colonization. Most were originally planned as parade grounds or pastures, or to serve recreational purposes. As time went by, landscaped gardens similar to those in England, France, and Germany became popular. Before 1864, however, no public reservation had ever been set aside purely for the purpose of preserving and protecting the natural scenery for the enjoyment of the citizenry. Therefore, in February of that Civil War year when the proposal was advanced to establish Yosemite Valley and the Mariposa Grove as a pleasuring ground for all the people, the concept was unprecedented.

The principal advocate of the idea was Captain Israel Ward Raymond, the California representative of the Central American Steamship Transit Company of New York. Raymond (1811–1887) first came to California in 1850 and again, permanently, to San Francisco in 1862. He visited Yosemite Valley and was struck by its singular beauty. A public-spirited citizen, he was alarmed by the trend toward private exploitation in the Valley and the threatened destruction of its trees. On February 20, 1864, Raymond addressed a decisive letter to the junior senator from

Englishman Eadweard Muybridge, who began photographing Yosemite in 1867, took this picture of his "Flying Studio," consisting of a portable developing tent and an assortment of boxes and bottles.

Carleton Watkins made this self-portrait while seated in the cave at the foot of Upper Yosemite Fall about 1867. The small peaked canvas enclosure behind him is his developing tent.

Captain Israel Ward Raymond originated the Yosemite Grant idea.

California Senator John Conness (1821–1909) introduced the historic Yosemite Grant bill in the United States Senate. Conness was a member of the California legislature in 1853–54 and again in 1860–61 before serving as U. S. Senator in 1863–69. Mount Conness in the High Sierra was named for him by the Whitney Survey in 1863 because "he deserves, more than any other person, the credit of carrying the bill organizing the Geological Survey of California through the Legislature."

California, John Conness, urging Congress to grant to the state of California "that cleft or Gorge in the granite peak of the Sierra Nevada . . . known as the Yo Semite Valley . . . to prevent occupation and especially to preserve the trees." Further, he asked that the Mariposa Grove of Big Trees be similarly conferred.

In his letter, Raymond furnished much of the description and language that was later used in the actual legislation, including the extraordinary proviso that the property be granted to the state for "public use, resort, and recreation . . . inalienable forever."[14] He also had the foresight to send Conness a set of Watkins' mammoth-plate views, which demonstrated the uniqueness of the Yosemite landscape more graphically than any words.

Senator Conness forwarded Raymond's letter to the Commissioner of the General Land Office (GLO) asking him to devise suitable legislation to carry out the proposal. The GLO promptly provided the desired material, and on March 28, 1864, Conness introduced the historic Yosemite Grant bill in the Senate. The Senate Committee on Public Lands reported favorably on the measure on May 17. Conness then asked for its immediate consideration and was granted his request.

The proposition had come to him, the Senator told his colleagues in an eloquent speech, "from various gentlemen of California, gentlemen of fortune, of taste, and of refinement." The sole objective of the bill, Conness said, was the "preservation of the Yosemite Valley and the Big Tree Grove . . . for the benefit of mankind." He emphasized that the area contained nothing of commercial value and would not require an appropriation from the federal government. No mention was made of the nine pre-emption claims, two hotels, and assorted other structures that had already been in place in Yosemite Valley for some years.

The bill passed the Senate with little discussion, went to the House Committee on Public Lands on June 2, passed the House on June 29, and was signed into law by President Abraham Lincoln on June 30, 1864. The act stipulated that the Yosemite Grant be managed by a board of nine commissioners, serving without compensation, who would be appointed by and include the governor of California.[15]

Other than I. W. Raymond, we know very little about the identity of the "gentlemen of fortune, of taste, and of refinement" to whom Conness referred in his presentation. Although no testimony has been found regarding their participation, the most likely candidates are the men Raymond and Conness suggested as prospective Yosemite commissioners in their proposal to the General Land Office. Raymond nominated George W. Coulter, founder of Coulterville, and Josiah D. Whitney, the California State Geologist. Conness added Raymond's name, along with Professor John F. Morse, a well-respected physician from San Francisco, and Stephen J. Field, a former member of the state legislature who was then chief justice of the California Supreme Court and later an associate justice of the U. S. Supreme Court.

Raymond also recommended Frederick Law Olmsted, co-developer of New York City's Central Park and one of the foremost landscape planners in the country, as a commissioner. Olmsted had come to nearby Bear Valley, California, in October, 1863, to manage the gold mines on John C. Frémont's former 44,386-acre Mariposa Estate for the new Eastern owners of the property, but according to the compilers of Olmsted's voluminous papers, he had no part in advancing the Yosemite legislation:

Frederick Law Olmsted was twenty-eight years old when this portrait was taken in 1850. Eight years later he began the development of New York's Central Park.

"It has often been assumed that Olmsted was one of these gentlemen, but the editors have found no evidence to support the claim. Olmsted made no reference to the Yosemite Grant in any surviving correspondence prior to his report to his father on October 16, 1864, that he had been appointed to the commission, and he said nothing in that letter about being previously involved in any way. Moreover, he gave no indication in any later correspondence that he had played a role in creating the reservation. Olmsted could not have had firsthand knowledge of the scenery at the time Raymond sent his proposal to Conness. Although Olmsted visited the Mariposa Big Tree Grove in November, 1863, he did not reach the Valley until [six weeks] after Congress authorized cession of the land to the state of California in June. Raymond's letter to Conness did propose that Olmsted be appointed a member of the commission, but Olmsted's reputation as a landscape architect would have been sufficient reason for that."[16]

ACCEPTANCE OF THE YOSEMITE GRANT

The Yosemite Grant Act, as legislated by Congress, consisted of two parts: Section 1 (called the Yosemite Valley Grant) comprised 36,111.14 acres (about fifty-six and one-half square miles) in and around the Valley itself; Section 2 (called the Mariposa Grove Grant), a noncontiguous area of 2,589.26 acres (four square miles) about twelve and one-half air miles to the south, contained the Mariposa Big Trees. The total reserved territory was 38,700.4 acres in all, or more than sixty square miles.

Because the terms of the grant required acceptance by the California legislature, which met only every other year and had already adjourned until early 1866, Governor Frederick F. Low issued an interim proclamation of the state's approval on September 28, 1864, and appointed the eight other commissioners mandated by the act. They were William Ashburner, mining engineer and former member of the California Geological Survey;[17] Alexander Deering, lawyer and one-time Mariposa County district attorney (later district court judge); Erastus Saurin Holden, druggist and mayor of Stockton, 1859–61; George W. Coulter; I. W. Raymond;[18] Galen Clark; J. D. Whitney;[19] and Frederick Law Olmsted.[20] The governor served as the ninth member *ex officio*. On April 2, 1866, the legislature officially accepted the grant for the state of California and ratified the governor's actions.[21]

SIGNIFICANCE OF THE YOSEMITE GRANT

Although the act setting aside the Yosemite Grant as a trust for the state of California was the first instance anywhere in the world of a central government preserving an area purely for the protection of scenic values and the pleasure of the people as a whole, it caused little stir at the time in a nation deeply involved in a terrible war. Only in more recent years has the unique import of the 1864 legislation been accorded due recognition by historians. As one writer put it: "It is clear now that the reservation of Yosemite marked perhaps the most significant event in the changing relationship of Americans to the land they live on.[22]

The Yosemite Grant was far more than just the first state park. It was really the birth of the whole national park idea.[23]

NOTES AND REFERENCES

1. Lafayette H. Bunnell, *Discovery of the Yosemite and the Indian War of 1851 Which Led to That Event,* 4th ed. (1911; reprint, with a preface by Hank Johnston, Yosemite: Yosemite Association, 1990), 300–1.

2. *The Mariposa Indian War, 1850–51. Diaries of Robert Eccleston: The California Gold Rush, Yosemite, and the High Sierra,* ed. C. Gregory Crampton (Salt Lake City: University of Utah Press, 1957), 66.

3. The activities of the Madera Flume and Trading Company and its successor operation are described in Hank Johnston, *Thunder in the Mountains,* 2d ed. (Glendale, CA: Trans-Anglo Books, 1985).

4. From a dated inscription carved on one of the trees and additional sources, it appears likely that at least two other non-Indians preceded Dowd in exploring the Calaveras Grove. An in-depth discussion of the matter can be found in Rodney Sykes Ellsworth, "Discovery of the Big Trees of California" (master's thesis, University of California, Berkeley, 1933). Regardless of who was first, however, it was Dowd's discovery that brought the Big Trees to the attention of the world.

5. Hutchings tells of Dowd's adventure in several of his publications, notably *Hutchings' California Magazine* (March, 1859); *Scenes of Wonder and Curiosity in California* (San Francisco: Hutchings & Rosenfeld, 1860); and *In the Heart of the Sierras* (Oakland and Yosemite: Pacific Press Publishing House, 1886).

6. Grover's account is examined in Hank Johnston, "The Mystery Buried in Bridalveil Meadow," parts 1 and 2, *Yosemite* 54, no. 2 (spring 1992): 1–6; no. 3 (summer 1992): 11–13.

7. In their accounts of this incident, both Bunnell and Hutchings call the hunter "Mr. Hogg." The name, however, is correctly spelled "Ogg." Information about Ogg is sketchy, but it is known that he was dead by the time Clark and Mann discovered the Mariposa Grove in the spring of 1857.

8. What criterion Clark used to count his "large sequoias" is not clear. In 1867 the California Geological Survey reported that there were 365 Big Trees "over one foot in diameter in the main grove, besides a great number of smaller ones." Other non-Indians may have seen the Mariposa Grove before Clark and Mann came upon the Big Trees. Clark himself said that he found the "remains of a well-equipped miner's camp very near the grove." Clark's long and interesting life is described in Shirley Sargent, *Galen Clark, Yosemite Guardian* (Yosemite: Flying Spur Press, 1981).

9. Some writers have stated that the great burns in the bases of many of the sequoias were caused by years of Indian campfires ("the vandal hands of Indians," Hutchings said), but there is no proof of this. Most authorities are now persuaded that the blackened areas are the result of innumerable natural fires over the centuries.

10. A report of the Cogswell party's discovery appeared first in the San Francisco *Daily Evening Bulletin* of May 17, 1858. The *Mariposa Gazette* and other area newspapers soon carried stories that corroborated the find. The Tuolumne Grove was known as the "Crane Flat Grove" for some years. It is so designated in J. D. Whitney, *The Yosemite Guide-Book* (Sacramento: California Geological Survey, 1869).

11. The Merced Grove is situated about six air miles north of the Merced River and about two air miles southwest of Crane Flat.

12. Born in New York State, Charles Leander Weed (1824–1908) was working as a photographer in Sacramento by 1854, and in early 1858 took charge of a branch studio in that city run by Robert H. Vance, San Francisco's leading daguerreotyper. Before his Yosemite trip, Weed successfully tested the new "wet-plate process" on a field trip up the American River. Weed made a second trip to Yosemite Valley in 1864, this time with a "mammoth plate" camera and took a number of views, of which twenty-nine signed photographs are now in the New York Public Library. In 1865 he left San Francisco for Hawaii, then journeyed on to Hong Kong and perhaps Europe before returning to San Francisco in 1871. After a brief association with a number of San Francisco photographic studios during the 1870s, Weed turned to photoengraving about 1880, a profession he practiced until his death in Oakland.

13. Carleton E. Watkins (1829–1916), the son of a New York State innkeeper, came to California during the 1849 gold rush. By 1853 he was employed as a carpenter in Sacramento. The next year he moved to San Francisco and, like Weed, became acquainted with Robert Vance, who hired him as a temporary employee at Vance's branch studio in San Jose. Although he knew nothing about photography, Watkins quickly mastered the technique of making daguerreotype portraits after some basic instruction from Vance.

Intrigued by the potential of the new "wet-plate process," Watkins eventually turned to large-scale scenic photography and soon received international recognition for his panoramic Yosemite prints. In 1867 he opened his Yosemite Art Gallery in San Francisco. When the studio prospered, he undertook a series of extensive field trips into Oregon, Utah, and the Cascades in search of new subjects. He also returned again and again to photograph Yosemite.

A poor businessman, Watkins lost his studio and most of his prints and negatives to creditors during the financial panic of 1873–74, including more than a hundred mammoth plates and nearly two thousand stereographs of Yosemite. Undaunted, Watkins gamely began revisiting the Valley in a determined effort to reproduce all his earlier views. Labeling his work "Watkins' New Series," he was successfully back in business with another San Francisco gallery by 1880.

During the next decade, Watkins' eyesight began to fail and his photography gradually came to an end. One last disaster remained for Watkins: the great fire that followed the San Francisco earthquake of 1906 demolished his studio and burned up all his remaining prints and negatives. A helpless old man unable to function on his own, Watkins spent the final six years of his life in the state hospital at Napa, California. Mount Watkins in the Yosemite high country honors his memory.

14. Raymond's letter to Conness is reproduced in full in Hans Huth, "Yosemite: The Story of an Idea," *Sierra Club Bulletin* 33, no. 3 (March 1948): 47–78.

15. The Yosemite Grant Act of June 30, 1864, is reprinted as Appendix B.

16. Frederick Law Olmsted, *The Papers of Frederick Law Olmsted, Volume V, The California Frontier, 1863–65,* ed. Victoria Post Ranney (Baltimore: Johns Hopkins University Press, 1990), 513.

17. William Ashburner (1831–1887) grew up in Stockbridge, Massachusetts, and studied at the Lawrence Scientific School of Harvard and in Paris. He joined the California Geological Survey as a field assistant in 1860. After steady field work proved too strenuous for his health, Ashburner opened private practice in 1862 as a confidential mining consultant for some of the leading bankers of San Francisco. In later life he was a professor and regent at the University of California and a trustee at Stanford University. Frederick Law Olmsted, who worked with Ashburner during the first year of the Yosemite Board of Commissioners, called him "a very nice fellow, cheerful and unobtrusive."

18. Mount Raymond, elevation 8,546 feet, a few miles east of the Mariposa Grove, was named for Israel Ward Raymond by the Whitney Survey.

19. Josiah Dwight Whitney (1819–1896) was a native of Massachusetts and a graduate of Yale. He received some European education and subsequently engaged in geological surveys in New Hampshire, Iowa, and Wisconsin. A man of high reputation in his field, Whitney was named state geologist of California by an act of the state legislature, approved April 21, 1860, with authority to appoint his assistants. The California Geological Survey, which provided the first extensive mapping of the Sierra Nevada, functioned until 1874, when antagonism developed between Professor Whitney and Governor Newton Booth.

Despite his scientific training—or perhaps because of it—Whitney gave some very wrong geological opinions over the years, most notably in his public disagreements with John Muir about the formation of Yosemite Valley. Nonetheless, he made important contributions to earth science during his California tenure and later served as professor of geology at Harvard. Mount Whitney, elevation 14,495 feet, in the southern Sierra, the highest mountain in the contiguous forty-eight states, is named in his memory.

20. Frederick Law Olmsted (1822–1903) was born in Hartford, Connecticut; attended lectures at Yale University (childhood eye problems prevented regular college study); traveled widely observing horticultural techniques in other countries; and eventually took up farming and gardening on Staten Island. In 1858 he was appointed superintendent of Central Park, then under development in New York City, after his design was selected in competition with about thirty others. With partner Calvert Vaux, Olmsted prepared a compre-

hensive plan for the park that was for the most part carried out. This was the first great park in the United States and is an excellent example of Olmsted's skill. After a disagreement with the park board, he resigned in 1861 and became head of the U. S. Sanitary Commission, the largest charitable organization in the history of the country, overseeing the health of the volunteers in the Union army.

On August 10, 1863, Olmsted accepted the position of superintendent of John C. Frémont's Mariposa Estate and embarked for California to assume his new job the following month. (His California experiences are described in Chapter IV.) Olmsted returned to New York in November, 1865, and again joined with Vaux in the development of Central Park. He later designed the park system and Capitol grounds in Washington, D. C.; laid out the grounds for the World's Columbian Exposition in 1893; and in all, planned more than eighty important public parks in major cities across the country.

Olmsted married Mary Perkins, the widow of his younger brother John, who died of tuberculosis in 1857, thereby becoming stepfather as well as uncle to his brother's three children. He and Mary later had children of their own, one of whom was Frederick Law Olmsted, Jr. (1870–1957), who also distinguished himself as a landscape architect and city planner. In 1928 the younger Olmsted was appointed chairman of the National Park Board of Expert Advisors for Yosemite and served with distinction until his death. A viewpoint on the Tioga Road about one and one-half miles southwest of Tenaya Lake was designated "Olmsted Point" by Superintendent John Preston in 1961 in recognition of the Olmsted family's contributions to Yosemite.

21. The state legislature's act of acceptance of the Yosemite Grant is reprinted as Appendix C.

22. Harold Gilliam, "Centennial of a Pioneer's Dream," *San Francisco Chronicle* (June 28, 1964).

23. It seems to have been presumed by all concerned with the 1864 legislation that state administration of the Yosemite Grant was the proper way to accomplish the desired purpose. At that time, the federal government's policy was to pass the burden and expense of management of areas in the public domain to the citizens of the states involved wherever possible. That Yellowstone was set aside only eight years later, in 1872, as the first *designated* national park does not necessarily represent a change of position by Congress in this regard. Nor should it in any way diminish Yosemite's claim as the first park. Wyoming did not achieve statehood until 1890, and there was no effective local government in the territory at the time to assume responsibility for the property. Its reservation by the federal government was therefore deemed the only practical method of attaining the objective. Congress promptly proved its lack of interest in its new scenic wonder by providing it with no appropriations whatsoever for the first five years of its existence.

Early Years of the Yosemite Grant
(1864–1874)

FREDERICK LAW OLMSTED: THE FIRST ADMINISTRATOR

During the eighteen months between Governor Low's proclamation of acceptance of the Yosemite Grant and the state legislature's ratification of the act, the duly appointed Yosemite Board of Commissioners existed more or less in name only—a group with no ability to requisition funds and no legal authority to enforce rules and regulations.[1] Nonetheless, Frederick Law Olmsted, the functional head of the board, took his unspecified responsibilities seriously, making a number of fact-finding visits to the Mariposa Grove and Yosemite Valley during 1864–65. He also assumed the task of drawing up a comprehensive management plan for the state's new preserve. Although Olmsted was never officially designated "chairman" of the commissioners, his name led the list of appointees, and he was singled out in the governor's proclamation of September, 1864, as the one to whom "all propositions for the improvement of the aforesaid tracts of land or for leases should be made."

In the summer of 1864, the foothill heat engendered by a severe California drought prompted Olmsted to take his family into the nearby Sierra on a seven-week camping trip. The elaborate party that departed the Mariposa Estate on July 14 comprised Olmsted and his wife Mary; the couple's four children, aged two to eleven; Harriet Errington, the children's English governess; Bell, a black combination cook, groom, and guide; and soon-to-be fellow Yosemite commissioner William Ashburner and his wife Emilia. It required twenty-one horses and mules to transport the travelers and their baggage to a base camp of four tents set up in a dusty meadow near Galen Clark's station on the Merced South Fork. Here the group remained for a month, during which time Olmsted visited the Mariposa Grove on at least four occasions ("exploring, and measuring cones and stumps") and also rode with Clark to the Fresno Big Trees fourteen miles to the southeast.

"We live mainly on trout and mutton, several flocks having been sent up here from the plains," Olmsted said in a letter to a friend on July 24. "We share our water privileges with a few Indian families—perfect savages scarcely at all touched by civilization."

On August 14, Olmsted entered Yosemite Valley for the first time and established a permanent camp somewhere opposite Yosemite Falls. Nine days later, on one of his several hurried trips back to Mariposa to attend to business affairs, Olmsted met William Brewer, the thirty-five-year-old field director of the California Geological Survey, at Clark's Station and arranged a mutual excursion into the high country above the Valley. On August 28, Brewer, Olmsted, and Olmsted's eleven-year-old stepson John Charles rode up the Coulterville Trail to Crane Flat, turned east along the old Mono Trail, and eventually reached Tuolumne Meadows. They continued on nearly to the summit of the peak just south of

Mount Dana and named it Mount Gibbs for Olmsted's friend Oliver Wolcott Gibbs (1822–1908), professor of science at Harvard. The travelers came back to Yosemite Valley on September 2 by way of Cathedral Peak and Nevada Fall. Their guide on the six-day junket was Stephen Cunningham, a recent returnee from Civil War duty. According to Brewer, Cunningham "knew all the localities."

On September 28, 1864, even before formal word of his appointment reached him in Bear Valley, Olmsted hired at his own expense two young members of Brewer's geological survey crew to survey and map the boundaries of the Yosemite Grant, as required under the federal act, before winter snows set in. "We have no money," Olmsted wrote his father, "but I have got a surveying party at work on the chance of being paid two years hence by the legislature." The surveyors were James Gardner[2] and his friend Clarence King, both twenty-two-year-old former students at Yale's Sheffield Scientific School who had traveled overland to California the previous summer. With some expedient field work, Gardner and King completed their task of running a boundary survey around Yosemite's walls before the first big winter storm drove them out in November. The scale map drawn by Gardner from the party's notes was engraved and first published in 1865. It was subsequently reproduced in *The Yosemite Book* (1868) and *The Yosemite Guide-Book* (1869).[3]

Frederick Law Olmsted, Mary Perkins Olmsted, and Schuyler Colfax were photographed in 1865 by Carleton Watkins near their camp in Yosemite Valley.

Clarence King worked with James Gardner to establish the boundaries of the Yosemite Grant in 1864. His survey of the Valley floor was subsequently called "a complete sham" by State Geologist J. D. Whitney.

By the end of 1864, Olmsted's position as superintendent of the Mariposa Estate had become extremely tenuous. Because of matters largely beyond his control, the company was deeply in debt; employees, including Olmsted himself, had gone unpaid for many weeks; and day-to-day operations were virtually at a standstill. On January 9, 1865, Olmsted arrived in San Francisco to await instructions and working capital from his superiors in New York. When word finally came in April, Olmsted received the disheartening news that his salary had been suspended and he was to come home at once.[4]

Ignoring the order, Olmsted remained in California for another six months. In the interim, he worked on his management plan for the Yosemite Grant and finished up two independent landscaping projects—a cemetery and a college in Oakland. Early in July he returned to the Valley to receive the first Eastern dignitaries to visit the new park. They were Schuyler Colfax,[5] Indiana congressman and Speaker of the House, and a party of friends from the East and from San Francisco. Included in the group of three women and seventeen men were Samuel Bowles, publisher of the *Springfield Republican;* Albert D. Richardson, distinguished war correspondent for the *New York Tribune;* Charles Allen, attorney general of Massachusetts; and William Bross, lieutenant governor of Illinois and senior editor of the *Chicago Tribune.*

The Easterners had traveled across the plains to California over the recently established overland mail route "simply to see the country and to study its resources." Bowles, who had been interested in the Yosemite legislation, later wrote favorably about the grant: "The wise cession and dedication by Congress and proposed improvement by California. . . furnishes an admirable example for other objects of natural curiosity and popular interest all over the Union."

On August 7, after camping with his family for two weeks along the Merced South Fork, Olmsted met informally with Commissioners Galen Clark and William Ashburner at Clark's Station. Two days later, on August 9, 1865, he read his Yosemite report to Commissioners Clark, Ashburner, George Coulter, and Alexander Deering at his camp in the Valley. Despite its somewhat labored syntax, the fifty-two-page, nearly eight-thousand-word treatise was an extraordinary document, one that went far beyond the business at hand in its philosophical scope.[6]

OLMSTED'S REPORT ON THE YOSEMITE VALLEY AND THE MARIPOSA GROVE

"It is the main duty of government, if it is not the sole duty of government," Olmsted said, "to provide means of protection for all its citizens in the pursuit of happiness against the obstacles, otherwise insurmountable, which the selfishness of individuals or combinations of individuals is liable to interpose to that pursuit."

Olmsted noted that although the rich were able to furnish their own recreational opportunities, it was the government's obligation to set aside and safeguard "natural scenes of an impressive character" where the great body of its citizens could go for contemplation and relief from ordinary cares. He described in a lengthy passage how such activity would benefit man's physical and mental well-being.

"It employs the mind without fatigue," Olmsted said, "and yet exercises it; tranquilizes it and yet enlivens it; and thus, through the influence of the mind over the body, gives the effect of refreshing rest and reinvigoration of the whole system."

Olmsted then became more specific about the state's responsibilities concerning the Yosemite Grant. "The main duty with which the commissioners should be charged," Olmsted said, "should be to give every advantage practicable to the mass of the people to benefit by that which is peculiar to this ground and which has caused Congress to treat it differently from other parts of the public domain. This peculiarity consists wholly in its natural scenery. The first point to be kept in mind then is the preservation and maintenance as exactly as is possible of the natural scenery; the restriction, that is to say, within the narrowest limits consistent with the necessary accommodations of visitors, of all artificial constructions and the prevention of all constructions markedly inharmonious with the scenery or which would unnecessarily obscure, distort, or detract from the dignity of the scenery."

Olmsted predicted with remarkable prescience that although present

William Ashburner was a Yosemite commissioner and a member of the three-man Executive Committee from 1864 until 1880. He also served as secretary of the board between 1868 and 1880.

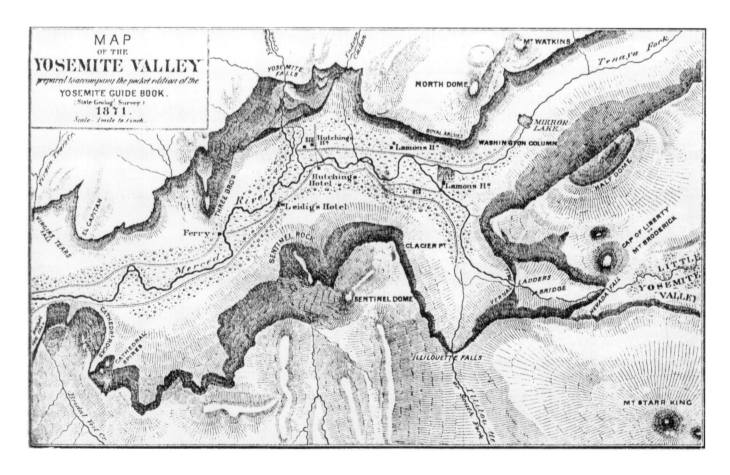

visitation totaled only a few hundred persons each year, it would eventually "become thousands, and in a century the whole number of visitors will be counted by the millions. An injury to the scene so slight that it may he unheeded by any visitor now, will be one of deplorable magnitude when its effect upon each visitor's enjoyment is multiplied by these millions."

Olmsted recommended that a high, scenic access road be built to Yosemite Valley and asked for an appropriation of twenty-five thousand dollars to aid in its construction.[7] The road would connect with the Mariposa Grove and be carried completely around it as a "barrier of bare ground to the approach of fires."

Within the Valley itself, Olmsted proposed to lay out a double trail that would make a complete circuit of the broader parts of the Valley, "reaching all the finer points of view to which it can be carried without great expense." Such a trail could be easily made suitable for vehicles when the access road was completed. For accommodations, Olmsted advocated spending two thousand dollars for the erection of five cabins at "points in the valley conveniently near to those most frequented by visitors. . . These cabins would be let to tenants with the condition that they should have constantly open one comfortable room as a free resting place for visitors, with the proper private accommodations for women, and that they should keep constantly on hand in another room a supply of certain simple necessities for camping parties, including tents, cooking utensils and provisions. . ." Olmsted asked that thirty-seven thousand dollars be appropriated by the legislature at its earliest opportunity to carry out his proposals. As it turned out, the large amount of the request proved to be the major undoing of his plan.

Three days after presenting his report, Olmsted departed Yosemite Valley, never to return.[8] On October 13, 1865, he set sail from San Francisco for New York to rejoin partner Calvert Vaux in the further development of Central Park. Olmsted resigned from the Yosemite Board of Commissioners in October, 1866, and was replaced by Henry Cleaveland.[9]

Late in November, 1865, Commissioners Ashburner, Whitney, and Raymond met in unofficial executive session in San Francisco to discuss the merits of Olmsted's Yosemite plan and decide whether or not to push for its implementation. They came to the unanimous conclusion, as stated in their letter to Governor Frederick Low on November 29, "that it is not expedient at present to lay the report before the legislature [which was going through a period of severe budget cutting resulting from the near bankruptcy of the state government], or to call for an appropriation so large as $37,000, the sum demanded by Mr. Olmsted."[10] The governor evidently concurred with their opinion, for Olmsted's proposal never went beyond his office. (In both 1867 and 1869, the legislature refused to make any appropriation to meet the grant's basic requirements, even though the commissioners requested $5,000 on each occasion.)

Other factors besides its high cost may have contributed to the pigeonholing of Olmsted's plan. His recommendation that the present board of commissioners immediately resign to be superseded by a

The Colfax party in Yosemite Valley in July, 1865. Samuel Bowles stands at top left; Schuyler Colfax sits third from left in the middle row; Frederick Law Olmsted, fifth from left in middle row; William Bross, third from right in middle row; Mary Perkins Olmsted, third from left in front row; William Ashburner to her left; Albert Richardson to Ashburner's left.

This map of Yosemite Valley appeared in the 1871 edition of The Yosemite Guide-Book. *It is a corrected version of King and Gardner's original 1865 map, which had errors in the meanders of the Merced River.*

A party of tourists stands for the camera in the meadow across from Yosemite Falls on June 20, 1870.

new board—selected annually and not restricted to California citizens, of which at least four of the eight members must be "students of natural science or landscape artists"—would not have appealed to Ashburner, Whitney, and Raymond, who took considerable pride in their Yosemite appointments. Moreover, Olmsted's lengthy treatise failed to address, except in a most general way, the problem of what to do about the hotels, cabins, and other claims that were extant in Yosemite Valley before state ownership. During the grant's formative years, the subordination of private holdings to the public interest turned out to be the commissioners' biggest headache.[11]

THE COMMISSIONERS TAKE CONTROL

On May 21, 1866, seven weeks after the legislature validated the state's acceptance of the Yosemite Grant, the Yosemite Board of Commissioners held its first official meeting in San Francisco. The commissioners elected officers (the governor was named president *ex officio*), formulated by-laws,[12] and "resolved that Galen Clark be appointed Guardian of the Yosemite Valley and Big Tree Grove with power to appoint a sub-Guardian of the Valley, and that the combined salaries of said Guardian and sub-Guardian be five hundred dollars ($500) per annum," the maximum authorized by the legislature.

The board drew up an eight-page handwritten letter of instructions detailing Clark's responsibilities: to patrol and prevent depredations; build roads, trails, and bridges and maintain them; bestow and regulate leases for hotels and other concessions; use the income from these rentals for improvements; and serve as the commissioners' liaison with local residents. Clark afterward hired former innkeeper Peter Longhurst as sub-guardian to supervise the Valley; he himself took responsibility for the Mariposa Grove, which was near his residence and business on the South Fork.

In the act accepting the grant, the legislature appropriated two thousand dollars from the state treasury for the two-year period beginning July 1, 1866, to cover the guardian's salary and the incidental expenses of the commissioners. The board used the residue of the fund to reimburse Olmsted, make minor trail improvements, and build two bridges across the Merced River: one where the Coulterville Trail entered the Valley near the foot of El Capitan; the second above Vernal Fall at the Silver Apron, which facilitated the trip to the bottom of Nevada Fall. The Valley bridge was swept away during the great winter of 1867–68 when high water destroyed every bridge on the lower Merced River.[13]

The act also authorized the state geologist to further explore the grant and the surrounding Sierra Nevada "as may be necessary to enable him to prepare a full description and accurate statistical report of the same." Two editions of a book resulted from the survey. The first, called *The Yosemite Book* (1868), with twenty-eight photographs (twenty-four by Carleton Watkins), was limited to 250 copies, "as only a small number of prints could be obtained from the photographic artist." The second, *The Yosemite Guide-Book* (1869 and later editions), printed without photographs, was intended as a general guide to the Valley and surrounding mountains (see note 3).

For the next forty years, the commissioners met annually each fall in

James Hutchings battled the Yosemite commissioners in the courts for nearly a decade in an effort to sustain his Valley claim.

San Francisco (later changed to each June in Yosemite Valley) and occasionally at other times throughout the year. Most of the routine business was handled by the Executive Committee, which held informal sessions in San Francisco as often as two or three times a month.[14]

This enlargement of a section of the frontispiece shows James Hutchings sitting on the rock in the center of the picture. Wife Elvira leans against the building to his immediate left. The date is probably 1865.

LEGISLATION AND LAWSUITS CONCERNING SETTLERS' CLAIMS

Charged by Congress with preserving the Yosemite Grant for "public use, resort, and recreation. . . inalienable for all time," the commissioners faced the immediate predicament of how best to deal with three individuals who had taken up or purchased pre-emption claims in the Valley before the land was set aside by federal decree. They were James Lamon, who began full-time residency in Yosemite in 1862; James M. Hutchings, proprietor of the Upper Hotel since May, 1864; and Alex G. Black, who bought the Lower Hotel from Steve Cunningham in 1861. Others had also filed on quarter sections before state ownership, as described in Chapter II, but these claims were either sold or abandoned prior to 1864.

The commissioners conceded that Hutchings and Lamon would eventually have been able to consummate their claims had Yosemite not been withdrawn from the public domain. Black's rights were less certain because he had leased out his property rather than living on it as required by the pre-emption law. Recognizing that Lamon and Hutchings had

Elvira Sproat Hutchings (1842–1917) rests in the manzanita armchair made by husband James. The chair was willed to daughter Cosie by Hutchings. Cosie donated it to the Yosemite Museum in 1941. James Garfield, Horace Greeley, Ralph Waldo Emerson, Helen Hunt Jackson, Joseph LeConte, and many other notables sat in this chair during their Yosemite visits.

Taken when she was about fifteen, this is the last known photograph of Florence (Floy) Hutchings. Florence died in an accident in Yosemite (described in Chapter VI). (Shirley Sargent collection)

significant investments in their holdings, the board was sympathetically disposed to grant the two men the most generous terms permissible under the Yosemite act. In Lamon's case, his upper Valley location was relatively inconspicuous, and his fruit had "found a ready market in the valley among the visitors." The commissioners therefore offered him a ten-year lease on his premises for the token sum of one dollar a year.

As for Hutchings, knowing that his hotel—even though it occupied a prime location—was not a very lucrative enterprise, the board offered him a similar ten-year lease of his land and buildings "at a mere nominal rent." Hutchings, however, insisting that he held valid claim to his property, stubbornly refused the commissioners' accommodating proposition and persuaded Lamon to do the same.

"The Board," Hutchings said, "notified Mr. J. C. Lamon and myself—the only *bona fide* settlers—that we must take a lease of the premises occupied by us from them, on or before a given time; or, failing to do this, they would lease them to other parties, 'and early in the ensuing spring take all necessary measures for installing the new tenants into possession.'

"Under the beguiling hallucination that the Preémption Laws of the United States were a sacred contract between the Government and the citizen, I took the liberty of notifying the Secretary of the Board, in reply, that in my judgment it would be time enough for the Commissioners of the Yo Semite Valley to exercise authority over my house, or my horse, or anything I possessed, *after* they had proved a better title to either than I had."[15]

Hutchings' intractability impelled the commissioners to file a suit of

ejectment against him and Lamon in 1867 as a test case for all land claims in the Valley. In their *Biennial Report* for 1866–67, the commissioners said they "had no alternative but to begin legal proceedings against both these gentlemen as trespassers."

Faced with possible expulsion from their homes, Hutchings and Lamon took their case to the state legislature, asking that it grant them title to the land they occupied in Yosemite Valley under the federal Preemption Law and the Possessory Law of California. In February, 1868, both the state house and senate overwhelmingly passed Assembly Bill 238, which awarded Hutchings and Lamon full possession of their 160–acre claims subject to approval by Congress. The act contained the proviso that the state could lay out roads, bridges, paths, and anything else necessary for the convenience of tourists.

Governor Henry H. Haight, the *ex officio* president of the Yosemite Board of Commissioners, vetoed the bill in a strongly worded message. Haight called it "a repudiation by the state of a trust deliberately accepted for public purposes, and an appropriation of the whole Yosemite Valley to private ownership." Unpersuaded by the governor's words, the legislature easily carried the measure over his veto in March, 1868, and petitioned Congress for ratification.

The act also enjoined California Surveyor General John W. Bost to determine the exact boundaries of the settlers' claims. Bost reported that Hutchings' plat was laid out in the form of a cross to include good meadowlands, and "reached from mountain to mountain, completely blocking the valley; and the claim, or rather claims, of Lamon, are taken in three detached pieces more than half a mile apart." (Lamon, who

Gertrude (Cosie) Hutchings (1867–1956) at about age twenty-three. After attending college in the East, Cosie worked at a variety of jobs (including schoolteaching) in and near Yosemite until 1899 when she married William E. Mills. The Mills moved to Vermont in 1907 and thereafter lived in New England. Cosie visited Yosemite Valley every summer between 1941 and 1949. (Shirley Sargent collection)

originally purchased or filed on a total of 378 acres, cut his claim down to the maximum quarter-section by splitting off enough acreage to cover both his orchards, which was technically illegal.)

On June 3, 1868, George W. Julian of Indiana, chairman of the House Committee on Public Lands, introduced H. R. 1118 in the Fortieth Congress, "an Act to confirm to J. M. Hutchings and J. C. Lamon their pre-emption claims in the Yosemite Valley." Julian, whom Hutchings called "an uncompromising friend of the settler," depicted the two claimants as courageous pioneers who had staked their fortunes and "faced hardships in a life remote from society and civilization." He conveniently neglected to mention that Hutchings had taken up innkeeping in the Valley only six weeks before the enactment of the Yosemite Grant. Other supporters spoke for the measure in similar fashion. "The bill passed the House," Hutchings said, "without a dissenting vote."

By 1872 Hutchings had improved his hotel by adding a porch and additional upstairs windows. Rock Cottage appears at the right, just behind the edge of the finished timber bridge Hutchings built in 1868 to replace Gus Hite's original bridge, which washed away in the great flood of December, 1867.

In the Senate, however, the Committee on Private Land Claims issued an adverse report and moved to postpone consideration of the bill indefinitely, which effectively killed the legislation. "The valley had never been surveyed," the committee spokesman said in his report to the full Senate, "and thus had never become subject to pre-emption or private sale . . . The passage of the bill before the Senate would be to give up the idea of the public enjoyment of the valley, and surrender it wholly to the purposes of private speculation." Meanwhile, the suit of ejectment brought by the Yosemite Board of Commissioners against Hutchings and Lamon was decided in the defendants' favor in the Thirteenth Judicial District Court of California. The commissioners appealed the verdict to the California Supreme Court. Fearing a possible reversal of the lower court's ruling, Hutchings made the long train trip to Washington over the new transcontinental railroad in 1870 to lobby Congress to approve the action of the California legislature. He financed his six-month sojourn in the East by giving eighty-seven stereopticon (magic lantern) lectures on Yosemite in cities as far away as Boston.

In January, 1871, Representative Julian introduced a new bill supporting Hutchings' and Lamon's claims in the Forty-first Congress. The measure again passed the House without objection, only to be blocked once more by the Senate committee after a close vote.

Later the same year, Hutchings suffered a second blow to his hopes when the state supreme court reversed the favorable ruling of the district court on the grounds that pre-emption

The main room of Hutchings' cabin contained a fireplace formed of four huge granite slabs, a bookcase holding several hundred volumes, and various items of furniture, including the celebrated manzanita armchair at the left.

James Hutchings lounges in the doorway of his cabin on the north side of the Merced River during the early 1880s. Hutchings was forced to give up his cabin after completing his term as guardian in 1884 (described in Chapter VI). Each year, beginning in 1890, he applied for a lease on the unused building at the annual June meetings of the Yosemite commissioners. Permission was repeatedly denied because "no portion of the valley is to be devoted to merely personal residence." After five such denials, Hutchings appealed to the state legislature, which gave him approval to occupy the cabin for one year or more beginning in 1895. The commissioners refused to grant Hutchings the two hundred dollars he requested to put the place in order (John Muir reported in 1895 that the cabin was "dilapidated"), and the proposed lease was cancelled in 1897. The neglected structure stored hay in the early 1900s. From 1906 until 1909, Gabriel Sovulewski (the park supervisor) used it as a residence, after which it was removed.

claims established on unsurveyed lands were not valid. In December, 1872, Hutchings lost his ultimate appeal in the United States Supreme Court *(Low v. Hutchings).* "The Act of California, of February, 1868," the Court said in its decision, "was inoperative unless ratified by Congress . . . and it is not believed that Congress will ever sanction such a perversion of the trust solemnly accepted by the state."

The Big Tree Room became a parlor in later years. The two guests appear to be minding their own business.

With California's ownership of Yosemite Valley now firmly established, the legislature took up the question of financial compensation for the displaced Yosemite settlers during its next session. In March, 1874, a bill was passed appropriating sixty thousand dollars to indemnify the several claimants in exchange for all rights and title to their properties and improvements. Experts from the state board of examiners were assigned to apportion the funds. On March 20, the *Mariposa Gazette* reported that "Hutchings and Black, who were present during the vote, were made happy. Hutchings' face was positively radiant."

In September, 1874, after taking testimony from all parties involved, the examiners awarded the following sums: J. M. Hutchings, $24,000; J. C. Lamon, $12,000; A. G. Black, $13,000; and Ira B. Folsom, who owned a bridge and two buildings near the Lower Village, $6,000—a total of $55,000. The balance of $5,000 was returned to the state treasury (see note 31).

The Yosemite commissioners considered the large settlements to be inappropriate. In the board's *Biennial Report* for 1874–75, Secretary William Ashburner stated that "when legislation [regarding Yosemite Valley] is necessary, information should be obtained from the Commissioners appointed to the charge and management of this great national trust, and not as has been the case in the past, from the ex parte statements of interested persons [read Hutchings]. What the Commissioners here suggest, they confidently think, would, at least, be productive of economy, if no other advantages result from it. As evidence of the correctness of the view here advanced, the Commissioners would state in this connection, that in 1866, Mr. Lamon would have been glad to have taken $3,000 for his claim. Messrs. Black and Folsom only asked $1,000 apiece for theirs, while Mr. Hutchings would have been obliged to rest satisfied with all he could get. . .

"The Commissioners would further add that they have never heard but one expression of opinion with regard to the amounts which all the above parties have received, namely: that the state has dealt by them most munificently."

In retrospect, the actions of the California legislature during this early period indicate that its members never really understood the concept of the Yosemite Grant. Besides enacting the shortsighted bill in favor of Hutchings and Lamon and later awarding the claimants excessive compensation, the legislature failed to provide the funds necessary for the protection and enhancement of the Valley. After the initial grant of two thousand dollars in 1866, two successive legislatures made no appropriations whatsoever to enable the commissioners to carry on their work. And a third, the legislature of 1872, allocated only two thousand dollars for the two years ending June 30, 1874. Guardian Galen Clark received no pay for four full years (1868–72). One critic of the legislature wrote that it "was almost childish to hope to do anything with [such amounts] in this great valley, when Golden Gate Park took $100,000 annually just to keep the grass green!"

YOSEMITE TOURISM INCREASES

Despite the expense and discomfort of the demanding journey to Yosemite, visitation grew steadily in the years following the establishment of the state grant. After averaging only eighty-five persons annually prior to 1865, Valley tourism climbed to more than six hundred in 1868, and nearly twice that number in 1869, the year the transcontinental railroad was completed. In 1873 Yosemite visitation exceeded twenty-five hundred persons.

To accommodate the growing influx of sightseers, the two Valley hotel owners, Hutchings and Black, continued to aggressively improve and expand their facilities all through the decade of judicial and legislative wrangling. New operations also opened for business under state lease. By the summer of 1874, three hotels provided accommodations on the Valley floor, two others stood on higher ground within the grant, and five more adjoined the two main trails leading into the Valley.

John Muir operated Hutchings' sawmill in 1870–71. The two men parted company in July, 1871, on decidedly unfriendly terms.

HUTCHINGS HOUSE (THE UPPER HOTEL)

When James Hutchings arrived in Yosemite in May, 1864, to take possession of Gus Hite's failed Upper Hotel, he was forty years old and a novice at the innkeeping trade. With him was his fragile, dreamy, pregnant wife of four years, Elvira, aged twenty-two, and her hard-working, capable mother, fifty-three-year-old Florantha Sproat. The "hotel" was then a two-story rough frame building, sixty by twenty feet, consisting of two very long rooms, one upstairs and one down. The doors and windows were covered by cotton cloth.

"When our first guests arrived," Hutchings said, "the ladies were domiciled upstairs, and the gentlemen down. This arrangement we felt not only had its inconveniences, but was contrary to law, inasmuch as it sometimes separated man and wife." To provide a semblance of privacy for his guests, Hutchings packed in bolts of muslin and hung cloth dividers around each guest's sleeping area. A visitor who arrived only weeks after the Hutchings House opened for business described the premises as follows:

"No partition between the dining and sitting rooms; no plastering, no chairs, except one rocking

River Cottage stood across the road from Hutchings' original hotel building. This view, taken between 1871 and 1875 from the north side of the Merced River, shows the picturesque location of the new facility where one could "listen at all hours to the grand violoncello tones of the mysterious waters." The building at the right is the Cosmopolitan saloon.

The two-story Rock Cottage contained ten small bedrooms and a parlor.

chair. We sat at table on long wooden benches, without backs, and at other times on ottomans or stools. Upstairs the rooms were only divided by pieces of cotton cloth, and were very small at that, containing a small bed, a small rough wash-stand, a rough bench, and no place to hang anything. The only choice being to go to bed with one's clothes on, or leave them under the bed on the floor. Of course, every word and movement were plainly audible and visible, and it required some little strategy to place the candle so that one's figure should not appear on the cloth partition, hugely magnified. . . We slept in unironed sheets, on rough, dry pillow-cases, and dried our faces on towels guiltless of attention, beyond a hasty washing."[16]

From all accounts, Hutchings was not a great success as a hotel proprietor. He had a deep store of knowledge about the Valley and approached his duties with enthusiasm, but he often forgot to furnish knives and forks to his diners, sometimes brought sugar when asked for salt, and occasionally refilled coffee cups with cold water.

"The genial host entertained his guests by lectures on the geology of the region and by conducting them on tours," said one observer. "Unfortunately, however, his accommodations were not on a par with his discourses, a circumstance that led one disgruntled early visitor to remark that guests would be better served if the proprietor paid less attention to describing the beauties and more to providing comfortable

beds and properly prepared meals." Nevertheless, most customers proclaimed the Hutchings House clean and the food satisfactory, thanks largely to the diligent efforts of mother-in-law Florantha Sproat.

Wife Elvira Hutchings, a shy, withdrawn girl, performed her hotel duties listlessly, far preferring to spend the time with her books, music, and painting, or studying the local flora. The couple's first child, a girl named Florence (called Floy), arrived on August 23, 1864. Three years later a second daughter, Gertrude (called Cosie), joined the household, and in 1869, son William Mason Hutchings completed the family. William was born with a deformed spine that severely limited his energy and activities. Most of the care of the children fell to grandmother Sproat, as Elvira had little interest in motherhood.

After spending one gloomy winter living in his hotel building, which received no more than two hours of sun each day, Hutchings—like Lamon before him—built a comfortable winter cabin on the sunny north side of the Valley about three-quarters of a mile southeast of Yosemite Falls. He was assisted in moving the heavy logs into position by Lamon and his two oxen. Here the family passed quiet winter evenings by the great stone fireplace, the women knitting and sewing, while Hutchings read aloud from one of the several hundred books in his library.

John Olmsted (apparently no relation to Frederick Law Olmsted), who visited Yosemite in 1868, described the premises as follows:

Hutchings' water-powered sawmill on Yosemite Creek worked "extremely well," according to sawyer Muir. The box-like cubicle fastened to the top front of the mill was Muir's "hang nest" where he kept his notes and other personal possessions (he slept in the mill itself). It had a hole in the roof "to command a view of the glorious South [Half] Dome," and a skylight that provided "a full view of the Upper Yosemite Fall." Muir said his "hang nest" study could be reached only by a series of sloping planks roughed by slats like a hen ladder, which served to "keep out people I dislike." (Painting by Herman Herzog, circa 1871)

Skilled in the family trade of carpentry and cabinetmaking, Hutchings fashioned his own rowboat for use on the Merced River.

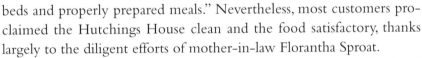

By the late 1860s, a second building (to the left, with addition) had been added to the Lower Hotel facilities. The original structure at the right and the tacked-on addition to the second building were razed when Black built his new hotel in 1870.

"Beyond the river we come to the winter residence of Mr. Hutchings— a large cabin made of hewn logs, warm and snug, a huge stone fireplace at one end; hanging shelves containing some two hundred and fifty volumes in the corners; fishing rods, guns, and rifles along the walls; and a pair of snowshoes, indispensable to that snowy region. . . Near the house are sheds and hay racks, and a fruit and vegetable garden of several acres—at least one acre in strawberries. In the rear of this house, and fronting the hotel, is the far-famed and beautiful Yo-Semite Fall."[17]

As time went on, Hutchings added lean-to rooms made of boards to three sides of the main log structure: a workshop-woodshed on the west, a kitchen-storeroom at the back, and a bedroom at the eastern end. A small attic served as an extra bedroom, and once as a place of refuge when the Merced River overflowed its banks in the winter of 1867–68.

Realizing that he needed lumber in order to improve his hotel accommodations, Hutchings hired two local men to make boards from logs using a primitive pit-saw. In pit-sawing, one man stood on a platform above the log and one in a pit dug beneath it, each grasping one end of a long two-handled saw. The men slowly worked their way lengthwise along the log, all the while alternately pushing and pulling the saw up and down until a usable board was finally created. The work was extremely tiring and tediously slow. According to Hutchings, only fifteen hundred board feet of lumber were cut during the entire summer, a total far short of his requirements.

Enough lumber was provided, however, for Hutchings to add a shed-like addition to the rear of his hotel building sometime before October,

1867. The structure was unique in that it was built around a large cedar tree that Hutchings could not bring himself to fell. The "Big Tree Room," as it became known, functioned originally as a combination kitchen and sitting room. It had a dirt floor and a stone fireplace equipped with cranes and Dutch ovens. The redoubtable Mrs. Sproat hung her pots and pans from a wire strung around the tree's great trunk. The room was later floored and used as a parlor.

About the spring of 1869, Hutchings had a water-powered sawmill packed in from San Francisco with the hope of improving his lumber output. Unfortunately, no one in the Valley could get the mill to operate. In late November, Hutchings solved his problem by hiring an itinerant thirty-one-year-old former sheepherder named John Muir, who arrived at the hotel looking for a job.

"I had the good fortune to obtain employment from Hutchings," Muir wrote in his memoirs, "in building a sawmill to cut lumber for cottages that he wished to build in the spring, from the fallen pines which had blown down in a violent windstorm a year or two before my arrival." (During the winter of 1867–68, about a hundred Valley trees, estimated by Galen Clark to contain more than a million board feet of lumber, had been leveled by severe storms.) Muir set up the sawmill on Hutchings' claim along the most easterly branch of Yosemite Creek, not far from Yosemite Falls. On March 20, 1870, he wrote his brother: "I have completed the sawmill here. It works extremely well." Muir sawed the prostrate yellow pines, which were often several feet in diameter, into shorter sections, drove iron pins into the centers, and with chains and Lamon's oxen hauled them to the mill.

Linnie Marsh Wolfe, Muir's biographer, described the 1870–71 construction work in her book, *Son of the Wilderness:* "As soon as enough lumber was piled up, building began. In this John had the help of two carpenters, but being more deft with hammer and saw, he was largely responsible for the improvements. He not only did much of the partition work in the hotel itself, but planned and built in large part the artistic River and Rock Cottages. . ."[18]

The River Cottage, which stood along the south side of the Merced just across the road from Hutchings' original building (later called Cedar Cottage), had eight small bedrooms on the first floor, seven bedrooms and a linen room on the second floor, and three rooms for employees on the third floor. The two-story Rock Cottage, "half hidden among huge mossy boulders and tall pines, a charming little cottage," contained five small bedrooms and a parlor on the ground floor, with five more bedrooms on the second floor.

In her book *Bits of Travel at Home,* noted author Helen Hunt Jackson told about her 1872 stay at the River Cottage:

"He who would like to open his eyes every morning on the full shining of the great Yosemite Fall; to lie in bed, and from his very pillow watch it sway to right and left under moonlight beams, which seem like wands arresting or hastening the motion; to look down into the amber and green Merced, which caresses his very door-sill; to listen at all hours to the grand violoncello tones of the mysterious waters, let him ask, as we did, for back bedrooms in the Cottage by the River.

"But if he is disconcerted by the fact that his bedroom floor is of pine

Former miner Alexander Gordon Black lived at Bull Creek along the Coulterville Trail where he operated a way station for Yosemite tourists until 1870 when he built his new Valley hotel.

Black's Hotel adjoined the newer of his two previous building (at left end of the long one-story wing). In this 1870 photograph, the upper porch railing remains unfinished and no advertising sign has yet been erected. The two-story section of the hotel was later doubled in length.

boards, and his bedroom walls of thin laths, covered with unbleached cotton; that he has neither chair, nor table, nor pitcher; that his washbowl is a shallow tin pan, and that all the water he wants he must dip in a tin pint from a barrel out in the hall; that his bed is a sack stuffed with ferns, his one window has no curtain, and his door no key, let him leave Ah-wah-ne the next day."

On July 10, 1871, Muir sawed his last log and quit Hutchings. In Muir's opinion, Hutchings was shallow, vain, and not quite fair in his dealings with him. On Hutchings' part, Muir's close rapport with Elvira Hutchings and his growing popularity as a Yosemite authority and guide created a jealousy that soon mounted into hatred. Hutchings had been considered "Mine Host" of the Valley from the day he began hotelkeeping. To share the spotlight with his sawyer was more than he could graciously handle. The two men parted company bearing mutually bitter feelings that endured for the rest of their lives.[19]

Soon after his two new cottages were completed, Hutchings changed the name of his establishment to "The Yosemite House." During 1873–74 he ran advertisements in the *Mariposa Gazette* using this description: "The Yo Semite House. Two neat and pleasantly located cottages have been furnished rooms for the accommodation of tourists in addition to the original hotel. J. M. Hutchings, Proprietor of the Yo Semite House." Rates were $3.50 per day, $20.00 per week, or $75.00 per month.

At the end of the 1874 season, ownership of "The Yosemite House" passed to the state of California. Hutchings took his twenty-four-thousand-dollar settlement and departed for San Francisco. In December, the Yosemite Board of Commissioners posted notices in Mariposa, Sonora, and four San Francisco newspapers that the lease on Hutchings' former facilities was now open for public bid.

BLACK'S "NEW SENTINEL HOTEL" (THE LOWER HOTEL)

Englishman Alexander Gordon Black migrated to the Coulterville area during the gold rush and became a principal in a quartz mine near Marble Springs. Sometime in the mid-1850s he sold his interest to a corporation and settled on a 160-acre claim along Bull Creek. After the Coulterville Trail was constructed through his property in 1856, Black and his wife Catherine furnished meals and lodging to Yosemite-bound tourists until the trail fell into disuse in 1870. One visitor described his stopover at Black's in this fashion:

"We reached Black's at half-past eight. . . I was a tired but happy man, as Black's white face and gray whiskers shone in the red light of a kerosene lamp; and as, soon after, the fragrant fumes of coffee and steak invited us to table; and most particularly happy when a spring mattress yielded gently to my weary pressure, giving promise of needed rest and repose.

"No lovelier Sabbath morning ever dawned over any spot of earth's paradise than greeted us in the little secluded valley at Black's on the 21st of June. But the sun was high in the heavens before, in answer to a summons to breakfast in half an hour, we looked out upon its splendor. We had lodged in a long, low building, one room deep, containing a nicely furnished parlor and several lodging rooms, all opening on a piazza.

Everything in the parlor of Black's Hotel had to be packed in on the backs of mules over rugged terrain before 1874.

This view of the two-structure Lower Hotel was taken in the late 1860s during the period that Fred and Isabella Leidig managed the enterprise for Black. The child is probably George Frederick Leidig, Jr., who was born in 1865. The man and woman flanking him are most likely his parents.

Leidig's rustic new two-story hotel was unpainted and the porch railing dangerously incomplete when J. P. Soulé took this photograph in 1870.

"Its rustic columns were wreathed with honeysuckles and running roses, while standard roses of great size and beauty looked through and over the balustrade. A clean, well-ordered garden was in front, abounding with fruit and vegetables, and irrigated by ditches of water brought from the mountain stream."[20]

In 1861 Black purchased the Lower Hotel in Yosemite Valley from Steve Cunningham, as earlier described. During the next decade, he leased the premises intermittently to Fred Leidig and others while he continued to accommodate guests at Bull Creek. After the Big Oak Flat stage road reached Crane Flat in 1870, however, Yosemite tourists no longer used the Coulterville Trail. Early that spring, Black and his wife moved to the Valley and took over their hotel in person. The expectation of a surge in Yosemite travel following the completion of the transcontinental railroad the previous year may have played a part in their decision.

Black immediately began the erection of an L-shaped addition to the end of the newer of his two existing small buildings (the other was razed). The longer part of the L, which adjoined the old structure, was single-story; each room opened onto a wood-planked porch. The shorter section, about thirty feet in length, had two stories and contained the kitchen, dining area, and parlor. Sometime later, Black doubled the length of the two-story wing, which increased his capacity to about seventy guests. One unfeeling critic likened the architectural style of the hotel to that of a bowling alley.

Further construction details are uncertain. It seems likely that Black hired carpenters and possibly bought lumber from Hutchings, whose Valley sawmill was in operation at the time. The rustic, shake-roofed, clapboard-sided hotel opened for business during the summer of 1870.

Bancroft's *Tourist Guide* for 1871 called Black's "a new house having excellent bath and other accommodations, with well-finished and furnished rooms." A visitor a year later reported that "two women and one man receive guests in their long wooden inn and dispose them separately in rooms, although attempt is made to utilize the second bed in each room. You eat in the long room on a table, the kitchen adjoining. Boots are blacked by a wandering German." An article in the *Mariposa Gazette* in 1874 described the virtues of the "New Sentinel Hotel of Mr. and Mrs. Black. Bathrooms are attached to the hotel itself, and there is a bar."

Unlike Hutchings, the Blacks obtained a lease to their premises after being bought out by the state in the fall of 1874. They continued to serve Yosemite visitors at their "New Sentinel Hotel" for six more years.

LEIDIG'S HOTEL

In the spring of 1866, German-born George Frederick Leidig, a twenty-eight-year-old former hoist operator at the Princeton Mine near Mount Bullion, arrived in Yosemite Valley from Coulterville with his nineteen-year-old wife, Isabella Dobbie, a "pretty dark-eyed Scotch maid," and their infant son, George Frederick, Jr. Many years later, another Leidig son said that his father came to the Valley to join James Lamon in the cultivation of his orchards, but the two men had a falling out. This report remains unsubstantiated.

In testimony before the Investigative Committee of the state assembly

Ralph Waldo Emerson visited Yosemite in the spring of 1871 and met with John Muir at Hutchings' sawmill. "I showed him my collection of plants and sketches," Muir said, "which seemed to interest him greatly." Emerson was talked out of Muir's invitation to camp out with him in the Mariposa Grove by the elderly transcendentalist's over-protective companions.

in 1889, Leidig said that he ran the Lower Hotel seasonally under a sub-lease from Black for four summers—1866 through 1869. The Leidigs spent the first two winters in Coulterville, becoming full-time Yosemite residents in April, 1868. During this period, Leidig built a rough log house, measuring fourteen by twenty-two feet and facing west, in a sunny area north of the Merced River at the edge of what is now called Leidig Meadow. Here the family passed the winter months until the tourist business resumed, usually sometime in March. The cabin burned to the ground about 1883.

Photographs taken in the late 1860s show that the Lower Hotel eventually consisted of two main buildings, each of which had been patched and added to over the years. A visitor gave this account of his stay there in 1869:

"It was a good house—this of Leidig's—or rather there were two of them. They hadn't mansard roofs, to be sure, and were only one-story high, but they were very comfortable. One contained kitchen, dining room, and barroom; the other had a parlor and several sleeping rooms. Some of the rooms were floored and had nails to hang clothes on. There were candles and a barrel of water with tin basins, and a long towel on a roller at the corner of the house, and fragments of a looking glass. A Digger Indian brought water from the river for the use of guests.

"The table was first-rate, with the juiciest and tenderest of mutton from Leidig's own flock, fine fresh trout from the Merced, excellent vegetables, plenty of fruit and berries, and the richest of cream, with good cooking and neat service. . ."

In the summer of 1869, Leidig tried to lease the Lower Hotel directly from the Yosemite Board of Commissioners, but was unsuccessful. The commissioners said they had no intention of disturbing any of the Yosemite claimants "until the question of title has been decided and the authority of the state recognized." At this point, Leidig said, "Black kicked me out." The commissioners then granted Leidig a lease on a hotel site of his own about four hundred yards southwest of Black's near the start of the present Four Mile Trail to Glacier Point. "I built my own place in 1869–70," Leidig said, "and occupied it in 1870. I stayed for the next eighteen years."

Son Jack Leidig afterward described the innkeeping project: "The old Leidig's Hotel consisted of twelve sleeping rooms upstairs, two sleeping rooms downstairs together with parlor, sitting room, and dining room. The kitchen was built on as an annex in the rear. The family's personal quarters were in a separate building behind the hotel, along with several small cottages and storage sheds.

"All lumber for the hotel, including tongue-and-groove flooring, was handsawed and ripped from logs on the property by father and three men. [Leidig said that Hutchings refused to sell him lumber from his sawmill.] The only things they didn't make were window glass, nails, locks, and hinges. Father used Lamon's two oxen to pull out willows. He put in rail fences, grew potatoes and corn, and planted timothy that grew five feet high." (Timothy is a tall, stout grass cultivated for hay and grazing.)

During the first two seasons of operation (1870–71), Leidig had a partner named Hugh Davanay, a prominent Mariposa mortgage broker. Leidig, who said his hotel cost "between $5,000 and $6,000 to build," ran short of funds midway through construction and sought financial help in Mariposa. Davanay offered to provide the $1,600 Leidig needed, in exchange for a half-interest in both the premises and the business. Leidig reluctantly agreed, and the two men became partners. Bancroft's *Tourist Guide* for 1871 extolled their accommodations:

"The new Yo Semite Hotel—Fred Leidig and Hugh Davanay, proprietors. A fine new hotel, two stories in height, roomy, new, and clean, with plenty of pleasant, airy bedrooms. The table is supplied with fresh mountain trout in abundance, in addition to fresh butter, milk, eggs, fruit, and every other luxury of the mountains. A splendid stock of ice has been laid in for the comfort of summer visitors—a luxury not to be had elsewhere in the valley. The bar is well stocked with the best qualities of wines, liquors, and cigars."

In May, 1871, Leidig and Davanay played host to famed transcendentalist Ralph Waldo Emerson, who visited Yosemite midway through an extensive tour of the West. "Leidig's is a neat and good tavern," said one member of Emerson's party, "very simple in its arrangements, but beautifully placed. I was waked one morning by the cackling of a hen that was walking over my bed in search of a nest."

Another customer who patronized the hotel during this pioneer period was not so complimentary about the facilities: "[Leidig's is] a house built of wood with two floors. The wood is so thin and the joints so imperfect that every sound goes right through the edifice. And the droll little rooms into which they contrive to stuff two people make me think of a row of large deal [board] bonnet boxes insecurely fastened together and arranged in a row."

Besides the superb view of Yosemite Falls from the front porches, upstairs and down, the hotel's biggest asset was Isabella Leidig, whose cooking and housekeeping skills were widely praised. Mother of eleven children, the popular, hardworking "Belle" somehow found time and energy to set a first-rate table and maintain a spotless establishment even as she bore and reared her many offspring.[21] Husband Fred, who was appointed sub-guardian for Yosemite Valley by Galen Clark in June, 1869, seems to have been far less involved than his wife in day-to-day duties at the hotel.

Co-proprietor Hugh Davanay left the business after the second year. Acrimonious relations between the two partners led to an ultimatum by Davanay that he would either buy out Leidig's interest or Leidig would buy out his. The result was that Davanay sold out to Leidig sometime before the summer of 1872, taking a lien on the building as collateral for his sixteen hundred dollar investment.[22]

The sale of all Valley claims to the state in 1874 had no effect on the Leidigs. The arrangement by which they operated their hotel on government property under lease was really the prototype of a concession policy still practiced in national and state parks throughout the country.

> **LEIDIG'S YO-SEMITE HOTEL,**
> **YO-SEMITE VALLEY.**
>
> *This popular Hotel is now open for the reception of Visitors, and parties stopping at this House can depend on receiving every attention while visiting this Wonderful Valley.*
>
> **LEIDIG & DAVANAY, - Proprietors.**

An advertising card issued by Leidig and Davanay during their partnership in Leidig's Hotel in 1870–71.

Albert Snow erected his original
"Alpine House" in 1870 near the
base of beautiful Nevada Fall.

SNOW'S HOTEL (LA CASA NEVADA)

Except for the original two-thousand-dollar allotment provided in 1866, all legislative appropriations to the Yosemite Board of Commissioners before 1878 were limited to the commissioners' expenses and the guardian's salary, and even these basic compensations were not always readily forthcoming. As a consequence, when it became imperative to improve and expand the few existing trails within the Yosemite Grant, the commissioners awarded toll rights to independent contractors who were willing to finance the projects. The leases stipulated that the state could buy back the routes when funds became available.

Under this arrangement, Stephen Cunningham obtained permission from Guardian Galen Clark on October 3, 1869, to construct a horse trail upward from Register Rock, a huge boulder along the Vernal Fall Trail, to a point somewhere near the base of Nevada Fall. The agreement authorized the charge of a "reasonable toll." A few months later, Cunningham acquired a partner in the person of Albert Snow, who had been granted a lease by the commissioners to build and operate a hotel on the rocky flat north of the Merced River at the base of Nevada Fall. Cunningham's trail, which crossed the river via the rustic bridge erected above Vernal Fall by the state in 1866, provided access to the site. Snow agreed to put up three hundred dollars in cash, or supply tools, provisions, and labor of a like amount. Each man was considered an equal owner entitled to half the toll receipts. The commissioners' minutes indicate that Cunningham built most of the lower portion of the trail,

while Snow completed the section above Vernal Fall.

Albert Snow (1825–1891) and wife Emily Topple Snow (1823–1889) were native Vermonters, born and reared near Lake Champlain. The date of their arrival in California is uncertain, but Albert was the owner of the Washington Hotel in Garrote (Groveland) for a time in the 1860s. The Snows had one daughter, Maria, who married Colwell Owens Drew, a well-known Groveland-area rancher and a silent partner in the hotel project. During their Yosemite years, Albert and Emily wintered in Groveland near their daughter's family.

Early in the spring of 1870, Snow packed in enough material to put up a one-story, barn-like building somewhat grandiosely called the "Alpine House." The structure stood in full view of spectacular Nevada Fall, and so close to the roaring cataract that "in some winds half the piazza is drenched with spray." Entries in the three-volume guest register now in the Yosemite Museum indicate that Snow's unpretentious hotel, elevation 5,360 feet, opened for business on April 28, 1870. It soon became a favored lunch stop for Yosemite visitors who rode or hiked up from the Valley to see the falls. Hardier travelers stayed overnight while journeying to or from Little Yosemite Valley and other outlying destinations.

Hostess Emily Snow was an excellent cook. Her doughnuts, bread, and elderberry pie drew special praise, as did her ability to "cook all the popular dishes." One early visitor reported that she was "delighted and considerably astonished at the excellence of the abundant meal. We felt as deeply humiliated as Sunday school children at the end of a tea-fight

By the summer of 1875, Snow had doubled the size of his first building, added a wrap-around porch, and completed an attractive two-story chalet nearby. Mr. and Mrs. Snow are shown here with daughter Maria (right).

Emily Topple Snow's prim looks belied her wit and character.

Guests at Snow's chalet enjoyed the sight and sound of booming Nevada Fall.

when we were compelled to hurt the feelings of the highly conversational landlady by the assurance that we really were unable to do further justice to her apple pies, hominy cakes, turnovers, and concluding trifles."

Emily possessed a dry wit and a small stock of jokes of her own making that she delivered in a distinct New England twang while waiting table. "Well, you folks would hardly think it," she often said, "but there is eleven feet of snow here all summer." When asked how that was possible, she replied, "My husband is near six feet tall and I'm a little over five. Ain't that eleven?"[23]

In the fall of 1871, Snow added an extension to his existing Alpine House, thereby doubling the size of the original structure. His efforts went for naught, however, after a great earthquake, centered in the Owens Valley east of Yosemite, caused extensive shaking in and around the Valley on March 26, 1872. Rock slides and avalanches were common, and a prominent peak in back of Hutchings' hotel fell with a terrible crash. Snow's Alpine House moved two inches to the east, and the new addition was so badly wrecked it had to be torn down and rebuilt.

"The most remarkable results of the quake occurred at Snow's," Galen Clark said in his "Guardian's Report." "Mr. Snow, on hearing the terrible rumbling noise preceding the shake, rushed out of his house somewhat alarmed. The night was very light and he being in plain view of Nevada Fall, distinctly saw that the water ceased to flow over the fall for at least half a minute. A large mass of rocks, which would weigh thousands of tons, fell from the west side of the 'Cap of Liberty' about a thousand feet above its base. When this mass of rocks struck the earth, Mr. Snow says that he was instantaneously thrown prostrate to the ground. . . The earth around Snow's place is still completely covered with dust from the pulverized rocks. I think that the prostration of Mr.

Snow and perhaps the moving of the main house and the wrenching apart of the timbers of the addition was probably more the result of the concussion of the atmosphere when the rocks fell than the effects of the earthquake."

Undaunted, Snow rebuilt his damaged Alpine House in 1872. During the next three seasons he continued to improve his facilities even though every item on the premises from nails to beds had to be packed in on the backs of mules. By the fall of 1875, Snow's establishment consisted of the original building and addition, which now contained twelve rooms; an attractive, well-furnished chalet—completed that summer—with ten bedrooms and a parlor; a woodshed; ice house; log cabin; and stable. All told, La Casa Nevada (the Snow house), as the expanded hotel was called, could accommodate about forty overnight guests.

CLARK'S STATION

Galen Clark (1814–1910), a latecomer to the California gold fields, arrived in San Francisco from the East in November, 1853. He took up prospecting in Mariposa County but achieved no particular success. In August, 1855, Clark was a member of one of the four pioneer tourist parties that visited Yosemite Valley that year. Captivated by the mountains, Clark filed a pre-emption claim on 160 acres along the Merced South Fork at present Wawona on March 19, 1856. Thirteen months later, he built a windowless twelve-by-sixteen-foot log cabin in a meadow on his property.

Travelers passing to and from the Valley via the Mann brothers' Mariposa trail soon began stopping at Clark's rude residence asking for food and lodging. "I began to give entertainment at my place," he said, "and as travel increased, I increased my accommodations." By the late 1860s, "Clark's Station" had grown into a full-fledged though very rustic inn. A visitor in 1868 described the operation:

"Clark's ranch was built more for use than show, and is capable of indefinite extension without hurting its proportions. It is a long, narrow building of one story, facing south and west, about twenty by one hundred and twenty feet, with covered stoops front and rear, and doors opening onto them from each room. The west room is used as an office, and a receptacle for certain compounds for the inner man. . . The east end of the house is cut up into bedrooms."[24]

As a hotel proprietor, Clark was well received by his guests, who wrote laudatory accounts of his hospitality, honesty, and wit. Unfortunately, his financial ability did not match his sociability, and he was almost constantly overextended. In December, 1869, Clark sold an undivided half interest in his property, hotel, and toll bridge across the South Fork to Edwin "Deacon" Moore, the recently deposed Mariposa County Recorder, for two thousand dollars. "I sold a half interest in my place to raise money to pay off some indebtedness incurred in building," Clark said. "[I sold it to Moore] because I wanted a partner who had a wife."

Moore was no better than Clark at business matters. The partners shortly took on new obligations by building a sawmill and a twelve-mile carriage road from Mariposa to the South Fork. At the end of 1874, unable to meet their mortgage payments, Clark and Moore sold out to

Clark and Moore's one-story facility, photographed about 1871, was capable of "indefinite extension," according to one visitor.

Henry Washburn and associates, their principal creditor, for twenty-one thousand dollars. Only a thousand dollars actually changed hands; the remaining twenty thousand dollars paid off the partnership's many debts. Washburn owned a Mariposa livery stable, a stage line running from Merced to the South Fork, and the saddle-train business from there into Yosemite Valley. As years went by, Washburn and his two brothers developed Clark's former wayside stop into the celebrated Wawona Hotel, called by some "the finest hotel in all the Sierra."

Clark and his new wife Isabella moved to a small house in Yosemite Valley early in 1875. His innkeeping days were over, but his position as guardian remained unchanged.

PEREGOY'S MOUNTAIN VIEW HOUSE

Charles Edward Peregoy (1827–1904), a sailor from Baltimore, arrived in California in July, 1849, aboard the schooner *Orpheus* bound for China. During a stopover in San Francisco, he jumped ship to seek gold. He went first to Calaveras County, then to Mariposa where he became a partner in a mining operation. In 1860 he married Mary Agnes Cochran. The couple eventually settled with their four children on a ranch near Mormon Bar. From 1865 to 1868, Peregoy served as Mariposa County Treasurer.

During this period he claimed 160 acres along the present Glacier Point Road at Bridalveil Creek and began running cattle in the summer.[25] Using fir and pine logs he felled himself, Peregoy erected a small log building in a verdant, picturesque meadow, elevation seven thousand feet. Travelers passing between Yosemite Valley and Clark's Station on the old Mann brothers' trail, which ran through his property, so often requested meals and lodging that Peregoy decided to go into the

innkeeping business after being deposed as county treasurer.

In 1869 he enlarged his log building into the "Mountain View House," consisting of a kitchen, dining room, office, and sleeping area for about sixteen. All furniture, bedding, and supplies came by mule back from Mariposa, thirty-five miles away. The accommodations were rustic (one guest said that wallpaper had been put over the cloth-lined log walls, and the "ceiling of cloth flops up and down when the wind draws through"), but tourists uniformly extolled both the setting and Mary Peregoy's genius in the kitchen.

"We dined and dined sumptuously at Paragoys [sic]," a delighted visitor said, "the new halfway house, set under the pines in the greenest of mountain meadows, with rushing snows and rushing streams about it, and great white-headed mountains above it." Another traveler added that "although there is no style, no printed bills of fare or change of cloth at dinner, everything is good and enjoyable. There never were such steaks and such mutton-chops; and as for cream pies and wonderful cakes, they would be fit company for the nectar of the gods at the feasts in Olympus."

The Mountain View House was popular from the start. The hotel register, a copy of which is now in the Yosemite Museum, lists some five thousand entries from September 10, 1869, when the first five guests signed in, to October 24, 1874, when Peregoy closed down his short-lived venture. In 1870, the first full summer of operation, 514 persons stopped at the new inn for lunch or lodging. Meals were one dollar; overnight stays, fifty cents. More than thirteen hundred travelers arrived in each of the next two seasons, including such notables as Bret Harte, Horace Greeley, Albert Bierstadt, John Muir, Joaquin Miller, Mark Hopkins, and botanist Asa Gray. The Mariposa County assessment roll

Completed in the spring of 1879, the new two-story Wawona Hotel (so-named in 1882) was 140 long by 32 feet deep. It had a lobby, sitting room, dining room, and office downstairs, and twenty-five small guest rooms upstairs. A covered porch ran around both stories of the building. This William Henry Jackson photograph, taken soon after the hotel opened, shows a string of stages parked on the road in front of the grand new structure. The Wawona Hotel is still a primary stopping place for Yosemite tourists.

Charles Peregoy operated his Mountain View House on the trail to Yosemite from 1869 through 1874.

Mary Peregoy was acclaimed as a "genius in the kitchen."

for 1871 showed Peregoy with a building and outhouses valued at $500; one wagon, $50; furniture, $200; one horse, $30; two hogs, $6; eighteen chickens, $6; and farming utensils, $20.

The following summer, Peregoy completed a second building, nearly fifty feet in length with a steep roof, this time using rough lumber packed in from Clark and Moore's new sawmill twelve miles distant. The structure contained a large living room and additional bedrooms. Regrettably, the new accommodations were not yet finished when fifty-six tourists crowded into the Mountain View House on June 4, 1872, during a freak, late-season snowstorm. Although many of the guests spent the night huddled around the kitchen stove, in view of the alternative, no complaints were recorded.

Visitation at Peregoy's fell to seven hundred in 1874, the year two stage roads were completed to Yosemite Valley from the north. A third road between Clark and Moore's and the Valley was in the process of construction. It became obvious to Peregoy that Yosemite's horse trail days were over, and so was the need for his hotel. On November 10, 1874, Peregoy's mountain holdings were offered at public auction. The *Mariposa Gazette* of November 14 reported the results: "C. E. Peregoy's property, sold Thursday last, consisted of a ranch and buildings on the trail between Clark and Moore's and Yosemite known as the Mountain View House, together with household furniture. The entire property realized about $700: cattle, $330; ranch, $270; and the balance for furniture. John Fritz bought most of the cattle. The rest was bid by S. Shane."

Charles and Mary Peregoy subsequently opened a public house for travelers and teamsters on their ranch along the Chowchilla Mountain Road near Cold Spring. Entries in the hotel register show that they received guests at least as late as June 5, 1878, when a party of twenty-two tourists from Oakland and the East signed the log. Among the group was Dioclesian Lewis, who later wrote a book about the journey (see note 29). Lewis' account verifies that the 1878 stopover was at Peregoy's foothill ranch and had no connection with the former Mountain View House, even though Peregoy obviously used the same register.

THE GLACIER POINT MOUNTAIN HOUSE AND FOUR MILE TRAIL

In 1871, James McCauley, an ambitious, hardworking Irishman, entered into a ten-year contract with the Yosemite Board of Commissioners to build and operate a toll trail from the Valley floor near Leidig's Hotel up to Glacier Point. (McCauley's background and subsequent Yosemite activities are described in later chapters.) It was reported that hotel own-

The only known photograph of Peregoy's Mountain View House, which stood in a beautiful meadow along the Mann brothers' trail at an elevation of seven thousand feet.

ers and other businessmen within the grant had encouraged the commissioners to authorize the venture.

McCauley hired John Conway, builder of many roads and trails in and around Yosemite, to survey the route. Beginning that fall, McCauley, working alone, completed about a half mile of trail before the first big snowstorm of the season halted his efforts. In the process he exhausted his capital of seven hundred dollars. During the winter of 1871–72, McCauley occupied himself obtaining loans totaling three thousand dollars from various friends as far away as Hite's Cove. The following spring he hired a crew of nine men and resumed work on the challenging project in earnest.

When a scenic outlook named Union Point, two miles from the summit, was attained in early summer, McCauley received permission from the commissioners to begin charging tourists who wished to visit the new viewpoint. Conway was injured about this time in an accident. Because he had already finished the survey to Glacier Point, trail work went on to completion without him in mid-1872.

McCauley then built a small combination tollhouse and residence at the foot of the trail and set about satisfying his many debts. Fred McCauley, one of James' sons, said many years later that his father paid off his thirty-five hundred dollar investment and began showing a profit in less than two years.

John Conway in his old age. Conway built many of the roads and trails in and around Yosemite.

J. J. Reilly photographed James McCauley (right) and his nine-man construction crew as they paused for lunch in 1872 part way up the Four Mile Trail. John Conway sits third from left (with beard).

Helen Hunt Jackson described her journey up and down the Four Mile Trail soon after its completion: "It is a marvelous piece of work. It is broad, smooth, and well protected on the outer edge, in all dangerous places, by large rocks; so that, although it is far the steepest out of the valley, zigzagging back and forth on a sheer granite wall, one rides up it with little alarm or giddiness, and with such a sense of gratitude to the builder that the dollar's toll seems too small."[26]

With convenient access to Glacier Point about to become a reality in 1872, Charles Peregoy decided to erect a small inn at the renowned overlook. John Muir, in a letter to a friend in June, 1872, wrote: "I hear Peregoy intends building a hotel at Glacier Point." Peregoy's great-granddaughter Beatrice said that construction of a rough, one-story building—"perched like an eagle's nest on a very commanding crag"—began that summer. Peregoy probably packed in the lumber from Clark's sawmill while he was enlarging his accommodations at the Mountain View House the same season. The shack-like structure was essentially completed by 1873, but apparently never furnished or utilized.

After the commissioners were awarded possession of all Valley claims in the fall of 1874, Peregoy signed over the rights to his Glacier Point shanty to the state in exchange for a ten-year lease on Black's New Sentinel Hotel. The following year the commissioners granted James McCauley a lease on Peregoy's former premises.

McCauley's Four Mile Trail was described as "a marvelous piece of work" by Helen Hunt Jackson.

HOTELS NORTH OF THE YOSEMITE GRANT

In the same fashion that Clark's and Peregoy's provided food and lodging for travelers entering Yosemite from the south, so did Gobin's, Hamilton's, and Gentry's along the northern approach to the Valley. All three were rough, impermanent stopping places that thrived briefly during the four years that the Big Oak Flat Road terminated near the edge of the Yosemite Grant. After it became possible to ride all the way to Valley hotels in a stage in 1874, the rustic wayside stops quickly fell into disuse. Details of the three operations are incomplete, and few photographs have been found, but the occasional accounts left by patrons provide a general idea of the facilities.

GOBIN'S HOTEL (CRANE FLAT)

In 1869 Louis D. Gobin, owner of a three-thousand-acre ranch in the foothills east of Knight's Ferry, began running sheep and cattle in the meadows surrounding Crane Flat during the summer months. He and his wife Ann erected a "rough log shanty" and soon began—as James Hutchings described it—"providing for the wants of the public." The

A guide leads two women riders along the Four Mile Trail. The trail provided excellent views of Yosemite Falls and other scenic landmarks. (Author's collection)

Gobins' cabin sat squarely on the county line so that one-half of the diners consumed their dinner in Tuolumne County, while those on the other side of the table ate theirs in Mariposa County.

A visitor in 1869 said that "Mrs. Gobin is a native of the Emerald Isle. She occupies a little shanty on the flat, while her leige lord looks after the sheep on the surrounding mountains. . . She entertains travelers to and from Yosemite in a truly magnificent style." The landlady's considerable culinary skills were obviously the best feature of Gobin's primitive hostelry. "The accommodations may have been scanty," another guest said, "but the hand that fed us was generous. Mrs. Gobin gave us plenty; she gave us that plenty hot; she gave it kindly; and she gave it to us clean."

Gobin's one-room facility consisted of wooden tables, benches, and six beds. The beds were separated from the center room by boards, four beds on one side, two on the other. Privacy was at a minimum, but "the landlady's heart was warm."

Ralph Waldo Emerson's party arrived at Crane Flat on May 4, 1871, and one of his companions later wrote:

"We found indeed the half-built shanty, the 'hotel,' as they called it: but the lord and lady of it were away. Two men, however, remained in charge. Nothing was ready: no bedsteads were up; there were no knives, forks, spoons, or towels. Candles were there, and bedding, and bales of new blankets never opened; some provisions, too; and the cook (an old official from a Panama steamer) contrived to give us a good dinner, which we, somehow, even with few implements, were able to eat. The seventeen horses were hitched to a fallen tree for the night.

"By a great roaring fire near by, some of the younger men made ready to camp, while the rest of us were to sleep on the floor within. It was a lovely evening; the moon was full, the air was cool, the great bonfire was blazing, and frogs were singing in full chorus in a pond in front. The pond, indeed, was bordered with snow; but the frogs already smelt the good season that was at hand. After dinner Mr. Emerson sat, with his shawl about him, sharing with W. and me our frugal puff of tobacco. 'I find this,' said he, 'a singular comfort.' One of the ladies soon came up to

speak with him, and we two withdrew to the kitchen and its blazing hearth, and lay down on the cook's bunk to finish our cigars. In a few minutes Mr. Emerson came in. 'Ah,' said he, as he spied us, 'these are the only philosophers!' and he sat down and fell into a talk with the cook."[27]

Billy Hurst's Crane Flat saloon, which stood directly across the road from Gobin's, served as a home away from home for the solitary sheep-herders, teamsters, ranchers, and Indians who traveled the mountain byways. "Warm, lighted, full of cheerful company, whiskey, noise, music, poetry of a sort, and a riotous kind of good fellowship" was one habitue's description of Hurst's rough-hewn establishment. The saloon functioned until Hurst's death in the winter of 1889–90.

Gobin's buildings burned in 1886, but were rebuilt two years later. The hotel operated on a limited basis until the early 1900s.

HAMILTON'S TAMARACK HOUSE

Alva Hamilton and wife Johannah established a rude stopping place at Tamarack Flat, five miles southeast of Crane Flat on the original Coulterville Trail, in 1870. Here the couple furnished meals and lodging for several summers to those intrepid travelers who departed the stage at the end of the road and mounted horses for the enervating journey into Yosemite Valley. In 1870, when it still required eighteen miles of equestrian transportation to reach the Valley, tourist Olive Logan described her stopover at the Tamarack House. Logan's party arrived in a heavy mountain rain, drenched and weary after a long day of travel.

"At Tamarack Flat the experienced Hamilton is ready," she wrote. "He is ready every time every saddle train arrives, for he knows the state the arrivers will be in—and he lifts poor tourist women off their horses. Our limbs are paralyzed. Some of us are barely alive. The good wife Hamilton does all she can for us. She offers wine—she rubs us with whiskey; and at last all of us, men, women, and children, married and unmarried, friends and total strangers, lie down in the one only room which composes their cabin, and pass the night in blissful disregard of civilization and modesty at once."

Soon after the stage road was completed to Yosemite Valley in 1874, fire destroyed Hamilton's Tamarack Flat house. Alva and Johannah moved permanently to their winter ranch at what is now Buck Meadows. As proprietors of the stage stop known as "Hamilton's Station," they accommodated travelers along the Big Oak Flat Road for a number of years.

GENTRY'S STATION

Situated near the brink of the great cliffs along the north side of Yosemite Valley, Gentry's Station, elevation 5,759 feet, was the last stop on the Big Oak Flat Road from 1871 to July, 1874. According to an undated item in the *Mariposa Gazette,* one John S. Gentry[28] claimed 320 acres at the terminus of the Big Oak Flat Road known as "Cascades' Flat" and erected a sawmill, hotel, and other buildings. The road reached the area in July, 1871, so construction probably began about that time (travelers in 1869 and '70 make no mention of Gentry's).

The main dwelling was a two-story, porchless affair with a steep roof to shed the mountain snow. Helen Hunt Jackson depicted the hotel after she stopped at Gentry's in 1872: "The pleasant little sitting room, with its bright carpet and lace curtains and melodeon; the bedrooms clean as clean could be and with two beds in each; the neat dining room and good dinner; the log cabin for a linen closet; the running spring water; the smiling faces and prompt kindliness of the landlord and his wife—what a marvel it was to find all these in this new clearing in a pine forest of the Sierra country, seven thousand feet above the sea!"

From his position at the very edge of the Yosemite Grant, Gentry had apparently planned to sell the output of his sawmill in Yosemite Valley in addition to running his hotel. On May 18, 1872, the *Mariposa Gazette* reported that "John S. Gentry has sold an undivided half interest in 320 acres at Cascades' Flat, valued at $400, with improvements thereon of $1,000, to William C. Stockird."

Whether for lack of patronage or financial overextension, Gentry and his partner failed to meet their mortgage obligations, and the venture went bankrupt after only three seasons. The *Mariposa Gazette* of May 22, 1874, carried this short notice: "John S. Gentry and William C. Stockird are forced to sell their 320 acres, together with Gentry's Hotel and other buildings at public auction. Sheriff John F. Clarke has set the sale for May 23." No further information about Gentry's has been found, but John Muir said the premises were deserted when he passed by during the summer of 1875.

Later History: In 1885 Joseph Hutchins (not to be confused with James Hutchings) took over the location and built a steam-powered sawmill to supply lumber used in the construction of the new government hotel (Stoneman House) in Yosemite Valley. Upon completion of the contract early in 1888, Hutchins dismantled his mill and moved to Fresno. The name "Gentry's" adhered to a checking station at the site until the old Big Oak Flat Road was superseded by the present highway in 1940.

John C. Smith owned successful saloons in both Yosemite Valley and Merced. He died in Merced in 1904.

THE COSMOPOLITAN

During the spring and summer of 1870, the disquieting sounds of saw and hammer became commonplace in Yosemite. All four hotels within the grant—Black's, Leidig's, Hutchings', and Snow's—were in the process of being built or greatly expanded; a privately financed toll bridge spanning the Merced River was under construction half a mile west of Leidig's Hotel; and the Cosmopolitan saloon, an edifice whose amenities equaled its worldly name, began taking shape along the south side of the Merced River near Hutchings' hotel.

Called the "wonder of Yosemite buildings" by one admiring tourist, the Cosmopolitan was the creation of John C. Smith, a resourceful, energetic California tavern owner of high reputation. Born in Ohio, Smith emigrated to San Francisco by way of Panama in 1850. After a period of mining and tavern-keeping at various places, he came to Yosemite in 1870 from the Riffle Saloon in Sonora and set about building a deluxe bathhouse and barroom in the upper Valley. The enterprise was hailed as "filling a great civic need, with the promise of a more abundant life for Yosemite visitors and residents alike."

"One of the great necessities of Yo Semite Valley during the past ten years has been a saloon such as will be owned and conducted there by Mr. John C. Smith and opened on or before the 1st of May next for the reception of visitors," said the *Sonora Union Democrat* in its issue of November 5, 1870. "Each year we hear of the complaints of travelers with regard to the accommodations and the absence of those refinements which are inseparable to celebrated watering places. . ."

Smith embarked on his project without approval from the commissioners, who voted on July 30, 1870, "to allow no further leases until it has been legally decided that the Commissioners have exclusive control of the grant." On August 3, 1870, the board instructed Guardian Galen Clark to "destroy any buildings in Yosemite Valley erected with-out permission, especially a certain billiard saloon said to be in the process of construction by one John Smith." Smith then belatedly

applied to the state for a lease, which the board refused to grant until the court decision was final. The commissioners ultimately allowed Smith to pay an annual use fee, an arrangement that continued until January 23, 1875, when he received a ten-year lease to his premises at $250 a year.

The billiard room of the Cosmopolitan contained two tables and an elaborate bar. Transporting the heavy tables on mules down the steep trail to the Valley floor must have challenged the skills of the packers.

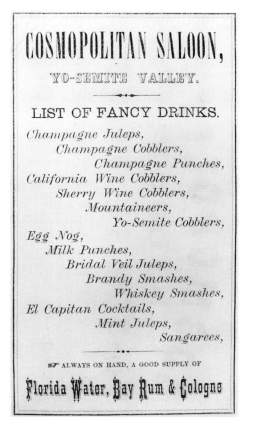

The Cosmopolitan's main building was eighty by twenty-five feet, with a ten-foot-wide covered porch along three sides. Helen Hunt Jackson described the structure in 1872:

"A long, low, dark-brown house, with a piazza on two sides . . . [it] consists of nine rooms. A billiard-room, where are two fine billiard-tables; a reading-room, where are the California newspapers, and a long writing table, with stationery ready to one's hand; a small sitting-room, furnished with sofas and comfortable easy-chairs, and intended exclusively for the use of ladies; and five small bath-rooms, perfectly appointed in all respects and kept with the most marvelous neatness. A small store-room at the end completes the list of rooms.

"The bath-tubs shine; the floors of the bath-rooms are carpeted; Turkish towels hang on the racks; soaps, bottles of cologne, and bay rum are kept in each room; a pincushion stands under each glass, and on the pincushion are not only pins, but scissors, needles, thread, and buttons of several kinds. Has anybody ever seen public bath-rooms of this order? And Mr. Smith mentions, apologetically, that the button-hooks for which he has sent have not yet arrived."

Hot water for the baths was heated by circulation in iron pipes running through a firebox stoked with wood. The billiard room contained a long, ornate bar, from which proprietor Smith dispensed a remarkable assortment of "gin slings, mint juleps, brandy cocktails, eye-openers, corpse revivers, and other potent combinations" in elaborate glasses. High quality wines and cigars were also stocked in abundance. For his visitors' further comfort, Smith built a half-mile-long walkway of four-foot planks from Black's Hotel to his building. The boardwalk stood four feet off the ground to provide a dry pathway during occasional high water and had benches at several places for weary pedestrians to rest.

The Cosmopolitan's grandeur was all the more remarkable in that at least some of the building material (Smith may have purchased lumber from Hutchings, whose sawmill was then in operation), and all of the equipment, furnishings, and supplies for the saloon had to be carried on the backs of mules from the terminus of the stage road, at that time a distance of perhaps fifteen miles. Ornate doors, full-length mirrors, even the billiard tables came down the steep cliff-side trail without mishap, although many of the bulky loads no doubt taxed the ingenuity of the packers.

The Cosmopolitan opened for business in the spring of 1871 to the gratification of exhausted travelers recovering from the long, dusty ride to the Valley. The saloon's comforts drew high praise from patrons ("A hot bath, shave, haircut, billiards, and fancy drinks—what more could anyone ask?"), and so did owner Smith, who quickly became a popular and well respected member of the community. On June 12, 1875, the *Mariposa Gazette* printed these words of praise: "John C. Smith. . . has won the distinction of being the most tasteful and expert saloon-keeper and bartender in California. He is now located at Yo Semite, and has established there the brag saloon of the State. . . 'See Paris and die' has passed into a proverb, but a better one is 'Visit Yo Semite and take a drink at Johnny Smith's saloon.'"

THE LICK HOUSE

The Lick House, a fourteen-by-twenty-four-foot wood-frame building with a lean-to addition at the rear, stood on the south side of the river road just east of Leidig's Hotel in the Lower Village. During the early 1870s, it served as a boardinghouse for guides employed by Henry Washburn and John McCready of Mariposa, who were partners in a saddle-train business transporting tourists from the end of the road at Clark's Station to the Valley floor. Washburn and McCready also owned the stage line running between the railroad connection at Merced and Clark's Station via Mariposa. The "Lick House" designation was a tongue-in-cheek reference to the luxurious San Francisco hotel of that name.

After the Wawona Road was completed from the South Fork to the Lower Village in 1875, the Yosemite Stage & Turnpike Company (successor to Washburn and McCready) erected a substantial two-story boardinghouse for its drivers and hostlers on the south side of the Merced River northeast of present Camp Curry. First called the Upper Lick House ("Upper" was dropped after the state razed the original Lick House in the 1880s), the new accommodations were part of a sprawling stable complex that by 1888 comprised a five-board corral, 80 by 128 feet; a barn, 48 by 60 feet; a coach house, 16 by 40 feet; and several smaller buildings. The barn accommodated thirty horses and their feed; the coach house provided shelter for four stages. The extensive operation endured until motor coaches replaced horse-drawn vehicles in Yosemite in 1915.

John Smith's Cosmopolitan is pictured here with a group of patrons gathered on the piazza. An advertising leaflet issued about 1874 described the premises as offering "a fine ladies' parlor, a gent's reading room, several superb billiard tables, hot and cold baths for ladies and gentlemen, a barbershop, bootblack stand, swings, quoits, shuffleboards, and a fine shooting gallery. Arrangements for laundry can be made."

THE VERNAL FALL LADDERS AND FOLSOM'S FERRY

When the settlement of Yosemite Valley by whites began in 1856, a primitive Indian path to the tops of Vernal and Nevada Falls already existed (probably up the general route of the present horse trail). The Mariposa Battalion followed this track while searching for Indians during the volunteers' first primitive expedition in March, 1851. Lafayette Bunnell described the initial exploration of the area in his book *Discovery of the Yosemite:*

"Gilbert and Chandler came in with their detachments just at dark from their tiresome explorations of the southern branches. Only a small squad of their commands climbed above the Vernal and Nevada Falls; and seeing the clouds resting upon the mountains above the Nevada Fall, they retraced their steps through the showering mist of the Vernal, and joined their comrades, who had already started down its rocky gorge. These men found no Indians, but they were the first discoverers of the Vernal and Nevada Falls, and the Little Yosemite."

After Stephen Cunningham took over the Lower Hotel in the spring of 1858, he and others built a toll route from the Valley to the top of Vernal Fall. They began by improving the old Indian trail running along the south side of the Merced River to the base of Vernal Fall. Here they erected a pair of elongated wooden ladders, which provided a wet and rather scary passageway up the vertiginous cliffs alongside the fall. On July 31, 1858, the *Tuolumne Courier* reported that "artificial steps are being prepared by Mr. Neal to get up Vernal Fall." John Neal was Cunningham's manager at the Lower Hotel that summer.

Cunningham was succeeded as proprietor of the Vernal Fall trail and ladders by Ira B. Folsom, who also acquired the Merced River ferry when Cunningham sold his hotel and other interests and took temporary leave of the Valley in the early 1860s. The commissioners reported in 1867 that "Mr. Folsom has a claim to the ferry and the ladders." The board noted that "the building of the new bridge at the lower end of the valley does away with the necessity for a ferry," and that "a set of steps, or staircase, should be erected at the Vernal Fall, in place of the present ladders, which are awkward and perhaps even dangerous for ladies to climb."

Accounts by tourists of scrambles up and down the slippery wooden rungs would give a modern safety expert nightmares. John Olmsted described his adventure in 1868:

"The real hard work was now to be done. Above us the path grew steeper and steeper, until it led along the face of a sloping rock partially covered with muck—where the wind blew furiously, and the spray from the fall was blinding. At this juncture I availed myself, for once, of the strong hand of the guide. On a slippery shelving rock, with a seething cauldron on our left, a precipice on our right, with a boggy, slushy path rising before us, a thick penetrating spray eddying around, filling our eyes and ears, the wind roaring, and bellowing, and lashing against us, and the thunders of the cataract booming on our ears—surely this was a position to be sought but once in a lifetime, and to be endured but once more, and that from necessity.

"Soon, however, the whole party were safely at the foot of a high

Carleton Watkins photographed the abandoned original ladders up to the top of Vernal Fall, and Snow's new stairway, which was built alongside the old ladders in 1871.

rock, parallel with the face of the fall, where stood a ladder about sixty feet long, nearly perpendicular. Stepping from the top round on to a ledge of rock, I found another ladder some twenty feet high, at right angles with the first, from the top of which a little smart climbing brought the party to a smooth expanse of rock at the very verge of the Vernal Fall."

Another early visitor said: "There is an awfully pokerish ladder fastened against the cliff on which you can go down and get very wet. It is painful and rather dangerous, but a great many persons escape, and they only charge you seventy-five cents."[29]

James Hutchings wrote about a trip up the ladders in 1869: "Still ascending and advancing, we are soon enveloped in a sheet of heavy spray driven down upon us with such force as to resemble a heavy storm of comminuted rain. . . In a few minutes we stand at the foot of 'The Ladders.' Beneath a large, overhanging rock at our right is a man who takes toll for ascending the ladders, eats, and 'turns in' to sleep upon the rock. The charge for ascending and descending is seventy-five cents; and as this includes the trail as well as the ladders, the charge is very reasonable."[30]

Ira Folsom sold the Vernal ladders and the rights to the Valley ferry to one Philip Coulter about 1868. The original ferry set up by Cunningham ten years earlier washed away in the great flood of 1867–68 which also took out both the state's new bridge and Hutchings' bridge. "All the bridges were carried away," Guardian Clark said, in describing the damage in the Valley, "and the ferry boat has gone altogether along with the tree to which it was fastened." In the absence of other means of crossing the Merced River, a toll ferry once again became a practical investment.

On August 4, 1868, the *Mariposa Gazette* reported that "the Mariposa County Board of Supervisors has issued a franchise to Philip Coulter to operate a toll ferry on the Merced River in Yosemite Valley. Tolls are set as follows: horseman and horse (or mule), $1.00; footman, 50 cents; loose horse or mule, 25 cents." Coulter was listed as the owner of the ferry, the ladders to Vernal Fall, and improvements in Yosemite Valley with an appraised valuation of three hundred dollars.

The intrepid John Olmsted crossed the Merced on Coulter's ferry in 1868: "Just above the base of 'The Captain' we had to cross the river in a scow, with our horses," he wrote. "As the river at this point swept close along the northern bank, we had no trouble getting on to the scow; but the difficulty was

The old ladders and Snow's stairway in the early 1880s. This George Fiske photograph first appeared in James Hutchings' In the Heart of the Sierras *in 1886.*

Snow's toll-collection cabin at "Register Rock" stood at the start of the two toll routes to Nevada Fall (stairway or horse trail). Photographer Carleton Watkins' developing tent can be seen under the overhang of the rock.

The bridge built by Phil Coulter in 1870 and later called the Folsom bridge. The structure fell into disuse after the state constructed the lower iron bridge in 1878.

THE YOSEMITE GRANT: 1864–1906

to get off—for the river had overflowed the flats on the other side, and the boatman had to hold the scow by the aid of a rope tied to a tree while he jumped our horses off the bow. The water was three feet deep and running swiftly. After much urging [my horse] took the plunge, giving me no greater wetting than soaked feet and a thorough sprinkling . . . and we soon reached dry land again."

In 1870 Coulter built a truss-type wooden toll bridge, 110 feet in length, just upriver from his ferry. The bridge stood until about 1890 when it was swept away by a spring flood, although the guardian reported in 1882 that the structure was "utterly unsafe." The county assessment role for 1870 showed Coulter as the owner of a bridge and residence on the Merced River near Leidig's Hotel, valued at one thousand dollars, and the ladders at Vernal Fall, valued at five hundred dollars.

At a meeting held August 3, 1870, the commissioners voted to notify the "parties in charge of the ladders to discontinue the collection of tolls or otherwise they will be indicted." They also passed a motion to "inform Phil Coulter that he may collect 50 cents toll on the bridge he has constructed without permission in the valley for a period of two years from June 1, 1870. If he declines he will be presented for indictment."

In 1872, unable to meet his debts, Coulter signed over the rights to his business to the mortgage holder, Ira Folsom, who assumed active management of "one bridge, known as Phil Coulter's Bridge, valued at $500; merchandise, $500; and one horse, $50." The "merchandise" most likely consisted of the contents of a small store and saloon that Coulter opened in a portion of his combination tollhouse-residence. Coulter's building, which measured about sixteen by thirty feet, stood near his bridge on the west side of the Merced River.

On January 6, 1871, the commissioners authorized Guardian Galen Clark "to make arrangements with Mr. Albert Snow for the construction of a stairway at the Vernal Fall with the privilege of collection toll thereon." During that summer, Snow, in partnership with son-in-law Colwell Drew, built a sturdy wooden stairway with railings to the top of the fall. Before the new access could be completed, Giacomo Campi, an Italian restaurateur from San Francisco, fell to his death in June, 1871, the only known fatality resulting from climbing the rickety old ladders. Snow collected tolls from travelers on the stairs and his horse trail to Nevada Fall until 1882 when the routes were acquired by the state. In the summer of 1874, Folsom erected a large new building north of Black's Hotel with the announced intention of installing a saloon, store, and dance floor. "Ira Folsom proposes to have his new establishment complete for next spring's travel," the *Mariposa Gazette* reported on September 5, 1874. "It is situated opposite Black's Hotel." The following month, when the state bought out all Valley claims, Folsom's bridge and buildings passed to the Yosemite Board of Commissioners.[31]

The upper iron bridge replaced Hutchings' wood-truss structure across the Merced River near his hotel in 1878.

THE DEATH OF JAMES C. LAMON

This ornate marker in the Yosemite cemetery denotes the final resting place of James C. Lamon, Yosemite's first white settler. Galen Clark stands third from the left.

James Lamon, Yosemite Valley's pioneer settler, was popular with tourists and residents alike. Hutchings called him a man of "uniform kindness and many virtues." In 1869 he built a "commodious" two-story log cabin (his third) near the site of the present Ahwahnee Hotel and cultivated the land around it. The *Mariposa Gazette* reported in April that "Mr. Lamon has been getting out material for a two-story hewed log house, and making a line fence on his lower boundary. He is now pruning his fruit trees, and showing the young buds which way to 'shoot.'"

A passive participant in Hutchings' lengthy litigation with the state, Lamon was elated to receive twelve thousand dollars for his claim in October, 1874, especially after the commissioners granted him a lease to his former property at a low rent. Lamon had only a short time to enjoy his newfound prosperity, for he died suddenly of pneumonia on May 22, 1875, at the age of fifty-eight. His grave in the Yosemite cemetery is marked by a tall monolith carved from local white granite by John Conway. The impressive monument was ordered and paid for at a cost of fifteen hundred dollars by Lamon's heirs.

THE FIRST WHEELED VEHICLES IN YOSEMITE VALLEY

In 1870 Guardian Galen Clark had a carriage taken apart and packed in pieces onto mules for transport into Yosemite Valley where it was reassembled. Horses were harnessed, and Clark gave free rides to all Valley residents. Repeated travel by the three-seat, nine-passenger vehicle widened some of the trails into crude roadbeds in the upper part of the Valley. Clark later hired his carriage out to tourists as a pioneer taxi, charging fifty cents to Mirror Lake and one dollar to the Cascades. (Clark's conveyance is now on display at the Pioneer History Center in Wawona.)

Not to be outdone, James Hutchings paid for a light two-horse stage to be carried in in sections the ensuing summer. The *Sacramento Daily Record-Union* reported its arrival on August 7, 1871: "A dispatch dated August 5 at Yosemite says that yesterday, J. M. Hutchings' new stage, 'The Pioneer,' was packed down the mountain on mules and made its first trip up the valley, arriving in front of the hotel. The advent of so useful a visitor was welcomed by prolonged cheers and the firing of guns. It is an event in the history of progress."

Hutchings then hired John Conway to build a road down the north side of the Valley to a junction with the horse trail near El Capitan. Here saddle-weary travelers could transfer to a four-wheeled carriage that would transport them in relative comfort to their destination farther up the Valley. Besides the income from the brief stage ride,

Hutchings had the great advantage of steering tourists directly to his hotel, a situation not appreciated by rivals Black and Leidig.

THE END OF THE GRANT'S FIRST DECADE

By 1875 Yosemite Valley had become a bustling summer community, with an annual visitation of some twenty-five hundred tourists. Activities centered in two separate settlements connected by John Smith's long boardwalk. The so-called Upper Village consisted largely of Hutchings' three hotel buildings, Aaron Harris' store, and the Cosmopolitan saloon and bathhouse. The larger Lower Village, seven-tenths of a mile west, comprised McCauley's toll house, two Folsom buildings, Black's and Leidig's Hotels, Flores' laundry, Westfall's butcher shop, the original Lick House, stables, and several residences and miscellaneous buildings. Year-round population averaged about twenty-five persons, nearly half of them children.

Skilled packers and sturdy, sure-footed mules were employed to carry all sorts of cumbersome loads to Yosemite Valley before roads were completed in 1874–75. William Henry Jackson's photograph of a similar conveyance illustrates how Galen Clark's wagon might have been arranged for transport in 1870.

NOTES AND REFERENCES

1. The governing body's legal title, as prescribed in the legislative act of April 2, 1866, accepting the Yosemite Grant, was "The Commissioners to Manage the Yosemite Valley and the Mariposa Big Tree Grove." The group was more commonly known as "The Yosemite Board of Commissioners."

2. In later life, James Terry Gardner (1842–1912) adopted an earlier family spelling, "Gardiner."

3. Gardner and Clarence King (1842–1912) were assisted in the grant survey by Dick Cotter, a packer and mountain climber, and four volunteers. Gardner was in charge of the boundary determination; King handled the topographical and geological material. King describes some of the survey's procedures and gives a

vivid and perceptive account of Yosemite's outstanding features in his book, *Mountaineering in the Sierra Nevada* (1872; reprint, with an introduction by James M. Shebl, Lincoln and London: University of Nebraska Press, 1970). After *The Yosemite Book* and *The Yosemite Guide-Book* were published, Charles Hoffmann, a young German engineer with a talent for map making and a member of the geological survey, found a number of errors in the topographical investigation of the Valley floor, which had been done by King and his assistant William Hyde.

The mistakes resulted in the meanders of the Merced River being incorrectly drawn on the survey's map of Yosemite Valley. On October 10, 1869, Whitney wrote to William Brewer about the matter: "Hoffmann and I have just been looking at the map of the Yos. Valley and find that all the part done by King, or pretended to be done by him—namely the bottom of the valley—has got to come out and be put in correctly for a new edition, as the whole of King's work there was a complete sham." When a revised edition of *The Yosemite Guide-Book* was published in 1870, it included a corrected map.

The vast difference in the two maps was a source of considerable embarrassment to Whitney and his associates. King's faulty work is discussed in Francis Farquhar, *Yosemite, the Big Trees and the High Sierra* (Berkeley and Los Angeles: University of California Press, 1948), 33–34; and Robert Harry Block, "The Whitney Survey of California, 1860–74, A Study of Environmental Science and Exploration" (Ph.D. diss., University of California, Los Angeles, 1982), 341–47.

4. The Mariposa Estate was private property, owned at first by John C. Frémont under a Spanish land grant, and later by two successive incorporated companies. Covering almost seventy square miles about the town of Mariposa, the estate included seven gold mines, four ore-crushing mills, two company stores, a railroad, water system, and a tenant population of three to five thousand miners. "A famous property," Horace Greeley said after an 1859 visit, "perhaps the finest mining property in the world." Nevertheless, the best days of the estate were already past when Olmsted assumed active management in October, 1863, for the New York capitalists who had acquired the property from Frémont earlier in the year and formed a new $10 million corporation.

A major cause of the company's problems was the administration of Trevor William Park (1823–1882), superintendent under Frémont from 1860 to 1863, who had been paid 5 percent of the gross income in addition to a handsome guaranteed salary. This resulted in Park's depletion of the richest, most easily reached veins while neglecting all expenses related to long-term development. At the end of his lucrative tenure, Park departed California with an estimated $1.5 million in cash.

Olmsted, who was not a mining expert, made some ill-advised decisions in his own right, spending nearly $250,000 on unproductive surface improvements and an abortive tunnel. The principal cause of the operation's untimely demise, however, was the culpability of the Eastern bankers who sold millions of dollars worth of stock to an unwary public, then diverted the proceeds to their own pockets rather than paying off the company's considerable debts. When the estate fell into receivership in November, 1865, the *Mariposa Gazette* called it a "great Wall Street swindle."

5. Schuyler Colfax (1823–1885) was born in New York City but moved to Indiana in 1836. Elected to the House of Representatives in 1854, he served seven terms. He was Speaker of the House (1864–69) and vice president of the United States during President Ulysses S. Grant's first term (1869–73). After becoming caught up in the Credit Mobilier of America scandal, in which Colfax and other high government officials, including some members of Congress, were accused of taking bribes, he departed public life.

6. Olmsted's monograph was unearthed and first brought to public notice by Laura Wood Roper in Frederick Law Olmsted, "The Yosemite Valley and the Mariposa Big Trees: A Preliminary Report, 1865," with an introductory note by Laura Wood Roper, *Landscape Architecture* 43 (October 1952): 12–25; also see "The Lost Report by Frederick Law Olmsted," *The Living Wilderness* (Winter, 1952–53).

7. Olmsted was overly optimistic in his estimate of the cost of a scenic road to Yosemite Valley. When the three toll roads were finished in 1874–75, during a time of severe national recession, the outlays for each road ranged from fifty-six to seventy-one thousand dollars.

8. Olmsted revisited the Mariposa Big Tree Grove in 1886, but for unknown reasons did not enter Yosemite Valley.

9. Henry William Cleaveland (1827–1919) practiced architecture in New York City for four years before moving to California where he resumed his profession in 1859. He may have met Olmsted in September, 1864, when both attended Henry Bellow's farewell dinner in San Francisco.

10. Whitney, Ashburner, and Raymond to Governor F. F. Low, November, 1865, in the California State Archives, Roseville.

11. Some writers have theorized that Whitney, Ashburner, and Raymond shelved Olmsted's plan because they feared it would compete with the California Geological Survey for funding in the legislature, but this assumption appears to be unwarranted. While it is true that Whitney was the state geologist, he also had a great affection for Yosemite Valley. Furthermore, Ashburner, whom Olmsted said he was "very close to—much more so than to anybody else in California," had resigned from the geological survey three years before to enter private practice. He was an ardent supporter of the Yosemite Grant. And it seems unlikely that Raymond, the instigator of the Yosemite legislation, would have had any reason to support such a scheme.

12. The by-laws of the Yosemite Board of Commissioners are reprinted as Appendix D.

13. "On December 23, 1867, after a snow fall of about three feet, a heavy down-pour of rain set in, and incessantly continued for ten successive days. . . The whole meadow land of the Valley was covered by a surging and impetuous flood to an average depth of nine feet. Bridges were swept away, and everything floatable was carried off." This eyewitness account appeared in James Hutchings, *In the Heart of the Sierras* (Oakland and Yosemite: Pacific Press Publishing House, 1886), 492.

14. The act of the California state legislature accepting the Yosemite Grant, approved April 2, 1866, specified that the commissioners "shall make a full report of the condition of said premises, and of their acts under this law, and of their expenditures, through the Governor, to the Legislature, at every regular session thereof." The reports, which contain minor variations in titles and printer's imprints, are biennial (except for 1880) because the legislature met only every other year. There are nineteen numbers in all from 1866–67 through 1903–04 (no report was published for 1899–1900 or 1905–06). Complete or nearly complete files can be found in the Yosemite Research Library, the California State Library at Sacramento, and the Bancroft Library in Berkeley. For a check list of the reports, see Francis Farquhar, *Yosemite, The Big Trees, and the High Sierra*, 89–94. The minute books (1864–1903) of the Yosemite Board of Commissioners, consisting of seventeen volumes, are on deposit in the California State Archives, Roseville.

15. Hutchings, *In the Heart,* 153

16. Quoted in Margaret Sanborn, *Yosemite, Its Discovery, Its Wonders, and Its People* (1981; reprint, Yosemite: Yosemite Association, 1989), 94.

17. John Olmsted, *A Trip to California in 1868* (New York: Trow's Print. and Bookbinding Co., 1880), 75.

18. Mrs. Wolfe erroneously said that Muir "also planned and built the 'Big Tree Room,' unique in that it was constructed around the bole of an enormous cedar." Perhaps Muir made some improvements to Hutchings' Big Tree Room, but it was definitely in place well before his arrival on the Yosemite scene in November, 1869. Cosie Hutchings, James Hutchings' younger daughter, said she was born in the Big Tree Room in October, 1867. John Olmsted, who stayed at Hutchings' in June, 1868, wrote: "The kitchen of the hotel is built around a cedar tree, seven feet in diameter and 200 feet high. . . a large rear room where an immense fireplace, filled with logs, was shedding its cheering, warming light."

19. John Muir was born at Dunbar, Scotland, in 1838. He migrated to America with his family when he was eleven years old; attended the University of Wisconsin, 1860–63; came to California in 1867, which was his home until his death. He visited Yosemite briefly in 1868, moved there in November, 1869, and remained for five years except for short intervals.

Muir's many influential articles, beginning with "Yosemite Glaciers" in the *New York Tribune* of December 5, 1871, stem from his Yosemite experiences and did much to popularize the Sierra Nevada. Muir's published writings are extensive, and writings about him equally so. The definitive biography is Linnie Marsh Wolfe, *Son of the Wilderness, the Life of John Muir* (New York: Alfred A. Knopf, 1945).

Hutchings' bitterness toward Muir became obvious in 1886 with the publication of his classic book, *In the Heart of the Sierras.* In all the nearly 150,000 words of text about Yosemite, Hutchings made not a single mention of Muir.

20. Olmsted, *A Trip to California,* 66–67.

21. The second of the Leidigs' eleven children, tiny daughter Agnes, born February 24, 1867, died on December 21, 1868, reportedly after eating some spoiled frozen peaches. First buried near the present Ahwahnee Hotel, she was reinterred some years later in the Yosemite cemetery. Son Charles Leidig (1869–1956) was the first white boy born in Yosemite Valley (March 8).

22. Under the terms of the lease, the state was the actual owner of Leidig's Hotel. Only the furnishings belonged to the proprietor. When the structure was razed by the commissioners in the summer of 1888, Davanay's note, with interest figured at 3 percent, amounted to more than thirty-three hundred dollars—a sum that neither the state nor Leidig felt obliged to pay. Testimony of William Coffman, a close friend of Davanay's, before the Investigative Committee of the state assembly in 1889.

23. Emily Snow's story of "eleven feet of Snow" appears in several places, notably Hutchings, *In the Heart,* 448. The version given here was related by M. Hall McAllister of San Francisco in a letter to Dr. Carl Russell dated January 31, 1927, copy in the Yosemite Research Library. In his letter McAllister describes a visit to La Casa Nevada in April, 1888.

24. Olmsted, *A Trip to California,* 91–92.

25. The King and Gardner Yosemite map of 1865 shows "Trail from Peregoy's," which indicates that Peregoy was running cattle at that early date.

26. The National Park Service considerably altered Conway's original route and eased the grades in the 1920s, so that the trail—although still called the Four Mile Trail—is now nearly five miles long.

27. James Bradley Thayer, *A Western Journey with Mr. Emerson* (1884; reprint, with a foreword and notes by Shirley Sargent, San Francisco: The Book Club of California, 1980), 66.

28. In their book *The Big Oak Flat Road to Yosemite* (1959; reprint, Fredericksburg, TX: Awani Press, 1986), 239–40, authors Irene Paden and Margaret Schlichtmann have a brief account of Gentry, the only historical description I have found. They call him "Colonel E. S. Gentry," which may be correct, but all three newspapers accounts used in this text give the name as "John S. Gentry."

29. Dio Lewis, *Gypsies, or Why We Went Gypsying in the Sierras* (Boston: Eastern Book Company, 1881), 170–71.

30. James Hutchings, *Scenes of Wonder and Curiosity in California,* 3rd ed. (New York and San Francisco: A. Roman and Company, 1870), 131–32.

31. Folsom's ferry, toll bridge, and buildings were probably built on land leased from Alexander Black, which Black had earlier acquired from Steve Cunningham. When the state bought out the Valley claimants in 1874, Black was originally awarded twenty-two thousand dollars, out of which he was to pay Folsom. When the two could not agree on a division of funds, the state made the final determination: Black, thirteen thousand dollars; Folsom, six thousand dollars. It appears that the inflexibility of the two men cost them three thousand dollars.

Ira Blaisdel Folsom (1832–1934) was born in Gilford, New Hampshire, where his family had lived since 1639. He emigrated to California in 1855; mined for several years with some success on the Feather River; and came to Yosemite Valley in the 1860s after hearing of its wonders. Folsom left Yosemite in 1875; served four years as a deputy sheriff in Fresno County; moved to Mariposa about 1880; and was employed in that county as a deputy sheriff for a number of years. Married with three children, Folsom later lived in Coulterville and Spring Gulch, and eventually acquired a store in Big Oak Flat. Called "a man with many friends and no enemies," he died in Big Oak Flat in 1934 at the age of 102.

Folsom Street in San Francisco and the town of Folsom (the location of Folsom Prison) were named for Ira Folsom's second cousin, Joseph Folsom, who came west before the gold rush and acquired considerable property in the area where the town is now situated.

CHAPTER V

Stage Roads Reach Yosemite Valley (1874–75)

THE YOSEMITE COMMISSIONERS ENCOURAGE TURNPIKE CONSTRUCTION

During the first nineteen years after James Hutchings' pathfinding tourist party of July, 1855, a period when horse trails provided the only access to Yosemite Valley, fewer than thirteen thousand persons visited the new scenic marvel. The effort and expense of the arduous journey limited sightseers, according to the Yosemite commissioners, to that "small leisure class who have the time to spend in travel for recreation. . . the larger portion of the population being busily engaged in the accumulation of wealth."

The advantages of a carriage road to the Valley had been noted by Frederick Law Olmsted as early as 1865, but the state legislature, which failed to appropriate enough money to pay even the guardian's small salary in those beginning years, was clearly not about to underwrite such a costly endeavor. Facing more immediate problems within the grant itself, the commissioners adopted a hands-off policy regarding access roads.

"We do not consider it any part of our duty to improve the approaches to the valley or Big Trees," they said in their initial report to the legislature in 1867. "This may safely be left to the competition of the counties, towns, and individuals interested in securing the travel." The commissioners did offer to grant franchises for the construction of roads within the grant, in return for which the builders would be authorized to collect tolls for use of their rights-of-way. It was specified, however, that these roads would pass to the state and become free whenever the legislature appropriated sufficient funds for their purchase. By the late 1860s, three turnpike companies were in various stages of formation in the rival foothill communities of Mariposa, Coulterville, and Big Oak Flat, their backers well aware that the first stage route to reach Yosemite Valley would be heavily used.[1]

ORGANIZATION OF THE BIG OAK FLAT ROAD

On September 19, 1868, a group of prominent citizens in Tuolumne County headed by George E. Sprague, L. E. Stuart, and John B. Smith formed the Chinese Camp and Yo Semite Turnpike Company, with the declared intent of building a toll road from Chinese Camp, through Big Oak Flat, First and Second Garrotes,[2] across the Pilot Peak Ridge, through Crane and Tamarack Flats, to a point on the summit overlooking Yosemite Valley. On February 20, 1869, the state of California granted the company a franchise to run for fifty years.

A month later, on March 19, the group met again and elected permanent officers. Abraham Halsey of Chinese Camp was named president, and plans were formulated to issue eight hundred shares of stock at

twenty-five dollars a share. In September, 1869, the company obtained exclusive rights from the Yosemite Board of Commissioners to build a wagon road within the Yosemite Grant, entering from the north side of the Valley. The privilege was contingent on the road's completion by July 1, 1871. On January 20, 1871, the company incorporated under the title of the Yosemite Turnpike Road Company, thus changing its status to that of a stock company.

In the spring of 1869, a "great army of workers," including many Chinese, began the challenging road-building project. Their tools were rudimentary: picks, shovel, axes, and wheelbarrows. Large quantities of black powder, which was hardly stronger than gunpowder, were used to blast out immovable rocks. In June, 1870, following basically along the path of the old Big Oak Flat Trail, the road reached Hodgdon's Station. Two months later it had been completed to Crane Flat, and by July, 1871, the road had been pushed through to Gentry's Station at the edge of the towering cliffs overlooking the Merced River Canyon at the northwestern corner of the Yosemite Grant. From there the company faced the daunting task of building more than three miles of twisting right-of-way down a mountainside so steep and unstable that the contoured roadbed would have to be shored up nearly all the way. Even though the commissioners extended the deadline for completion of the road by an additional six months, the Big Oak Flat group, lacking both

Beginning in August, 1871, tourists could ride along the north side Valley road, shown here, from the end of the Coulterville-Big Oak Flat Trail near El Capitan to their hotel in Hutchings' stage, which he packed in on the backs of mules. (Author's collection)

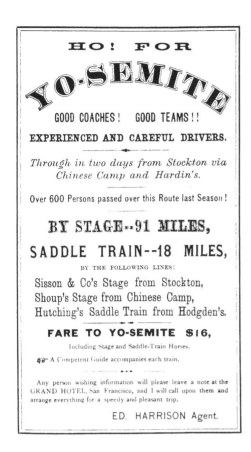

An 1870 poster advertised the virtues of the Big Oak Flat route during saddle-train days. (Author's collection)

Dr. John Taylor McLean completed the first stage road to Yosemite Valley in June, 1874, and squandered his entire fortune in the process. (Author's collection)

time and money, forfeited its exclusive franchise on January 1, 1872, and did not ask to have it renewed.

WORK BEGINS ON THE COULTERVILLE ROAD

Meanwhile, Coulterville businessmen had become painfully aware that they needed their own road into Yosemite Valley to stay competitive in the tourist business. In February, 1870, they organized the Coulterville Road Company and began advertising for laborers. By May a crew of more than forty men was grading a new right-of-way from the end of the public road at Bower Cave, a limestone cavern and later a tourist stop, east along the south slope of Pilot Peak to Hazel Green. (Different from the Big Oak Flat Road, the Coulterville Road did not follow the existing horse trail until the two routes converged just west of Hazel Green.)

On October 6, 1870, the Coulterville and Yo Semite Turnpike Company filed incorporation papers at the Mariposa County Courthouse, listing James Lindsey, president; J. W. Porter, secretary; and five others as directors. All seven men were prominent Coulterville-area settlers. The corporation's stated objective was to build a wagon road from Bower Cave through Hazel Green and Crane Flat to an unspecified point on the boundary line of the Yosemite Grant. Capital stock in the amount of twenty thousand dollars, divided into eight hundred shares at twenty-five dollars a share, was "certified to be fully subscribed, with 25 percent of said capital paid in."

"Coulterville people are pushing forward their road to Yosemite with great energy," the *Stockton Weekly Independent* reported on May 14, 1870. "The heaviest of the work is already completed . . . and by June 1 [the road] will reach Crane Flat, nine miles from the bluff." This estimate

proved inordinately optimistic, as it turned out. Soon reduced to a skeleton crew by financial shortages, Coulterville forces did not reach Crane Flat for another two years (August 13, 1872). Here they apparently intended to connect with the Big Oak Flat Road and share its route into the Valley just as the original trails had done for so many years.

A guide leads a group of tourists along the trail to Yosemite Valley. The women riding sidesaddle do not look very pleased with their journey.

THE MARIPOSA ROAD REACHES THE SOUTH FORK

Over on the south side of Yosemite, Galen Clark and his new partner Edwin Moore realized the necessity for developing easier access from Mariposa to their rustic hotel on the South Fork and eventually to the Valley itself. In February, 1870, they joined with others to organize the Mariposa Big Trees and Yo Semite Turnpike Company for the purpose of building a twelve-mile toll road from the end of the county road at Hogan's Ranch, east of Mariposa, to Clark and Moore's Station.

Construction began in the early spring of 1870 with John Conway in charge of the project. Grades were steep because twenty-eight hundred feet had to be ascended in five miles to reach the summit of Chowchilla Mountain. From the crest, the route plunged some seventeen hundred feet in a five-mile stretch to its terminus at the South Fork. By July, 1870, Conway had finished the road and travelers were using it. Toll charges, fixed by the Mariposa County Board of Supervisors, were one dollar for a hiker; two dollars for a carriage pulled by one horse; four dollars for two horses; on up to twelve dollars for a six-horse team. Clark and Moore collected the tolls, which they sorely needed, as the road had cost them more than twelve thousand dollars to construct, half of it in borrowed funds.

A HIATUS IN ROAD BUILDING

By the late summer of 1871, although no carriage road yet reached into Yosemite, the equestrian portion of the trip to the Valley had been reduced to twenty-three miles from Clark and Moore's on the south side and to only four and one-half miles from Gentry's on the north. Furthermore, after August, 1871, it was possible to ride from the bottom of the north side trail to the Upper Village in Hutchings' new stage, "The Pioneer," which had been packed in piecemeal and reassembled for use on the Valley floor.

"At last comes a gentler slope," one visitor wrote in 1871, "then a crystal spring, dense grove, and grass-covered plat, and we are down into the valley. Gladly we take the stage, and are whirled along in the gathering twilight."

With access to the Valley notably improved, the road-building flurry stopped abruptly in the spring of 1872. Along the Mariposa route, Clark and Moore were in such severe financial straits that they soon lost their holdings to their creditors. Over on the north side, backers of both the Coulterville and Big Oak Flat Roads had run out of funds, and further construction seemed unlikely for some time.

SADDLE-TRAIN DAYS

Once the Big Oak Flat Road reached Hodgdon's Station in June, 1870, regular stage service began over the new route, terminating wherever construction crews were working at the time. Travelers then transferred to James Hutchings' guided saddle train for the remainder of the journey to the Valley.

Hutchings soon had a rival in the person of Fred Brightman, a former employee, who started a competing saddle-train service about the time Gentry's became the end of the stage line in 1871. The greatly shortened horseback ride increased Yosemite visitation from the north

to such an extent that in 1873 Brightman utilized ninety-six horses to meet the demand.

The heyday of the saddle train was short-lived because stage roads were completed all the way to Valley hotels in June and July, 1874. Later that year, Hutchings' facilities were bought by the state. Brightman subsequently engaged in an abortive livery-stable venture in the Valley before taking a job with Henry Washburn's transportation company.

A buggy heads down the steep section of the Coulterville Road to the Merced River. Note the sheer drop-off at the right.

THE COULTERVILLE ROAD'S NEW OWNER

In June, 1872, Dr. John Taylor McLean, a prominent forty-eight-year-old physician from San Francisco, took over the Coulterville and Yosemite Turnpike Company and changed the face of Yosemite travel forever.[3] Dr. McLean first visited Yosemite in the summer of 1867. He, his wife Mary, and son Sterling journeyed by stage to Coulterville. There they mounted horses for the seventeen-mile ride to Black's Ranch on Bull Creek. Then came the wearisome thirty-three-mile ride through Hazel Green, Crane Flat, and Gentry's to the Valley floor. The trip proved so overwhelming for Mrs. McLean that she was confined to her bed for a week after reaching her hotel, and thus could not enjoy the sights she had come so far to see. Dr. McLean decided on that trip that the beauty of Yosemite Valley certainly justified an easier means of access.

In early June, 1872, when it became apparent that for financial and other reasons no road would soon be completed to Yosemite by any of the three interested groups, Dr. McLean "actively engaged himself in the road enterprise" by taking an option on the stock of the Coulterville and Yosemite Turnpike Company. He then petitioned the Yosemite Board of Commissioners for an exclusive franchise to extend a wagon road into Yosemite Valley from the north and to collect tolls for its use.

On June 16, 1872, the commissioners, who had heard nothing from Big Oak Flat Road officials in the six months since their franchise had

The Coulterville Road passed directly through the Merced Grove of Big Trees. This picture was taken in the early 1920s after automobiles had replaced horse-drawn vehicles. The cabin, built in 1915, was used for a time as a checking station by the federal government. A new cabin, erected in the grove in 1934, still stands. (Author's collection)

expired, adopted a resolution awarding an exclusive privilege to Dr. McLean for a period of ten years, and on August 13 entered into a formal contract. The commissioners were willing to grant this specific right because they doubted that anyone would put up the large sum needed for the enterprise without the assurance of being able to command all the travel from one side of Yosemite Valley. They also felt that the Mariposa business community would eventually construct a competing road from the south, and that one road entering the Valley on either side would suffice for years to come. The contract stipulated that a right-of-way suitable for a stage and four horses must be completed to the Valley within the year 1873.

Once the franchise was affirmed, Dr. McLean consummated his purchase of Coulterville and Yosemite Turnpike Company stock, ultimately acquiring 796 of the 800 outstanding shares. The price of approximately fifteen thousand dollars compensated the previous owners for the expense of building the nineteen-mile road from Bower Cave to Crane Flat. The original stockholders not only recouped their investment, but were assured of getting a road from Coulterville all the way to Yosemite Valley without any further cost to themselves.

In July, 1872, a "force of axe and linemen directed by a competent civil engineer prospected and surveyed" the best route for continuing the Coulterville Road to the Valley. "While making this survey," Dr. McLean later wrote, "a grove of big trees was discovered. . . It was determined to carry the road directly through this grove, which was named the Merced Grove of Big Trees by me because of its nearness to the Merced River."[4] The decision required abandoning six miles of existing roadway between Hazel Green and Crane Flat and created a more complex route to the Merced River Canyon, but Dr. McLean felt the attraction of the Big Trees justified the added expense of about ten thousand dollars.

From Hazel Green, elevation 5,665 feet, the serpentine right-of-way headed south through the Merced Grove of Big Trees, swung southeast past Buena Vista Gap where the first views of Yosemite loomed grandly in the distance, then proceeded on past Little Nellie Fall (named for McLean's daughter Mary Helen) on Little Crane Creek, before finally emerging from the thick pine forest onto the picturesque flat of Big Meadow. From a rise a mile south of here, the next two miles of the route dropped straight down a dizzying 16-percent grade into the Merced River Canyon, a half-mile west of the Cascades.

At the river junction, just below the "Blacksmith's Shop," the road turned sharply east and paralleled the river for four and one-half miles to the lower iron bridge where it joined the existing Valley road. (Before the lower iron bridge near El Capitan was constructed by the commissioners in 1878, stages crossed the Merced on Ira Folsom's bridge west of Black's Hotel, or continued up the north side of the river to Hutchings' bridge at the Upper Village. Hutchings had replaced Hite's original log bridge, which washed away in December, 1867, with a finished timber bridge.)[5]

Hutchings described the descent to the river canyon in his book, *In the Heart of the Sierras:* "This is made by a safe and excellent road, portions of the way having been blasted from the solid walls of the cañon. The passage of 'Devil's Gulch,' and other points of the bluff tell how formidable were the obstructions to be overcome when building this road. There is a cranny little spot at the foot of the hill known as 'The Blacksmith's Shop,' which consists of an irregular chamber formed entirely of huge bowlders that have toppled off and down from the surrounding cliffs, in the 'long, long ago.' Here the forge and anvil rung out their merry peals, while picks and drills and crow-bars needed on the road, were being sharpened." The Blacksmith's Shop was designated on Yosemite maps until 1938.

Dr. McLean's engineer had estimated that the cost of the eighteen-mile road from Hazel Green to the Valley floor would not exceed twenty thousand dollars. As it turned out, the actual figure was fifty-six thousand dollars! About twenty-four thousand dollars of this sum were spent blasting nearly four miles of roadbed out of solid rock between the top of the cliff and Cascade Creek.

The main Coulterville Road was thirty-one miles long from Bower Cave to the lower iron bridge in Yosemite Valley. With the six-mile branch to Crane Flat, plus a scenic three-quarter-mile wagon road built to the top of Pilot Peak, total construction encompassed nearly thirty-

A stage crawls up the steepest section of the Coulterville Road just above the junction with the Merced River. (John Fiske collection)

eight miles. The width averaged sixteen feet. In a few places where rock formations prevented the usual width, turnouts were built in plain view of each other. The average grade was about 8 percent, which included the final precipitous plunge to the Merced River. Cost of the project was seventy-one thousand dollars, an amount that his attorney later said "exhausted Dr. McLean's entire personal fortune."

During the late summer and fall of 1872, construction was pushed from both ends of the projected route. Crews working largely with hand tools and black powder cleared out rocks and trees from the winding right-of-way, then crowned and ditched the roadbed to the proper grade. Considerable cut and fill was required on the many miles of sidehill terrain. The last twenty-five hundred yards down to the Merced River were the most difficult. Here the tedious and dangerous process of setting powder charges, removing huge boulders, and erecting intricate retaining walls slowed progress to a crawl.

Compounding the problems was the unusually heavy winter of 1872–73. During the first six months of 1873, great drifts of snow stopped all work on the higher section of the route. When it became obvious that the road would not be finished by the deadline of December 31, 1873, an understanding board of commissioners heeded Dr. McLean's appeal and extended the contract for an additional calendar year.

By the end of August, 1873, the four and one-half miles of new road between the end of the existing Valley north side road and the Blacksmith's Shop west of Cascade Creek had been completed. On September 2, Hutchings' stage made the first trip over it to pick up tourists at the foot of the surveyor's trail running down to the river from the cliffs. By this time the upper end of the road, which stages were already using, had passed Big Meadow. This left only two miles of horse- or mule-back riding between San Francisco and the Valley hotels. The goal of a stage road all the way to Yosemite now seemed certain of attainment.

A small group of tourists enjoys the vista from the sharp zigzag turn on the Big Oak Flat Road, part way down the mountain from Gentry's Station. (Tuolumne County Historical Society collection)

THE BIG OAK FLAT ROAD RESUMES CONSTRUCTION

As the Coulterville Road drew ever closer to completion, Big Oak Flat Road officials knew they were in serious trouble. With a stage road that ended on top of a cliff, the Tuolumne County group could see that very few travelers would choose their route. Coulterville would be the overnight stopping place for tourists. Dr. McLean's company would operate the profitable toll gates. On August 29, 1872, the Yosemite Turnpike Road Company asked the commissioners for permission to build a road—not an exclusive right-of-way but just another toll road—

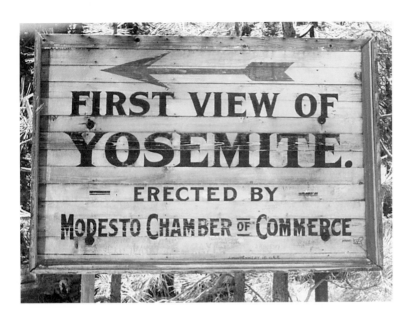

This sign at Buena Vista Gap greeted travelers on the Coulterville Road for many years until it burned in the forest fires of 1990. (Hank Johnston)

A surrey and a stage approach the Valley floor near the bottom of the descent from Gentry's on the Big Oak Flat Road. (Author's collection)

into Yosemite Valley. Because that privilege had already been granted exclusively to the Coulterville and Yosemite Turnpike Company, the board denied the petition, stating that the Coulterville Road involved a large expenditure, and its builders were counting on having sole entry rights from the north for a ten-year period in order to pay for it.

At the annual meeting of the commissioners on November 17, 1873, the Tuolumne group made a similar request and was again turned down. As a last resort, another petition was submitted by C. B. Cutting, president of the Yosemite Turnpike Road Company, to the Executive Committee of the board after the regular meeting offering to build a wagon road "forever free of tolls from Gentry's Station to the Yosemite Valley." This also met with failure.

Big Oak Flat directors now realized that their only option was to persuade the state legislature to override the commissioners' decision, just as it had done earlier in the matter of Hutchings' and Lamon's claims. The legislature was in recess, however, until early in 1874. The Tuolumne County group decided to use the intervening period improving the existing horse trail from Gentry's Station to the Valley. This would save time later if they were granted permission to build a road and would also show local legislators, whose support was essential, that the proposed route was practical. In October, 1873, the Yosemite Turnpike Road Company, through its secretary George E. Sprague, appealed to Guardian Galen Clark for authorization to "make certain trail improvements" within the Yosemite Grant. Clark granted the request.

During the next few months, working under the direction of Sprague, a surveyor by profession, crews labored along the steep mountainside between Gentry's and the Valley wherever snow allowed access. In some places, Sprague was obliged to erect a windlass and use ropes to lower and raise his chainman on the edges of the cliff so he could sight

Albert Henry Washburn was one of the most important men in Mariposa County during the last quarter of the nineteenth century.

the grade with his instruments. Despite the difficult going, Sprague's workmen moved steadily through the scrub and loose rocks and eventually contoured a winding right-of-way as nearly like a road as they dared. With its easy grades and unnecessarily wide curves, it had to have been one of the finest mountain horse trails in the state.

When the California legislature convened in 1874, Tuolumne County representatives introduced a measure granting the Yosemite Turnpike Company permission to enter the Valley on equal terms with the Coulterville Road. They contended in their presentation that the Yosemite commissioners had exceeded their authority in granting a monopoly to any one company. On February 17, 1874, over the strong objections of Coulterville partisans, the legislature passed the bill. The Tuolumne County group was back in the Yosemite road business.

Among those employed to improve the trail down from Gentry's were five Italian artisans, recent arrivals from Italy and wall builders by trade. The five told Sprague that if the company could raise sixteen thou-

A Yosemite Stage & Turnpike Company stage starts down the 12-percent grade below Inspiration Point heading for the Valley floor. (Author's collection)

sand dollars, they—along with others of their countrymen who were also experts at rock work—would expand the cliff-side trail into a road as rapidly as possible. Andrew Rocca of Big Oak Flat, the wealthy owner of the Golden Rock Water Company, lent the Yosemite Turnpike Road Company the required funds, agreeing to accept repayment out of toll receipts. Using the European technique of laying small rocks in wedge shape so they could not slip out, the skilled Italians cribbed up the steep sides of the twisting right-of-way without mortar. In just twenty weeks of labor, the clever wall builders completed the wagon road all the way to the Valley floor.

The thirty-four-mile toll portion of the Big Oak Flat Road began at the Tuolumne-Mariposa County line two miles northwest of Hamilton's Station (present Buck Meadows), and extended east through Hardin's Ranch, Hodgdon's Ranch, the Tuolumne Big Trees, Crane Flat, Tamarack Flat, and Gentry's Station, then dropped down the cliffs west of El Capitan to a junction with the Coulterville Road at the lower iron bridge. The road averaged thirteen feet in width, with an average grade of 8 percent and a maximum grade of 16 percent. Total construction cost was about fifty-six thousand dollars.

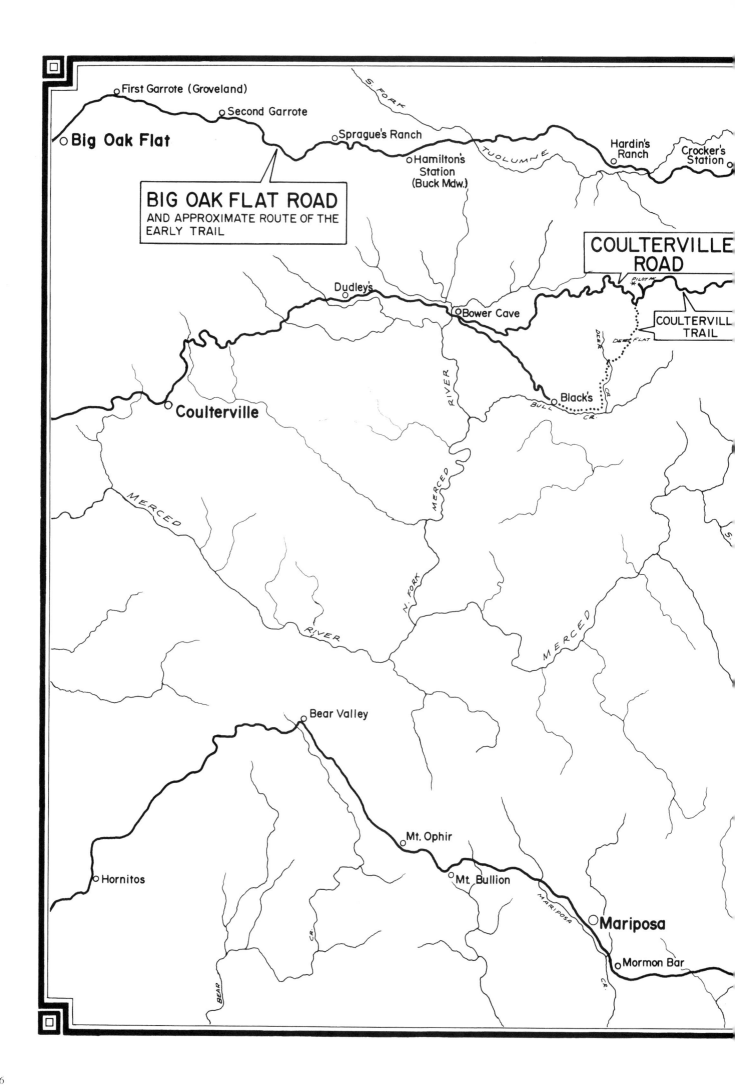

First Garrote (Groveland)

Second Garrote

S. FORK

Big Oak Flat

Sprague's Ranch

Hardin's Ranch

Crocker's Station

Hamilton's Station (Buck Mdw.)

TUOLUMNE

BIG OAK FLAT ROAD
AND APPROXIMATE ROUTE OF THE EARLY TRAIL

Dudley's

COULTERVILLE ROAD

PILOT PK.

Bower Cave

COULTERVILLE TRAIL

DEER FLAT

RIVER

Black's

BULL CR.

CR.

Coulterville

MERCED

MERCED

MERCED

N. FORK

RIVER

RIVER

S.

Bear Valley

Mt. Ophir

MARIPOSA

Hornitos

Mt. Bullion

Mariposa

BEAR CR.

CR.

Mormon Bar

CR.

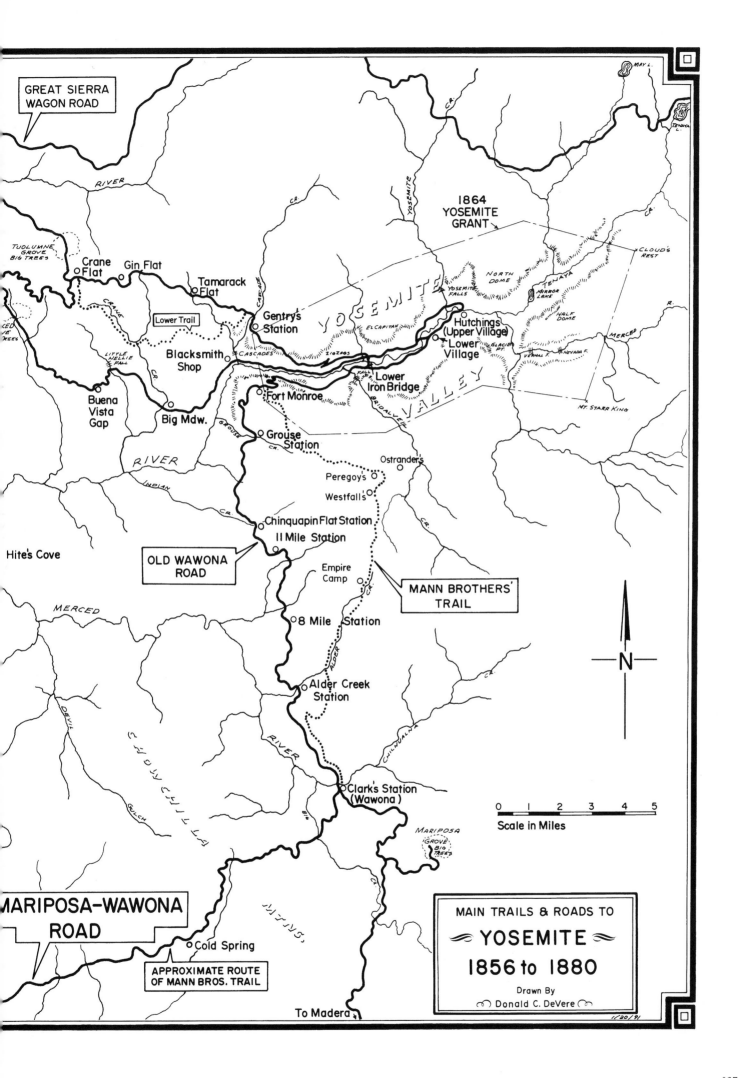

GREAT SIERRA
WAGON ROAD

TUOLUMNE
GROVE
BIG TREES

Crane
Flat

Gin Flat

Tamarack
Flat

Lower Trail

Gentrys
Station

Blacksmith
Shop

CASCADES

ZIGZAGS

Buena
Vista
Gap

Big Mdw.

Fort Monroe

Grouse
Station

Hite's Cove

OLD WAWONA
ROAD

MERCED

RIVER

INDIAN

CR.

CRANE

CR.

LITTLE
NELLIE
FALL

MERCED

CHOWCHILLA

DEVIL

GULCH

RIVER

B°

MTNS.

MARIPOSA–WAWONA
ROAD

Cold Spring

APPROXIMATE ROUTE
OF MANN BROS. TRAIL

To Madera

RIVER

CR.

CASCADE

CR.

YOSEMITE

YOSEMITE
FALLS

EL CAPITAN

VALLEY

FALL

BRIDALVEIL

1864
YOSEMITE
GRANT

MAY L.

TENAYA
L.

CLOUD'S
REST

NORTH
DOME

TENAYA

MIRROR
LAKE

HALF
DOME

MERCED

R.

Hutchings
(Upper Village)
Lower
Village

GLACIER
PT.

VERNAL F.

NEVADA F.

MT. STARR KING

Lower
Iron Bridge

Ostrander's

Peregoy's

Westfall's

Chinquapin Flat Station

11 Mile Station

Empire
Camp

CR.

8 Mile Station

ALDER

CR.

Alder Creek
Station

CR.

CHILNUALNA

RIVER

Clark's Station
(Wawona)

MARIPOSA
GROVE
BIG
TREES

CR.

MANN BROTHERS'
TRAIL

0 1 2 3 4 5
Scale in Miles

N

MAIN TRAILS & ROADS TO
≈ YOSEMITE ≈
1856 to 1880

Drawn By
Donald C. DeVere

1/30/91

Coulter and Murphy's Hotel (which succeeded Hutchings' Yo Semite House) was bedecked with signs, flags, and banners for the formal opening of the Wawona Road on July 22, 1875.

THE RACE TO THE VALLEY FLOOR

As soon as the legislature authorized its entry into the Yosemite Grant in February, 1874, the Yosemite Turnpike Road Company engaged the rival Coulterville and Yosemite Turnpike Company in a bitter, head-to-head struggle to be the first into the Valley. All through the early spring, in every kind of weather, the booming sounds of construction resounded up and down the Merced River Canyon from El Capitan to Cascade Creek. Along the precipitous route below Gentry's, George Sprague's Italian craftsmen wielded picks and hammers with full dispatch as they hurriedly widened the existing trail down their winding grade. A few miles west, Dr. McLean's forces doggedly blasted out the final rock-filled section between the north side cliffs and the Merced River junction at the Blacksmith's Shop.

The contest ended in June, 1874, when—with the Big Oak Flat Road still six weeks from completion—the Coulterville and Yosemite Turnpike Company announced that regularly scheduled stage service to Yosemite Valley over its new road would begin on June 18. This time Dr. McLean had achieved an honor that even the state legislature could not take away: his Coulterville Road would be forever remembered as the pioneer stage route to Yosemite Valley. On June 17, McLean and his supporters met to prepare for the formal opening of the road the following day.

"A meeting was held at Smith's Cosmopolitan Saloon on June 17," the *Mariposa Gazette* reported, "and a Committee of Arrangements was appointed consisting of fifteen men and six ladies. The meeting was addressed by J. M. Hutchings, in his happiest style, followed by Dr. J. T. McLean. It was determined that every wheeled vehicle, horse, mule, and jack in the valley should be put to use by the people, who would one and all go out and meet the Coulterville delegation. The meeting adjourned with three cheers and a tiger for Dr. McLean . . . who made it possible for the magnificent valley to be reached without involving horseback riding.

"We understand that fifty carriages passed over the road on June 18, and the procession was over a quarter of a mile long. Great enthusiasm prevailed. Giant powder, as well as other fireworks, was brought into requisition, making the grand old heights luminous and ringing. Flags were flying, and the entire valley was illuminated by bonfires on the cliffs. The exercises were all highly interesting and long to be remembered. The completion of a wagon road into the valley is a consummation of which Mariposa County can well feel proud."

The Coulterville monopoly on Yosemite stage travel lasted just twenty-nine days. On July 17, 1874, the completion of the rival Big Oak Flat Road set off a celebration by Tuolumne County citizens equal to the Coulterville gala a month earlier. On the morning of the 17th, a caravan of fifty-two vehicles, trailing nearly a mile back along the road, assembled at Gentry's Station led by the stage containing the eight-piece Sonora band and various notables. George Sprague gave the command, "Forward, march!" and the procession slowly began to descend the circuitous grade. The Sonora band made music all the way down the mountainside, and not even the great clouds of dust stirred up by the various participants could dim the pleasure of the excited throng. "It was a sight," an eyewitness later recalled, "that I shall never forget."

At the foot of El Capitan, the triumphant cavalcade was greeted by most of the visitors and residents of the Valley, with James Hutchings acting as host. Hutchings was exuberant that his dream of a stage road to the Valley had been fulfilled twice within a month. The cheering crowd then crossed the river via Folsom's bridge and moved slowly up the Valley to Black's Hotel where the band was "most royally entertained." The celebration continued unabated at various Valley saloons and hotels well into the evening. It was subsequently reported that the sale of "libations and restoratives" to the assorted merrymakers had nearly exhausted the local supply of spirits.

THE WAWONA ROAD REACHES YOSEMITE VALLEY

The completion of the two northern stage roads in the summer of 1874 finished off Clark and Moore's tenuously financed operation on the Merced South Fork. Even the lure of the nearby Mariposa Grove was insufficient to entice travelers to endure twenty-three debilitating miles astride a horse to reach the Valley floor when they could now ride all the way to their hotel in a stage over the northern routes. By the end of 1874, Clark and Moore's assets had been taken over by Henry Washburn, the principal creditor. Washburn and his associates were practical businessmen with both capital and enterprise. They felt confident that the South Fork location, once better facilities were con-

structed and the stage road finished into Yosemite Valley, would quickly capture a major share of Yosemite tourist travel.

In November, 1874, the Mariposa County Board of Supervisors granted Washburn's firm a permit to construct a twenty-mile toll road from the South Fork north to the edge of the Yosemite Grant. On January 1, 1875, the Yosemite Board of Commissioners signed a contract allowing Washburn to extend the road from the grant boundary to Leidig's Hotel in the Valley on the same terms as those given the Coulterville and Yosemite Turnpike Company three years before. John Conway, Yosemite's veteran road and trail builder, surveyed the road and supervised construction.

Under him were the Ridgway brothers of Mariposa, who took direct charge of the more than three hundred Chinese laborers. One crew, directed by James Ridgway, began from the Valley end of the route at Leidig's in the Lower Village; the second crew, headed by Josephus (Joe) Ridgway, worked north from the South Fork. Construction thus proceeded simultaneously from both ends of the twenty-seven-mile road.

"The new road from the South Fork to Yosemite Valley is being pushed with determined zeal," said the *Mariposa Gazette* on January 9, 1875, "by men of indomitable energy possessed of ample means." Despite heavy snow and ice later in the winter, progress by the indefatigable Chinese was swift and certain. Using mostly hand tools and black powder, they averaged more than a mile and a half of roadway a week. Carpenters, following behind the road crews, erected stage stops consisting of a corral, barn, and keeper's cabin every four or five miles, wherever water and a level spot could be found. The stations were close together because teams had to be changed frequently on the steep grades.

On April 18, 1875, the road builders reached the last mountain shoulder high on the south rim of Yosemite Valley near Inspiration Point. Here, with only three hundred yards of right-of-way remaining to be built, a sharp 12-percent grade along a steep slope topped by loose boulders created an unexpected delay. It was clearly going to take many weeks to construct a firm roadbed across the unstable rock formation. Undeterred, resourceful Henry Washburn immediately began regularly scheduled operations over his new route. When a stage reached the bottleneck, passengers were disembarked to walk past the construction area. At the same time, workmen dismantled the stage and carried the pieces by hand to the opposite side of the incomplete section where it was speedily reassembled and sent on its way. The unique procedure continued for the two months required to complete the troublesome bit of roadway. Not only did passengers not seem to mind the inconvenience, it was reported that many travelers actually chose the southern route because of the novel portage.

On June 24, 1875, the twenty-seven-mile road between the South Fork and Lower Yosemite Village officially opened to through traffic. Formal dedication did not take place until nearly a month later, however, after three postponements. On July 22, 1875, a boisterous delegation of dignitaries, fortified by "stimulants and bracers," arrived by stage from Mariposa to join jubilant Valley residents who had massed near the base of Bridalveil Fall for the obligatory speeches and ceremonies.

"The procession was then formed in line by Grand Marshall G. W.

In 1878–79, under contract from the commissioners, the Yosemite Stage & Turnpike Company built a wagon road into the Mariposa Grove. An early tourist party is pictured here at the Grizzly Giant. (Author's collection)

Coulter," the *Mariposa Gazette* reported, "ably assisted by his several aides, each properly designated by their scarfs and batons. The procession was proceeded by a detachment firing minute guns. Then came the Yosemite Band followed by the residents of the valley on horseback, followed by the Merced Brass Band, who led the visitors in coaches, wagons, carriages, and horsemen.

"The procession as a whole was a beautiful sight and consisted of about 350 persons. The march ended in front of Coulter and Murphy's Hotel [formerly Hutchings']. All the hotels in the valley were appropriately decorated. After several orations and a poem titled 'Yosemite,' with excellent music by the band between speakers, the entire throng repaired to the Cosmopolitan saloon where the celebration continued throughout the night. All vote the road, procession, and celebration a grand success."

The South Fork to Yosemite Valley toll road, soon to be known as the Wawona Road, cost fifty-one thousand dollars, including a 130-foot-long covered bridge across the South Fork.[6] Stations on the road were at Alder Creek, elevation 4,800 feet; Eight Mile, 5,500 feet; Eleven Mile, 5,750 feet; Chinquapin Flat, 6,039 feet; Grouse Creek, 5,110 feet; and Fort Monroe, 5,540 feet.[7] From here the road descended down a 12-percent grade to Yosemite Valley.

Later History: On November 1, 1877, Henry Washburn, who had bought out his partners earlier in the year, filed incorporation papers for the Yosemite Stage & Turnpike Company to maintain a freight, express, passenger stage, and livery business extending from Madera and Merced to Yosemite Valley and points between. Washburn, by far the largest stockholder, was named superintendent.[8] The corporation ultimately built or controlled more than 130 miles of roads, but only the roads within Mariposa County were operated as toll routes. These comprised sixty-seven miles, as follows: Wawona to Yosemite Valley, twenty-seven miles, cost $51,000 (1875); Fresno County line (became Madera County in 1893) to Wawona, eleven miles, cost $17,000 (1879); Chinquapin Flat to Glacier Point, fourteen miles, cost $8,000 (1882); Four-mile Junction to Big Trees Grant line, two miles, cost $1,250 (1879); and Cold Spring to Wawona (Galen Clark's Mariposa Road), thirteen miles, cost $15,500 (1870). Total construction cost was $92,750. Grades on the various routes ran up to 14 percent in a few places, with the major portions averaging about 6 to 8 percent. Widths of the several roads ranged from eight to twenty feet, and teams could pass on all but a few short sections.

THE WINTER ROUTE VIA HITE'S COVE

Although the newly completed stage roads greatly facilitated Yosemite visitation, sections of all three routes passed over high terrain where deep snows prevented winter travel. The so-called "Hite's Cove Route" came into use in 1874–75 as a partial answer to the need for all-year access to the Valley.

In 1862 John Hite, brother of Gus Hite who built the Upper Hotel, discovered a rich deposit of gold on the Merced South Fork a few miles upriver from James Savage's first Yosemite-area trading post. Hite ran tunnels into the mountainside for several thousand feet in various directions, hired a crew to work the operation, and soon achieved vast wealth. The facilities at Hite's Cove, as the area became known, eventually included a water-powered forty-stamp mill, a good hotel, a store, numerous outbuildings, and a two-acre vegetable garden. Washburn's

Hite's Cove was bustling when this photograph was taken about 1881. The two-story hotel at top left was built in 1879 to replace an earlier hotel. The Mariposa Gazette *reported on April 19, 1879, that the completion of the new hotel was celebrated by "a party lasting forty-eight hours, during which 300 bottles of champagne were consumed." Hite's forty-stamp mill is the large structure near the center of the picture. Tourists stayed overnight at Hite's hotel while traveling to Yosemite Valley via the "winter route." (Author's collection)*

"THE YOSEMITE FLYER"

stage line provided regular service from Mariposa over an eighteen-mile wagon road. Yosemite travelers took the stage to Hite's Cove, stayed overnight at the hotel, then journeyed the remaining eighteen miles to the Valley via horseback up the Merced River Canyon.

"The new river trail is now open for travel from Mariposa to Yosemite year round," said the *Mariposa Gazette* in January, 1875. "A good carriage road extends from Mariposa to Hite's Cove where hotel accommodations can be obtained... Fred Leidig, proprietor of the new Yo Semite Hotel, says that his house will be kept open during the entire winter for the convenience of visitors using the canyon route."

From all accounts, the Hite's Cove route was not heavily utilized. Most Yosemite sightseers preferred the relative comfort of being transported to their destination in a stage during the more temperate months.

YOSEMITE VISITATION DECLINES

With the completion of the three stage roads in 1874–75, merchants in the Valley and along the routes of entry confidently anticipated an immediate increase in tourist travel. To their surprise and dismay, the exact opposite occurred—the result of a severe national depression that began in 1873 and endured until 1880. The expensive journey to Yosemite—despite the improved access—was one of the luxuries that many people were obliged to pass up during the six-year depression. From a record high count of 2,711 tourists in 1874, visitation to the Valley dropped each ensuing year until it bottomed out at 1,183 in 1878, the smallest figure since the completion of the transcontinental railroad in 1869. Not until 1883, in fact, when 2,831 persons entered Yosemite, did travel to the Valley exceed the 1874 high.

COMPETITION AMONG THE ROAD COMPANIES

The scenic Wawona Road, with access to the Mariposa Grove and Glacier Point, attracted more than 60 percent of Yosemite tourist traffic right from the start. Henry Washburn not only had the most popular route to the Valley, he also had the great advantage of owning the stage line that traveled it. Washburn's Yosemite Stage & Turnpike Company soon grew into an enormous operation consisting of a dozen or more

After stage roads reached Yosemite Valley in 1874–75, materials and supplies were transported by heavy freight wagons pulled by teams of ten or more mules. (Author's collection)

The completion of the seventy-eight-mile Yosemite Valley Railroad from Merced to El Portal in May, 1907, marked the effective end of the horse-drawn stage era, although stages continued to run on a limited basis until 1915. In 1908, the first full year of rail service to Yosemite, 8,850 visitors entered the Valley. All but 1,469 arrived by train. Engine number 23 of the Yosemite Valley Railroad is shown here at the El Portal station. (Author's collection)

stables, nearly seven hundred horses, twenty-five resplendently red stages, plus numerous carriages, freight wagons, water cars, and other vehicles.

North of the Valley, the Yosemite Turnpike Road Company (reorganized on June 3, 1879, as the Big Oak Flat and Yosemite Turnpike Company) carried more than twice as many passengers over its route as the rival Coulterville and Yosemite Turnpike Company. Although not nearly so well patronized as the profitable Wawona Road operation, the Big Oak Flat Road managed to eke out enough revenue over the years to justify its construction. The stage line that transported passengers over the road from the railhead at Milton to the Valley via Chinese Camp functioned independently of the road company under an exclusive contract. About half of the Big Oak Flat Road directors were also involved in the stage company at various times.

Unlike its two competitors, the ill-fated Coulterville and Yosemite Turnpike Company lost money from its very inception, thanks primarily to the state legislature's ruling in February, 1874, which overturned the Yosemite Board of Commissioners' exclusive franchise agreement with Dr. McLean.

"The result of this action," the commissioners said in their 1874–75 *Biennial Report,* "was that the road property of the Coulterville and Yosemite Turnpike Company, on which they had expended, as we learn, between fifty thousand dollars and sixty thousand dollars, relying upon the good faith of the Commissioners, has been rendered almost or quite valueless. The Commissioners think that any disinterested person, after reading the various acts cited in the early part of this report, can hardly fail to reach the conclusion that in allowing the franchise to the Yosemite Turnpike Road Company the legislature exceeded its authority."

A bitter John McLean was even more vehement about the unfairness of the state's abrogation of his exclusive contract. "I would have seen them all in Tophet [Hell] before I would have put a dollar in a road if I knew another road would be allowed on the same side of the valley," McLean said, "but I had already spent $40,000 on the road from Hazel Green when the action took place. I had no choice but to finish my road."

Adding to McLean's troubles was the murder of George Ezra Boston, the Coulterville Road's toll collector at the Cascades in the Merced River Canyon near the Yosemite Grant's western boundary. The toll house stood against a large rock that had a straight face on one side, using the rock as the back wall. On the night of August 12, 1875, passers-by found the building burned to the ground, with Boston's body lying "horribly burned and crisped" in the smoldering ruins. Two weeks later, a notorious Indian renegade named Piute George, who had been seen standing in the doorway of the toll house talking to Boston with a six-shooter in his belt a short time before the fire, was captured in Yosemite Valley by deputies.

"Piute George resisted arrest," said the *Mariposa Gazette,* "and was dangerously shot, a charge of buckshot entering low down on each side of his backbone, coming out just below the groin, in the front part of each thigh. In addition to this, his breast and shoulders are riddled with shot. He is an athletic Indian, not more than 21 years of age, and must be possessed of extraordinary vitality to have survived his injuries." Tradition has it that an old Indian woman took an eagle feather with bear grease on it and worked the feather through the four or five holes that went clean through Piute George. He was then put in a wagon on a mattress and taken to Mariposa.

Three other Indians named Zip, Tom, and Lame George, who were suspected of being Piute George's companions on the night of Boston's murder, were arrested at separate times during the next few months and lodged in the Mariposa jail. All four Indians pleaded not guilty, and after several delays, trial began on April 22, 1876, in the Mariposa District Court before an overflow crowd of Indians and townspeople. On April 27 the jury found Piute George guilty of murder in the first degree. He was sentenced to life imprisonment at San Quentin where he remained confined until his death some years later.

The following day, Lame George, who had demanded a separate trial, was acquitted of being involved in the Boston murder.[9] The cases against Zip and Tom were dismissed for lack of evidence. George Ezra Boston, a popular, respected member of the Yosemite community, was buried in the Yosemite cemetery. A modest National Park Service marker denotes the approximate grave site.

Later History: In March, 1891, after five years of lobbying, John McLean finally persuaded the state legislature to pass an act, effective March 31, permitting the "Coulterville and Yosemite Turnpike Company to sue the state of California for the damage sustained by it by the construction of a road by the Yosemite Turnpike Company, under the act of February 18, 1874, that granted a right-of-way over the Yosemite Grant to said Yosemite Turnpike Company, thereby conflicting with the exclusive privilege of the plaintiff to construct and maintain a wagon road on the northerly side of the Merced River." Without this legislation, the state could not be sued.

On December 8, 1891, McLean's attorneys filed a claim against the state for $125,000, charging that the Coulterville Road had been so little used because of the action by the legislature in allowing the Big Oak Flat Road to enter Yosemite that it had suffered great loss and damage.

The case was heard in the Placer County District Court by Judge E. W. Prewett, who on August 3, 1892, ruled against the plaintiff. Judge Prewett said that the legislature was constitutionally empowered to enact the bill that permitted entry into the Valley by the Big Oak Flat Road, and the plaintiff therefore did not have an exclusive contract. Without an exclusive franchise, the Coulterville company could not have its rights invaded by a rival company, and thus had no grievance. McLean appealed the decision to the Superior Court of Sacramento County without success, and ultimately to the California Supreme Court, which on October 2, 1894, affirmed the judgment in favor of the state.

Dr. John Taylor McLean died on July 17, 1902, at the age of seventy-eight. According to his attorney, his 796 shares of stock in the Coulterville and Yosemite Turnpike Road Company represented his entire estate. McLean spent approximately $105,000 in building, maintaining, and improving the Coulterville Road over the years. His income during the same period totaled less than $45,000, which included a $10,000 payment by the state in 1885 for the four miles of road within the Yosemite Grant. This left McLean some $60,000 out of pocket at the time of his death—a significant sum in the late nineteenth century when $100 was a handsome monthly wage.

THE ONSET OF THE STAGE ERA

The three privately built toll roads—Coulterville, Big Oak Flat, and Wawona—accommodated nearly all Yosemite travel for more than thirty years. Their domination of Valley tourism endured until the completion of the Yosemite Valley Railroad in the summer of 1907.[10]

NOTES AND REFERENCES

1. For further information about early Yosemite roads and trails, see Hank Johnston, *Yosemite's Yesterdays Volume II* (Yosemite: Flying Spur, 1991). This chapter is basically a condensation, with additional material, of pages 31 through 58 of that book.

2. Modern Groveland was formerly called Garrote (death by strangulation) because a Mexican was reportedly hanged from a tree there in 1859 for having stolen two hundred dollars from two miners. A similar incident in a camp two miles southeast led to naming it Second Garrotte. By 1879 First Garrote had adopted the name Groveland.

3. John Taylor McLean (1823–1902) was born in New York City. A graduate of Wesleyan University at Middletown, Connecticut, he studied medicine in New York and later studied and practiced medicine in New Orleans. Dr. McLean came to California in February, 1850, at the height of the gold rush. Until 1860 he practiced medicine in Marysville, where he became one of Yuba County's most respected citizens. At the start of the Civil War, President Lincoln appointed McLean, a staunch and active Republican, Surveyor of the Port of San Francisco. After the war, he served as a special agent of the Treasury Department in San Francisco. In 1874 he moved across the bay to Alameda as Health Officer, a position he held for more than twenty-five years.

4. As mentioned in Chapter III, McLean's party provided the first documented visit of non-Indians to the Merced Grove, but others—notably the Walker party of 1833—may have made earlier sightings.

5. In the fall of 1878, the commissioners paid the Pacific Bridge Company of San Francisco six thousand dollars to erect two iron bridges across the Merced River in Yosemite Valley (three thousand dollars each). The eighty-foot-long lower iron bridge was constructed at the El Capitan crossing near the junction of the Coulterville and Big Oak Flat Roads (about a half-mile west of the present El Capitan bridge). The upper iron bridge, with a ninety-six-foot span, replaced Hutchings' old timber bridge at the Upper Hotel. In 1879 Guardian Galen Clark dynamited out the glacial moraine below the lower iron bridge, which had created a natural dam there, so that flood waters could rush down river instead of overflowing meadows and roads. The increased flow eventually caused detrimental erosion.

6. Henry Washburn, a native of Vermont where covered bridges were common, added sides and a roof to Galen Clark's open span across the Merced South Fork in 1875 using boards cut in the sawmill Clark and Moore had erected. The bridge continued to carry all traffic—foot, horse, stage, and motor vehicle—until replaced by a modern concrete structure on the new Wawona Road in 1931. After suffering major damage during the flood of December, 1955, the historic old bridge was restored by the National Park Service under the ambitious MISSION 66 program. The focal point of the Yosemite Pioneer History Center at Wawona since 1964, it stands today as the only covered bridge left in any national park.

7. George F. Monroe was a black man who worked as a stage driver and guide for Henry Washburn for many years. The "fort" was actually a stage stop and had no military connection. Monroe was reportedly taken with army life and frequently talked about it, hence the name "Fort Monroe" in his honor. Monroe, who had an outstanding record and reputation as a stage driver, died in 1886.

8. Albert Henry Washburn (1836–1902) was born in Putney, Vermont; moved to Mariposa County in the 1850s; became a partner in a Mariposa livery stable and later a stage line with John McCready; joined with William F. Coffman and Emery W. Chapman to take over Clark and Moore's South Fork holdings in 1874 and build a stage road from there to Yosemite Valley (McCready died suddenly in 1874). On March 8, 1877, Coffman and Chapman sold their interest in the operation to Washburn, but remained his friends and supporters. Coffman, who had been a miner and county assessor, opened a livery stable in the 1880s in Yosemite Valley in partnership with George W. Kenney. He continued in that business—first in the Lower Village, and after 1888 at the Royal Arch Farm—until his death in 1898. Chapman was a pioneer businessman in Madera. He served as a Yosemite Valley commissioner from 1884 until 1888.

9. On July 30, 1887, the *Mariposa Gazette* reported that Lame George had been killed near Eleven Mile Station on the Wawona Road. "The caretaker, Mr. Wood, stepped out of the Station and Lame George entered and took his money," the *Gazette* said. "George went for his pistol and Mr. Wood had to retreat. As the Indian rode off, Mr. Wood fired at him. He was later found dead with a fatal wound in the head. Mr. Wood was let off without charges."

10. The story of the Yosemite Valley Railroad (1907–1945) is contained in Hank Johnston, *Shortline to Paradise,* rev. 5th ed. (Yosemite: Flying Spur Press, 1986); and Johnston, *Railroads of the Yosemite Valley* (Long Beach: Johnston-Howe Publications, 1963, and later editions).

Years of Controversy and Change
(1875–1890)

THE COMMISSIONERS EVICT HUTCHINGS

In the fall of 1874, after a decade of acrimony and litigation, the commissioners finally gained legal control of all Valley claims following the state's "munificent" indemnification of the last four settlers, as described in Chapter IV. The properties consisted of Ira Folsom's bridge and buildings; Black's Hotel; James Lamon's cabins, barn, and orchards; James Hutchings' cabin home, sawmill, outbuildings, and hotel; and Charles Peregoy's unoccupied shanty at Glacier Point.

At a commissioners' meeting held November 27, 1874, in Sacramento, Hutchings asked for a lease on his former premises, "but most positively declined to make any offer." According to Secretary William Ashburner, Hutchings said "he had been forced to take much less than the property was worth. He was then asked if he would pay a fair interest by way of rental upon the sum which had been paid him. This proposition he rejected as one utterly unworthy of his consideration. Being unable to come to any terms with him, the Executive Committee of the Board were instructed to advertise the premises for lease. This was done December first, and the advertisement appeared for three weeks in a Mariposa and Sonora paper, as well as in four San Francisco papers, three of them dailies."

Instead of submitting an application, Hutchings published his own announcement in which he threatened legal action against anyone who attempted to lease his erstwhile hotel from the "so-called Commissioners." His warning may have had the desired effect, for the board received only one proposal to lease the property—this from George W. Coulter, a charter member of the commission. Coulter resigned his position before making the offer. His associate in the venture was Andrew J. Murphy, a long-time friend. In their application, the partners informed the board that they "possessed $4,000 with which to pay the necessary expenses incidental to opening the hotel."

"To these two gentlemen a lease has been granted for the premises for ten years," the commissioners announced, "at one thousand dollars per annum, the lessees also agreeing to keep the bridge in front of the house in good order."[1]

When Hutchings stubbornly refused to surrender his premises, the commissioners filed a writ of eviction in district court. Hutchings countered by applying to the state attorney general for a stay in the proceedings, alleging "fraud" on the part of the commissioners because of "inadequate notice." The attorney general—without investigating the merit of the charges—thereupon instructed the sheriff not to serve the writ. On or about April 14, 1875, Hutchings returned to the Valley, opened his hotel, and announced that he was "ready to serve guests as before." Governor Romualdo Pacheco finally put an end to the charade by ordering the attorney general to rescind his stay, thereby empowering the sheriff to forcibly remove Hutchings from the property.

On May 22, 1875, the *Mariposa Gazette* reported that "James Hutchings was evicted on Monday last [May 17] by the Sheriff. . . On Tuesday last, George Coulter, his wife, and daughter, together with Mr. Murphy, immediately took possession and are now dispensing good cheer."

Meanwhile, the irrepressible Hutchings persuaded Guardian Galen Clark to let him "store" his furniture in Ira Folsom's unoccupied new building, which had recently been acquired by the state. Too late, Clark learned that Hutchings had removed the telegraph apparatus, post office, and Wells Fargo office from his hotel and set them up in the Folsom structure. He then took up residence with his family and turned the place into a hotel.

"He promises to remain in his new abode until hell freezes over," said the *Mariposa Gazette*, "and the devil can take a trip to Yosemite on the ice." In June, Hutchings was officially requested to hand over the premises to Guardian Clark, which he defiantly declined to do. "He accompanied his refusal," Secretary Ashburner reported, "with language too profane to repeat." Not wishing to stir up further adverse publicity, the commissioners tolerated Hutchings' illegal enterprise until the close of the 1875 season, when he reluctantly moved back to San Francisco.[2]

Gustavus Fagersteen photographed the main building of Barnard's Yosemite Falls Hotel sometime between 1877 and 1882, when the complex was renovated. (Author's collection)

COULTER & MURPHY'S HOTEL

Soon after taking over from Hutchings, Coulter and Murphy began construction of a substantial two-story building fronting the Merced River immediately east of River Cottage along the north side of the road. The lower floor contained an office, bar, dining room, and kitchen; the upper story consisted of thirteen small bedrooms. On June 3, 1876, the *Mariposa Gazette* reported that "Coulter & Murphy's 'new hotel' is now open for business." An advertising card printed about this time described the partnership's expanded facilities:

"Coulter & Murphy's Hotel has been opened with entire new furniture and fixtures and is connected with J. C. Smith's celebrated hot and cold bathing establishment [the Cosmopolitan]. We are the only Hotel in this Valley with cottages separate from the main building and located immediately on the margin of the beautiful waters of the Merced River. Our dining room—also on the river, looks out under shady trees and over green lawns, with a grand view in a direct line of the Yo-Semite Fall, 2,634 feet high [actually 2,565 feet]."

Coulter and Murphy could hardly have picked a worse time for their costly new venture. Instead of the sizable increase in Yosemite tourism anticipated following the completion of stage roads in 1874–75, travel fell more than 34 percent between 1874 and 1876 because of a severe nationwide depression. Hotel patronage suffered a similar sharp decline.

At the end of the 1876 season, unable to meet their obligations, Coulter and Murphy abandoned their enterprise and departed the Valley owing the state $1,289 in back rent. They also left unpaid a labor bill of $777 owed to two workmen, A. Lancy and W. C. Holmes. In their *Biennial Report* for 1878–79, the commissioners said: "The claim was for carpenter work done upon one of the buildings used as a hotel in the Yosemite, and which had been ordered built without the consent and against the wishes of the Commissioners by Messrs. Coulter and Murphy, lessees of the premises. These parties failed in business, and being unable to pay their debts or their rent, the Legislature generously appropriated a sum sufficient to pay Messrs. Lancy and Holmes for the work done by them."

Coulter returned to Coulterville and resumed the operation of his two-story hotel in that foothill community. Murphy's later activities are unknown. In December, 1876, the commissioners leased the property to John K. Barnard, a Merced businessman, for eight years effective January 1, 1877, at an annual rent of one thousand dollars.

BARNARD'S YOSEMITE FALLS HOTEL

On March 20, 1877, John Barnard married Adelaide Weldon Crippen in San Francisco and soon after journeyed with his bride and her four daughters from a previous marriage, aged ten to seventeen, to Yosemite Valley to take over Coulter and Murphy's hotel. Adelaide was the widow of Joshua Crippen, sheriff of Mariposa County from 1857 until his death in 1870.[3] The Barnards later had two children of their own, a daughter Tisayac (the Indian name for Half Dome), and a son Guy. Barnard finished up Coulter and Murphy's new building, changed the name of the four-unit complex to Barnard's Yosemite Falls Hotel, and settled into a successful sixteen-year proprietorship.

The Barnards brought an excellence to their spacious, river-view dining room heretofore unseen in Yosemite. The tables were covered with fine white linen cloths, upon which sat English crockery and cut glass goblets. A crew of black former Pullman car waiters served a variety of tasty dishes with a style and grace worthy of San Francisco's finest restaurants.

The hotel's sleeping quarters were considerably less fancy. Whenever possible, Barnard crammed two persons into each of his tiny rooms, thereby providing accommodations for about a hundred guests. One visitor said the "chambers were no bigger than a steamboat stateroom." Each room contained two small beds, a washbowl, pitcher, soap dish,

---

Coulter & Murphy's Hotel,

YO-SEMITE VALLEY, CAL.

◆

The above named Hotel has been opened with entire new furniture and fixtures, and is connected with J. C. Smith's Celebrated Hot and Cold Bathing Establishment.

◆

We are the only Hotel in this Valley with cottages separate from the main building, and located immediately on the margin of the beautiful waters of the Merced River. Our dining room—also on the river, looks out under shady trees and over green lawns, with a grand view in a direct line of the Yo-Semite Fall, 2,634 feet high.

GEORGE W. COULTER.   ANDREW J. MURPHY.

glass, candle, and towels. Toilet facilities consisted of several strategically situated privies. Constance Gordon-Cumming, a literate, observant Scottish Lady, wrote this description of the Yosemite Falls Hotel after her three-month stay in the early summer of 1884:

"The main bungalow, which is surrounded by a wide verandah, has on the ground floor a minute post-office, booking office, and bar; a large dining room, with a row of windows on each side, occupies almost the entire space, and opens at the farther end into a clean, tidy kitchen, where a Chinese cook attends to our comfort. An outside staircase leads to another wide verandah running round the upper story, which consists entirely of bedrooms. A separate wooden house [River Cottage] stands just beyond it—also two storied—and all divided into minute sleeping rooms. . .

"The rooms are rough-and-ready, and the partitions apparently consist of sheets of brown paper, so that every word spoken in one room is heard in all the others.

"On the opposite side of the road is the Big Tree Room, which is the public sitting-room, and takes its name from a quaint conceit—namely, that rather than fell a fine large cedar, which stood in the way of the house, Mr. Hutchings built so as to enclose it, and its great red stem now occupies a large corner of the room! Of course it is considered a very great curiosity, and all newcomers examine it with as much interest and care as if it were something quite different from all its brethren in the outer air! It certainly is rather an odd inmate for a house, though not, as its name might suggest, a *Sequoia gigantea*.

"It stands near the great open fireplace, where, in the still somewhat chilly evenings, we gather round a cheery fire of pitch-pine logs, which crackle and fizz and splutter, as the resinous pine-knots blaze up, throwing off showers of merry red sparks. It is a real old-fashioned fireplace, with stout andirons such as we see in old English halls. Round such a log-fire, and in such surroundings, all stiffness seems to melt away; and the various wanderers who have spent the day exploring scenes of beauty and wonder, grow quite sympathetic as they exchange notes of the marvels they have beheld."[4]

In the fall of 1882, the commissioners gave Barnard's a "thorough renovation and painting." Five years later they constructed an addition "costing over $1,000" to the east end of the main building. In their *Biennial Report* for 1887–88, the commissioners reported that "Barnard's Hotel, as is well known, has been patched and patched until it quite resembles an architectural crazy quilt, but it is now in a good, safe, and comfortable shape, thanks to some necessary and substantial improvements that have recently been made."

In April, 1886, Barnard moved the bathhouse equipment from the Cosmopolitan after that enterprise ceased business and installed it in a building constructed for the purpose immediately east of Cedar Cottage. A windmill, elevated water tank, and wood-fired boiler with heating coils supplied hot water to the facility.[5] Barnard wasted no time in advertising his enhanced accommodations:

"BARNARD'S YOSEMITE FALLS HOTEL—Hot and cold baths at all hours. First-class barbershop. Strictly first-class! Location unsurpassed. Terms as reasonable as any hotel in the Valley. Invalids and parties who cannot endure horseback riding can see all the principal points of interest from the portholes of this hotel."

Although obviously a big improvement over a washbowl and pitcher, Barnard's bathrooms were considered by one hard-to-please patron as "a bit on the rough-and-ready side, certainly without the deluxe luxuries of Johnny Smith's former establishment."

In 1882 the commissioners awarded Barnard—"a provider of most satisfactory service"—a new ten-year lease to his property. As time went on, however, serious disagreement arose between the two parties concerning rent and repairs upon the premises. This eventually led to "long and vexatious litigation" that terminated in Barnard's expulsion from the Valley.[6] At the close of the 1892 season, the Barnards moved permanently to their winter residence in Merced. The family later bought a fig orchard and went into the fruit business.

BLACK'S NEW SENTINEL HOTEL

On February 13, 1875, the *Sonora Union Democrat* reported that the Yosemite commissioners had leased Alexander Black's New Sentinel Hotel to Charles Peregoy for a ten-year period at an annual rent of five hundred dollars. The lease was awarded to Peregoy in exchange for his unoccupied building at Glacier Point. Peregoy promptly sold the lease to

Black for $1,500. Peregoy, who disposed of his Mountain View House at Peregoy's Meadow in the fall of 1874 and left the Yosemite area, may have felt that it would be easier to sell the lease to Black's Hotel than the rights to his Glacier Point shanty, hence his trade with the commissioners. His ensuing transaction with Black was probably prearranged. On March 6, the *Mariposa Gazette* noted that "A. G. Black and Mrs. Black are preparing to reopen their New Sentinel Hotel in Yosemite for the coming summer."

Despite its scenic location directly opposite Yosemite Falls, Black's unadorned, L-shaped hotel had considerably less architectural appeal than its two Valley competitors. Constructed of the cheapest kind of material—"the most room for the lease amount of expenditure," according to the commissioners—the bare-bones structure evoked more and more criticism from visitors as time went by.

"There were always six or seven inches of powdered dirt all around the place, which Black seldom watered," said one disenchanted patron in 1879. "When a stage arrived, great clouds of dust covered the premises like a shroud." Another guest described the hotel as "so barn-like that I half-expected to see the cows come home every evening."

At the close of the 1880 season, after twenty years as Yosemite Valley entrepreneurs, the Blacks sold their lease to Walter B. Cooke and George M. Wright of San Francisco and moved back to Bull Creek.

WRIGHT AND COOKE'S YOSEMITE VALLEY HOTEL

On May 19, 1881, the *Mariposa Gazette* reported that "Messrs. Wright and Cooke have purchased Black's Hotel in Yosemite Valley, changed the name to the Yosemite Valley Hotel, and are now open for business." George Wright was a son-in-law of John Jay Cook, Henry Washburn's

Artist Charles Dorman Robinson painted an elaborate advertising poster for Barnard about 1886. It illustrated the Yosemite Falls Hotel's main attractions, such as the dining room, bathhouse, Big Tree Room, and outlying cottages. (I. W. Taber)

Alexander Black doubled the length of the original two-story section of his hotel to sixty feet in the mid-1870s (compare with earlier photograph on page 80).

brother-in-law and close business associate. Washburn, the principal owner of the Yosemite Stage & Turnpike Company and the Wawona Hotel, was the most influential man in the county during the latter part of the nineteenth century. Perhaps Wright's family relationship helped him obtain the lease to Black's property.

Wright and Cooke endured only a single season as proprietors of the Yosemite Valley Hotel, and little is known of their affairs. In December, 1881, the *Mariposa Gazette* carried the following brief notice: "J. J. Cook, formerly of Mariposa, is reported to have taken charge of the Wright and Cooke Hotel in Yosemite Valley and will give it his attention the coming season."

COOK'S YOSEMITE VALLEY HOTEL

John Jay Cook was an affluent businessman from New York who came to Mariposa in 1862, opened a drug and variety store, and acquired the Wells Fargo agency. He later owned similar stores in Merced and San Francisco, as well as oil wells near Santa Barbara. In 1865, Henry Washburn married Jean Lindsay Bruce, a sister of Cook's wife Fannie. Soon after, Cook became actively involved in his brother-in-law's many ventures and remained so for the rest of his life.

Cook, a quiet, efficient man with a dry wit, operated his Yosemite Valley Hotel (more commonly called "Cook's") through the season of 1887. In January, 1888, he was granted a ten-year lease to the Stoneman House, the state's capacious new hotel at the east end of the Valley, which opened for business in the spring of that year. The vastly increased guest capacity provided by the grand new facility enabled the commissioners to raze Cook's ramshackle old building—one member of the board described it "as about to fall down"—and return the site to its natural condition. By the fall of 1888, hardly a trace remained of Yosemite Valley's pioneer Lower Hotel.

LEIDIG'S HOTEL

Fred and Isabella Leidig ran their compact, two-story hotel below Sentinel Rock for eighteen years—1870 through 1887—under lease from the state. No money ever changed hands. Instead, Leidig was required by the commissioners to make improvements averaging $120 a year.

From 1874 until the hotel shut down at the end of 1887, Leidig was the only Yosemite innkeeper who remained open all year to serve the scattering of tourists traveling the "all-year route" via Hite's Cove.[7] It was no great inconvenience for the Leidigs because the family, unlike the other hotel operators, lived in the Valley full time in a small two-room house just behind the main building.

Motherly Belle Leidig was, in the words of Galen Clark, "an exceptionally popular lady." A woman of remarkable energy, she bore a child every two years or so all through her busy Yosemite days, the last nine of her eleven offspring being born in the Valley. Belle's baked goods were legendary, and the warm, unpretentious atmosphere of the Leidig house drew stage drivers, guides, and other local residents to the premises nearly every evening. The hotel's superior table fare was noted by John Muir, who stayed at Leidig's with his wife in the summer of 1884. In a letter to his daughter Wanda, dated July 10, Muir described an unforgettable breakfast of fresh bread, milk, mush, ice cream, ham and eggs, trout, venison, and mutton!

Competition for patrons among the three Valley innkeepers remained keen during the 1870s and 1880s, and the methods employed by the rivals were not always the most ethical. After J. J. Cook took over Black's Hotel in 1882, Leidig repeatedly accused Washburn's stage drivers of diverting tourists to Cook's establishment. As a countermeasure, Leidig

Wright and Cooke erected a large new sign when they took over Black's establishment in 1881.

An advertising card distributed by Wright and Cooke in 1881. (Author's collection)

J. J. Cook utilized half of Wright and Cooke's sign after he assumed proprietorship of their hotel in December, 1881. The enterprising Cook thereby saved the cost of a new sign even though his name was misspelled.

sometimes sent runners to Bridalveil Fall or Inspiration Point to solicit incoming travelers by offering lower rates at his hotel.

Like Cook's, Leidig's became expendable following the opening of the Stoneman House in the spring of 1888. Refused a new five-year lease by the commissioners, Leidig sold his furniture and goodwill to Barnard and Cook, agreeing in return to abstain from innkeeping in Yosemite for ten years. On April 25, 1888, Leidig left the Valley for Southern California. "I decided to move to Los Angeles County," Leidig said, "where my wife would not have to work so hard and my girls would have more advantages." Two of the four Leidig sons, Charles, nineteen, and Jack, fourteen, chose to remain in Yosemite and were allowed to continue residing in the family's small house at one dollar per year rental.

At the annual commissioners' meeting held June 7, 1888, Albert Snow applied for a lease on Leidig's vacant hotel, but was turned down by the board. During the summer of 1888, the commissioners leveled Leidig's main building. "There was a unanimity of feeling," the board explained in its *Biennial Report,* "that the old shanties and other architectural bric-a-brac that have long done service for hotels and the like should be torn down, and the erection of more inviting and pretentious buildings . . . should be proceeded with."

Later History: The Leidigs returned to the Sierra in 1889, spending that summer managing Grant's White Sulphur Springs Hotel on the original road from Raymond to Wawona. In 1891 Isabella Leidig unsuccessfully petitioned the commission for a ten-year lease on Barnard's Yosemite Falls Hotel. The privilege was granted instead to A. B. Glasscock. The following year the Leidigs succeeded Glasscock as operators of Henry Washburn's hotel at Raymond. They continued in that capacity until the hotel burned down about 1897.

SNOW'S LA CASA NEVADA

James Hutchings wrote in 1886 that "Snow's La Casa Nevada has become deservedly famous all over the world, not only for its excellent lunches and general good cheer, but from the quiet, unassuming attentions of mine host and the piquant pleasantries of Mrs. Snow. I do not think that another pair, anywhere, could be found that would more fittingly fill this position; And, although they do not know whether the number to lunch will be five or fifty-five, they almost always seem to have an abundance of everything relishable. On one occasion—and this will illustrate Mrs. Snow's natural readiness with an answer—a lady, seeing so great a variety on the table, with eager interest inquired, 'Why, Mrs. Snow, where on earth do you get all these things?' 'Oh, we raise them!' 'Why! where can you possibly do so, as I see nothing but rocks around here?' 'Oh! madam, we *raise them*—on the backs of mules!'"[8]

With her high white collars, pulled-back hairdo, and floor-length dresses, quaint, eccentric Emily Snow seemed every inch the prim, sedate New England lady. In her leisure time she gathered lichen and pretty ferns for scrap books that she sold to tourists. Nonetheless, she was—according to old friend Pinkie Ross—"always stewed to the eyebrows." Certainly there was a generous supply of spirits available at the hotel as the rubble of broken bottles on the rocky flat attests today. One

Fred Leidig (with beard, sitting in front) and Isabella Leidig (wearing dark hat, just in back of Fred) were photographed about 1880 on the porch of their hotel with some of their children and employees.

guest signed the hotel register with this comment: "No person here is obliged to commit burglary to obtain drinks."

"Emily thought her husband Albert a perfect Apollo and was very jealous of him," said Pinkie Ross, "although there was no question that she was the boss. Albert was a large, loose-jointed, good-natured man with all his upper teeth out. I never heard of anyone wanting to run away with him."[9]

Snow made no monetary payment for the lease to his site and a nearby meadow where he kept several cows and other animals to supply the hotel table with milk and fresh meat. The commissioners credited his small annual fee against his labor in maintaining the trail into Little Yosemite Valley. In 1882 Snow's toll trail from Register Rock to Nevada Fall became the property of the state by expiration of the lease, and was made free. In June of that year the commissioners purchased the Vernal Fall stairway for three hundred dollars from Snow and his partner, son-in-law Colwell Drew. On July 1, 1890, the commissioners ordered the guardian to "close and bar the wooden ladders at Vernal Fall so their use in their present condition is prevented." Whether or not the stairs were subsequently repaired is uncertain, but by 1897 the present stone steps had taken their place.

After twenty years as Yosemite innkeepers, Albert and Emily Snow were forced by advancing age and failing health to relinquish the operation of their unusual backcountry stopping place in the fall of 1889. Following a brief illness, Emily died in Groveland on November 15, 1889, just nine days shy of her sixty-sixth birthday. Less than two years later, on October 13, 1891, Albert joined his longtime marital partner in death.

Later History: On June 28, 1890, the commissioners granted one D. F. Baxter, about whom very little is known, a lease on La Casa Nevada for the remainder of the year. A token rent of one dollar was established because of the lateness of the season, with the specification that the customary rate of one hundred dollars would apply in the future. The tenant was also required to make all repairs to the premises and deal with Snow on the personal property. According to the commissioners' minutes, Baxter ran the hotel during 1890 and 1891, after which he gave up his lease.

La Casa Nevada never formally reopened, although the commissioners unsuccessfully asked for appropriations from the legislature in both 1890 and 1892 to make needed improvements and repairs to the hotel. On March 28, 1892, a party of nine tourists led by guide John Baptiste wrote the following message above their signatures in the hotel register: "The season of 1892 is opened at this hotel by the undersigned on the twenty-eighth (28th) day of March. Ground, trails, and trees covered with snow six to twelve inches but the cascades and vertical rocks remain as before." A few other entries follow in May and early June, the last dated June 2, 1892. Perhaps the historic old register was saved for posterity at that time by Guardian Galen Clark.[10]

At the commissioners' annual meeting of June 1, 1892, A. B. Glasscock, who was awaiting possession of Barnard's Hotel pending the end of litigation between Barnard and the state, requested a lease of La Casa Nevada, "now unoccupied and closed." Glasscock said he would like to be engaged in some business in the Valley while he was marking time (see note 6). The board turned down his petition in part because his application required that Valley hotels "be prohibited from preparing box lunches because otherwise La Casa would have no business."

Accounts by passers-by during the next seven years tell the story of the hotel's gradual demise. A visitor in August, 1893, wrote: "Near the foot of Nevada Fall stands Snow's Hotel, which has been deserted with everything left in it, even to the table being set with all the dishes, and the beds having mattresses and pillows. One of the boys climbed

Albert and Emily Snow ran their pic-
turesque La Casa Nevada near the base
of Nevada Fall for twenty summers.

through a window and unlocked a door, and we went all through it. We might have taken a lot of things away, but they will never be taken away, as it would cost more to do so than they are worth. The roof is already broken in several places by snow."

On June 5, 1895, Julius T. Boysen, who later operated a photography and souvenir shop in the Valley for many years, applied to the commissioners for a permit to "occupy the buildings at the foot of Nevada Fall for the purpose of accommodating tourists with meals, lodging, refreshments, and horse feed." His petition, which specified that the state be responsible for putting the buildings in a habitable condition at an estimated cost of three hundred to four hundred dollars, was denied.

The following year a traveler reported the "buildings still standing, but in dilapidated condition with most of the doors and windows gone—a sad relic of earlier days."

J. J. Cook's granddaughter, Marjorie Cook, described the premises in 1899: "We stopped at the ruins of Snow's Hotel on the flat below Nevada Fall. The sagging doors, broken windows, and swaybacked roof intrigued me. There was even some sorry furniture and crockery and a sleepy owl in the wrecked interior. The winter after my visit, Snow's Hotel was flat. The last vestige of the place served as fuel under the coffee pot of some trail party."

D. J. Foley's *Yosemite Souvenir and Guide* for 1901 verifies Marjorie Cook's account: "La Casa Nevada was accidentally destroyed by fire during the season of last year. It had not been used as a hotel for nearly ten years. Those who have visited Nevada Fall before will note the hotel's absence with many regrets."

THE STONEMAN HOUSE

In their *Biennial Reports* for both 1880–82 and 1883–84, the Yosemite commissioners evinced serious concern about what they called "the inadequacy and discomfort of the three apologies that now provide hotel accommodations" within the Yosemite Grant.

"The buildings erected for the purpose by private enterprise, and lapsed to the State by the terms of their leases," the commissioners said, "are totally inadequate to the demands of a proper hospitality, and sadly at variance with their natural surroundings. The Yosemite Valley is pre-eminently the wonder of this continent. It is within two days ride of San Francisco, where are hotels rivaling the finest in the world. It is impossible, therefore, to convince the world's travelers that there is any cogent reason why this resort of the earth's most appreciative visitors should not have a hotel of an inviting capacity and class, commodious, solid, and furnished with the conveniences which modern civilization has exalted to the list of necessities...

"How, then, can such a hotel be secured? Private enterprise will not build it because the Act of cession from the United States to the State of California limits the term of all leases in the ceded area to ten years. The

A party of Southern California sightseers made a lunch stop by Snow's sagging buildings about 1899. (Author's collection)

The Stoneman House contained "every comfort and many of the luxuries of a San Francisco hotel," according to one satisfied visitor.

shortness of the term will not justify capitalists in making the necessary investment, however remunerative the business in itself. The uncertainty as to what would become of the property of the lessees at the termination of the lease will deter from the venture.

"The Commissioners deem it proper to express their conviction that the State of California, holding in trust so distinguishing and remunerative an interest, should itself build and own the only hotel to be allowed in the valley. We therefore unanimously ask the Legislature for an appropriation of $75,000 to erect and furnish a State-owned hotel suitable to the needs of the traveling public and creditable to the only State in the Union which can boast of a Yosemite."

On March 9, 1885, the Twenty-sixth California Legislature responded to the commissioners' petition by appropriating $40,000 for the hotel project. Although the sum was far short of the requested amount and resulted in an inferior wooden structure rather than the substantial native-stone lodge they had envisioned, the commissioners—in what seems a bit of an overstatement—called the grant the "wisest, most statesmanlike, and defensible appropriation ever made by a legislative body."

Construction of the new hotel by the well-known Sacramento contracting firm of Carle, Croly & Abernethy began in 1886 and was essentially completed by the spring of 1888. Lumber for the ornate, three-and-one-half-story edifice, described as being of "slightly modern gothic suspicion," was purchased from Joseph Hutchins' steam-powered sawmill at Gentry's on the northwest corner of the Yosemite Grant and transported to the site by freight wagon. Called the Stoneman House in honor of California Governor (1883–87) George Stoneman, who played an important role in obtaining the appropriation, the hotel stood at the south end of the large meadow directly in front of present Camp Curry.[11]

The rectangular front of the L-shaped building, 100 feet wide by 56 feet deep exclusive of porches, faced southwest. A wing, 34 feet wide by 68½ feet deep, adjoined the rear on the north, thus giving a total depth of 124½ feet along that side. The hotel interior contained ninety-two rooms, not counting closets, lavatories, or storage areas. The first floor's nineteen rooms included a large vestibuled parlor, spacious manager's office, reading and writing rooms, commodious kitchen, barbershop, four bedrooms, and dining accommodations for two hundred. The second floor had thirty-one bedrooms; the third floor, twenty-seven; and the gabled attic, fifteen. Bathrooms and toilet rooms for both sexes—the first indoor toilets in Yosemite Valley—were conveniently situated on each floor. Maximum occupancy was about 150 guests.

A short distance north of the hotel, a store, billiard parlor, and saloon occupied the front section of a long one-story frame structure; the rear of the building was used as sleeping quarters for employees. Later, a cold storage room, smokehouse, stable, and corral were added.

Besides the initial forty-thousand-dollar appropriation, the legislature provided another five thousand dollars to pipe water to the premises from an "inexhaustible spring" at the base of Glacier Point a few hundred yards away. "The spring is one of the finest in the world," said a state official. "The water is so clear and beautiful, four or five feet deep, that you could have seen a needle in the bottom."

In 1886 the commissioners asked the legislature for additional funding to furnish and equip the hotel. "At a low estimate, it will cost $15,000 to prepare the house for occupancy," the commissioners said. "At the end of a ten years' lease, the furniture, however valuable in its place, would not pay the expense of removal. Under such circumstances it will be difficult, probably impossible, to obtain a desirable tenant." The legislature failed to act on the request.

On January 1, 1888, the commissioners leased the Stoneman House "after careful and elaborate conferences, and examinations of bids and bidders, to J. J. Cook, a responsible man, and long a polite and painstaking hotel keeper in the valley, for the sum of $100 a month [3 percent of the $40,000 cost], the year round, for a term of ten years." Cook also paid $350 annually for "other privileges," which included the right to operate a store and saloon in conjunction with the hotel, and fence in a portion of the surrounding meadow for pasture and a vegetable garden. A major factor in Cook's acquisition of the much sought-after lease was his willingness to invest more than $10,000 to furnish the hotel. His close association with Henry Washburn may also have influenced the commissioners' decision.

The Stoneman House opened for business on April 1, 1888. When the season ended on November 15, more than twenty-two hundred guests had been accommodated—nearly three times the number that patronized rival J. K. Barnard's Yosemite Falls Hotel. Accounts indicate that the majority of visitors were delighted with the new facility. The commissioners' *Biennial Report* for 1888–89 quotes a number of letters from prominent visitors, which contain complimentary remarks, such as: "The Stoneman House is well kept and very comfortable." "Mr. Cook makes everything delightful for the traveler." "The furniture is nice oak and ash, light colored, and as good as I would want in any hotel. The carpets were splendid. There were bathrooms on every floor and plenty of hot water." "The bill of fare was fine and the terms most reasonable." "The courtesy of the proprietor, clerk, and servants was all that could be expected." "Every comfort and many of the luxuries of a San Francisco hotel."

There were some, however, who felt the hotel was "ugly and poorly located." John Muir thought the building "had a silly look amid surroundings so massive and sublime." The commissioners responded to the criticism by saying that "while the amount expended would not admit of an enchanting architectural display, it was quite enough to rear an exceedingly pretty structure—all that could possibly be got out of the $40,000 appropriation."

As it turned out, the Stoneman House proved a continual headache and source of expense to the state right from the start because of serious internal defects that occurred during construction. On August 22, 1889, engineer George D. Nagle submitted an inspection report of the building at the commissioners' request: "I find that the chimneys throughout have been constructed of a very poor quality of concrete," Nagle said. "It is a mixture of gravel, broken rock, and a limited quantity of cement. The chimneys are cracked horizontally, vertically, and obliquely in many places, the cracks in some of them being open a half inch clear through the chimney. It is only a question of time when the building will be destroyed by fire from defective chimneys. It is urgently recommended that all chimneys be taken down and rebuilt." Nagle estimated that it would cost nearly six thousand dollars to rebuild all fireplaces and chimneys with new brick pipe. Nagle's ideas were considered "absurd and extravagant" by the board, which bought a new fire hose instead.

"The contractors slighted their work in the most open and flagrant manner," the commissioners stated at their July 14, 1891, meeting, "owing to the Board's inability to appoint an inspector, and the State Comptroller refusing to pay the salary of same. We must now preserve the building to the best of our ability."

Unusually heavy snows in the winter of 1889–90—twenty-five feet on the Valley floor—exacerbated the hotel's shortcomings. Porch roofs were crushed, rafters and pipes broken, and ceilings displaced by the weight of the accumulated precipitation. In 1890 the commissioners

reported that the "Stoneman House needed and received extensive reparation." Two years later, another wet winter created more problems. "Night storms weighted the Stoneman House roof," the commissioners said, "and its sills and frame were damaged, making necessary very comprehensive repairs of the entire building."

Nevertheless, in spite of its inherent flaws, the innovative state-owned hotel set a new standard for public accommodations on government property at the time. During its nine-year existence, the Stoneman House provided a comfortable stopping place for thousands of Yosemite visitors.

McCauley's two-story Mountain House, built in 1875–76 at Glacier Point, was the highest stopping place in the Yosemite Grant. (Author's collection)

THE GLACIER POINT MOUNTAIN HOUSE

James McCauley (1840–1911), a roughhewn, Irish-born sailor, came to America at the age of seventeen as a stowaway on a British ship. After a brief stay in New York City, he stowed away again, this time on a vessel bound for South America. Disembarking at Panama, he journeyed overland to the Pacific Ocean and eventually found his way to Portland, Oregon. He spent a half-dozen years mining in Washington State and Montana before being lured to Hite's Cove in Mariposa County in 1865 by a fellow miner's tall tales of golden riches.

In the spring of 1870, McCauley left his job at the Pine Tree Mine near Bear Valley and obtained employment in Yosemite at James Hutchings' water-powered sawmill. When Hutchings packed in his two-horse stage in August, 1871, McCauley became the driver. Later the same year, he began his four-mile toll trail to Glacier Point, which he completed in 1872.

Following the state's acquisition of Charles Peregoy's shanty at Glacier Point late in 1874, the commissioners leased the premises to McCauley

Twins Fred and John McCauley (at right on burros) rode down the Four Mile Trail from Glacier Point to Yosemite Valley to school. Mrs. Gallison (second from left) was the Yosemite schoolteacher when this picture was taken in 1894.

for ten years on condition that he build a suitable hotel on the site. McCauley devoted the summers of 1875 and 1876 to the construction of a greatly enlarged, two-story building. "Peregoy's shack was in tumbledown condition," McCauley said a few years later. "I practically rebuilt the structure, spending $2,000 to do so."

All wood used in the hotel came from trees felled in the nearby forest. Timbers were hewed on the ground with a broadax. Boards for flooring, doors, and window casings were cut by a three-man crew using a primitive pit-saw. It required a long day of arduous labor to produce seventy-five to a hundred board feet of usable lumber. Everything else needed for the remote project was carried up the Four Mile Trail from the Valley on the backs of mules.

McCauley completed his hotel after eleven months of strenuous work and immediately offered it for sale or lease to any interested party. It seems likely that McCauley, an uneducated, unmarried man, felt incapable of operating the business himself, but had undertaken the venture to boost travel over his trail. On August 5, 1876, the *Mariposa Gazette* carried the following advertisement:

"HOTEL FOR SALE OR LEASE. The hotel known as the Glacier Point Hotel, located near Yo Semite Valley, on the most commanding view of the Valley and the Nevada and Vernal Falls, is now offered for sale, or for lease, for a term of years. It is visited by all tourists, and acknowledged to be the most picturesque and beautiful spot in the region of Yo Semite Valley. The house is just completed, and is two-story high and contains fourteen bed-rooms, sitting room, dining room, kitchen, etc. It is furnished in first-class style, and is a very desirable stand

and a rare opportunity for anyone who wishes to engage in the hotel business. For further particulars address, JAMES McCAULEY, Yo Semite Valley."

In the spring of 1877, McCauley leased his new hotel, which was not nearly so grand as the advertisement implied, to Thomas and Elizabeth Glynn, a Massachusetts couple who had only recently come to Yosemite because of Mrs. Glynn's asthma ("I can't breathe in any other place," she often said). Mrs. Glynn, an industrious, somewhat eccentric woman, was an excellent purveyor of plain but appetizing food, which she served on her own Wedgewood china. This ability served the couple in good stead because most of their income derived from meals supplied to travelers who rode up the Four Mile or the Panorama Trail to see the spectacular view.

During the Glynn's three seasons of management (1877–79), few tourists elected to remain overnight in McCauley's rustic building, which had no bathing facilities and whose interior partitions and ceilings consisted of cloth and paper. Thomas Glynn transported all water used at the hotel in two ten-gallon kegs by wheelbarrow from a spring a quarter of a mile away. A few years later, McCauley piped water directly to the site from a better spring a half-mile distant. Naturally, all the heavy iron pipe required for the undertaking had to be packed up the steep trail on mules.

On November 18, 1879, James McCauley, age thirty-nine, married Barbara Wenger, a thirty-seven-year-old German woman who was employed at Leidig's Hotel. The new Mrs. McCauley had a four-year-old son named Jules, whom McCauley adopted. The following summer the couple took over operation of their unusual Glacier Point inn themselves and remained in place for eighteen seasons. Barbara, who was universally praised for her culinary artistry, prepared all the meals and did the housekeeping, assisted by a hired girl. James waited table, tended bar, handled the chores, and entertained the guests.

Twin boys were born to the McCauleys on November 4, 1880, in their winter residence at the foot of the Four Mile Trail. In 1883, a year after the state purchased his toll trail for twenty-five hundred dollars, McCauley bought the ranch of John Hamilton, a deceased Yosemite guide, which lay on a flank above the Merced River just west of present Foresta. He later homesteaded the surrounding 160 acres.

McCauley ran cattle in the El Portal area during the winter. Early each summer he drove his animals up the Four Mile Trail to Glacier Point and turned them out to pasture in several pleasant meadows nearby. The arrangement provided good forage for the stock as well as a plentiful supply of meat and fresh milk for the hotel table.

In 1882 the Yosemite Stage & Turnpike Company completed a toll road to Glacier Point. Built by John Conway at a cost of eight thousand dollars, the scenic, fourteen-mile spur joined the existing road between Wawona and the Valley at Chinquapin Flat. Patronage at the Mountain House was considerably increased by the coming of tourists who could not walk or ride a horse up the steep trails.

McCauley received three hundred dollars annually from the state for keeping the Four Mile Trail in good repair. From this, one hundred dollars was deducted as rent for the Glacier Point property. The agreement

McCauley accidentally began the famous "Firefall" in 1872 when he pushed his campfire over the sheer Glacier Point cliff. The Firefall, shown in this enhanced photograph, subsequently became a popular Yosemite tourist attraction.

was contingent on McCauley's making certain improvements at the commissioners' request. Over the years these included digging a basement under the building, completing the unfinished bedrooms, adding roofed porches, and replacing the flooring. McCauley accomplished the last-named item by clandestinely removing the floor boards from his former toll house, then under state ownership, and installing them in the Mountain House. The action did not endear him to Walter Dennison, the guardian at the time, who complained vociferously to the commissioners without success.

McCauley, a gregarious, fun-loving fellow, is generally credited with accidentally originating the famous Firefall, which became a Yosemite institution in later years.[12] "Father started the Firefall in 1872," son Fred McCauley said, "when he pushed his campfire over the Glacier Point cliff. He experimented with gunny sacks soaked in kerosene, fireworks, and even dynamite bombs for spectacular effects. In time, the firefall became almost a nightly event in the summer. . .

"When my brother and I were eight years old, father bought each of us a jackass. We attended school by riding our mules down the Four Mile Trail to the Valley. It took ninety minutes. If a tourist wanted a Firefall, we collected $1.50, the standard fee, before we rode back up the trail to Glacier Point. We had a pack animal that we used to carry provisions for the hotel on our return trip. On the Fourth of July, a collection often amounted to ten or twenty dollars. Then my brother and I were packing wood out to the point on our jackasses for at least two days. Father set off dynamite bombs along with dropping flaming gunny sacks. The noise reverberated like thunder around Yosemite Valley."[13]

All through the 1880s and beyond, the unsurpassed view from its porches and the cheerful efforts of the proprietors more than made up for the lack of amenities at the little Glacier Point hotel. During their lengthy tenure there, James and Barbara McCauley raised cattle, three sons, and the spirits of those fortunate sightseers who came to visit the highest stopping place in the Yosemite Grant.

THE COSMOPOLITAN

On November 18, 1874, John C. Smith, the genial proprietor of Yosemite's Cosmopolitan bathhouse and saloon, married Susan E. Hayes, a capable young Oakland woman who was employed as a telegraph operator in the Valley. Soon after their wedding, while Susan was helping her new husband close up the Cosmopolitan for the winter, a kerosene lamp exploded, catching her dress on fire and burning her severely. Although she slowly began to recover from her injuries, she could not be moved before the first big storm would close the roads until spring. Susan finally persuaded John to leave her behind and get out to Merced where he was sorely needed at his other saloon (also called the Cosmopolitan) in that city.

Full-time residents of the Valley such as Belle Leidig looked after Susan, who continued to mend over the winter. The following March, four burly men led by John Conway managed to pull her down the Valley to the Cascades, where the snow ended, on a specially made sled. There she was met by her husband with horses. From then on, the Smiths made their permanent home in Merced where they later reared

The Cosmopolitan functioned as a deluxe saloon and bathhouse in the Upper Village near River Cottage from 1871 through 1884, at which time it became the guardian's office and residence. (George Fiske)

Susan Hayes Smith moved to Merced with her husband in 1875 after being seriously burned by an exploding kerosene lamp at their Yosemite Valley saloon.

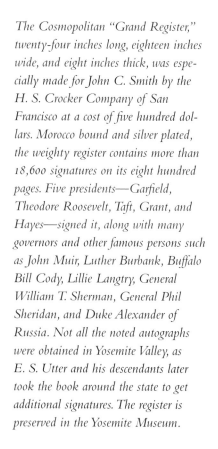

*The Cosmopolitan "Grand Register,"
twenty-four inches long, eighteen inches
wide, and eight inches thick, was especially made for John C. Smith by the
H. S. Crocker Company of San
Francisco at a cost of five hundred dollars. Morocco bound and silver plated,
the weighty register contains more than
18,600 signatures on its eight hundred
pages. Five presidents—Garfield,
Theodore Roosevelt, Taft, Grant, and
Hayes—signed it, along with many
governors and other famous persons such
as John Muir, Luther Burbank, Buffalo
Bill Cody, Lillie Langtry, General
William T. Sherman, General Phil
Sheridan, and Duke Alexander of
Russia. Not all the noted autographs
were obtained in Yosemite Valley, as
E. S. Utter and his descendants later
took the book around the state to get
additional signatures. The register is
preserved in the Yosemite Museum.*

*The "Grand Register" occupied a posi-
tion of honor on the front porch of the
Cosmopolitan. Tourists came to see the
signatures of famous people and to
inscribe their own. (J. J. Reilly)*

two children. Although they both loved Yosemite, too much physical
and mental anguish had occurred there for them ever to return.

In 1875 Smith turned over active management of the Cosmopolitan
to brother-in-law Ben Hayes, who successfully operated the business for
the next six seasons. According to commission records, Hayes grossed
between four and five thousand dollars a year in revenue during the
period, hired two employees, paid $250 annually for rent, and made his
own repairs to the building. On May 21, 1881, the *Mariposa Gazette*
reported that "the Cosmopolitan saloon and bathhouse has been sold to
Capt. E. S. Utter, and the firm heretofore known as Smith and Hayes
will hereafter be known as Smith and Utter." Hayes' reasons for selling
were not stated.

Eliakim Stannards Utter, a former ship captain, came to Yosemite
about 1875 and worked with Alex Black at the New Sentinel Hotel
until Black sold out in the fall of 1880 to Wright and Cooke. During
this interval, Utter married Elizabeth Coffman, stepdaughter of William
Coffman, a one-time associate of Henry Washburn's and later the proprietor of the Valley stable with George Kenney. From 1881 through the
early fall of 1884 when his lease expired, Captain Utter expertly provided fancy cocktails, hot baths, and other delectations to his
Cosmopolitan patrons in the same grand manner as Smith and Hayes
before him.

On November 18, 1884, Guardian Walter Dennison told the Yosemite
commissioners that "Mr. Utter, who has been occupying the
Cosmopolitan has sold out and decamped. The new parties, a Mr.
Contreras and a Mr. Baker, are now in occupancy and unwilling to pay
any rent due." Dennison recommended that the saloon be permanently
closed, and the premises taken over for the guardian's office. The commissioners approved Dennison's suggestion by a vote of seven to one,
giving the reason that "a saloon not run in connection with a hotel is
not a good thing in Yosemite Valley." Some local critics accused the

board of succumbing to pressure from Valley hotel owners who wanted guests to buy liquor at their own bars rather than the Cosmopolitan. Others charged that the state had arbitrarily taken over the building for its own purposes. In any event, Johnny Smith's remarkable, one-of-a-kind establishment had served its last customer.

Later History: From 1885 until 1897, the front section of the Cosmopolitan functioned as the guardian's office. The large main room near the center of the structure became a community meeting hall (even in Smith's time the saloon had often been the site of local gatherings). From 1887 until 1897, the building also housed the Yosemite Post Office and Wells Fargo office. Guardian Walter Dennison utilized the remainder of the premises as his family residence during his tenure (1884–1887).

According to Laurence Degnan, who lived nearby, after Galen Clark resumed the guardian's position in June, 1889, "his office, in the large, bright, cheery front room of the departed saloon, with its glass doors, became a sort of club or lounging room, well patronized by the men of the village and by visitors. Clark had a large table there, covered with newspapers and magazines, while a huge stove in the middle of the room was a popular attraction on cold winter evenings."

The living space formerly occupied by Dennison and his successor, Mark L. McCord, in the rear of the building (Clark had his own residence) was turned into a bunkhouse for workmen, a barroom, and barbershop, collectively known as the "Collar and Elbow." In 1897, following the destruction of the Stoneman House by fire, the commissioners extensively remodeled the Cosmopolitan into a fourteen-bedroom sleeping unit called Locust Cottage to provide additional accommodations for the Sentinel Hotel (formerly Barnard's). The building was later used as offices by the Yosemite National Park Company and the Yosemite Park and Curry Co. (concessionaires). On December 8, 1932, the rickety old structure burned to the ground.

THE MIRROR LAKE HOUSE

In the early spring of 1870, Peter Gordon, a veteran Yosemite guide, and Leonidas G. "Dick" Whorton,[14] who owned eighty acres at the Cascades, erected a small frame building called the Lake House on the western edge of Mirror Lake. An advertisement in the *Mariposa Free Press* of June 3, 1870, announced: "THE MIRROR LAKE HOUSE— Yosemite Valley, by Gordon and Whorton. Recently stocked with choice wines, fine liquors, and Havana cigars. Boats furnished for the lake."

On June 30, 1874, the commissioners ordered "the occupants of the building at Mirror Lake to vacate the premises for reason of having failed to comply with the conditions of the privilege." The board then leased the place to William J. Howard, a former county sheriff and later a state politician, who constructed a forty-by-sixty-foot platform out over the water for dining and dancing. Howard also built a mile-long toll road up Tenaya Canyon to his resort where he served meals, liquor, and rented out two flat-bottomed rowboats. On July 28, 1876, the *Mariposa Gazette* carried this glowing report of Howard's enterprise:

"A dance came off at Mirror Lake on Monday last. Bonfires were built around the lake, and the light, as it was reflected from its mirrored

surface, making distinct all objects, forming one of the most beautiful scenes imagination can well conceive. The boats as they were gently moved over the smooth water, with their lovely freight, the music as it fell on the ear with its soft cadence—all reminded those present, we are assured, of the stories they had read of the beautiful Naiads and their queens, as they rose out of the water. Why do not more people visit this lake? Life is short."[15]

On July 1, 1879, the state bought the rights to Howard's toll road for six hundred dollars and made it free. Soon after, the guardian, by order of the commissioners, demolished the Mirror Lake tavern and platforms and removed the accumulated rubbish. Howard, who had already taken out his personal property, received two hundred dollars in compensation for his dispossession. Howard was extremely upset about the commissioners' termination of his lucrative lease and very shortly got a measure of revenge. As a delegate to the Constitutional Convention of California in 1878–79, he helped push through the provision that state officials (such as the commissioners) be limited to four-year terms.

The rustic Mirror Lake House, built on the western edge of the lake by Dick Whorton and Pete Gordon, was still under construction when photographed in 1870. W. J. Howard later built a platform out over the water.

REPLACEMENT OF THE BOARD OF COMMISSIONERS

On April 15, 1880, ten months after California's radically restructured constitution took effect, the legislature established new regulations for the management of the Yosemite Grant.[16] A resolution accompanying the act declared all commission seats vacant and mandated Governor George C. Perkins to immediately select a replacement board. If possible, the governor was to appoint a majority of the new commissioners from "residents in the counties most affected by the actions of said commission."

In retrospect, the state's abrupt removal of the existing board was not really surprising. The commissioners had been at odds with the legislature on the issues of money and authority almost from the time they officially took office in 1866. For example, between 1866 and 1880, despite repeated pleas from the commissioners for sufficient funds with which to enhance Valley facilities, state lawmakers appropriated only $10,000 for improvements in the grant. Moreover, they reversed two of the board's important rulings during the period (Coulterville Road and settlers' claims), thereby causing its members considerable frustration and embarrassment.

The state's penny-pinching policy forced the commissioners to grant special concessions to private parties in order to provide trails, hotels, and supplies needed by visitors. This course of action eventually led to public charges, largely ill-founded, of favoritism and mismanagement by the board. The politically sensitive situation culminated in the commissioners' dismissal by the legislature in 1880.

On April 19, 1880, Governor Perkins appointed a new Yosemite Board of Commissioners consisting of holdovers I. W. Raymond and William C. Priest, and six other northern California businessmen. There is some evidence that the new regime was dominated by men favorable to the powerful Southern Pacific Railroad. One of its agents, William H. Mills, served for a time as a member of the Executive Committee. Furthermore, the commission almost instantly entered into harmonious relations with the railroad-dominated legislature. In contrast to its parsimonious record during the incumbency of the first commission, the legislature appropriated $169,000 in the 1880s for purchase, construction, and improvement of roads, trails, and bridges; erection of a large hotel, service buildings, and waterworks; and a number of other projects requested by the board.

Meanwhile, the deposed commissioners refused to recognize that they had been ousted, saying that the action of the legislature was in violation of the terms of the Yosemite Grant from the federal government. Secretary William Ashburner, who took genuine pride in his position on the board, instituted legal proceedings contesting both the state's new management regulations and Governor Perkins' right to appoint new commissioners. He took the case all the way to the United States Supreme Court, in the interim declining to surrender the books and records of the commission. As a consequence, from October, 1880, until March 21, 1881, when the court ruled in the state's favor,[17] there were two sets of commissioners and two guardians vying for control of the Yosemite Grant, an absurd situation that lessened public confidence in the state's administration of its spectacular property even further.

YOSEMITE GUARDIANS IN THE 1880S

One of the first acts of the new board on taking office was to dismiss long-time guardian Galen Clark and to replace him with none other than James Hutchings, the perennial adversary of the previous commissioners. The choice was not so incongruous as it might appear. Hutchings had an intimate knowledge of both the physical make-up and the historical evolution of the Yosemite Grant, a background the new commissioners sorely lacked. In addition, despite his many problems with the original board, his singular devotion to Yosemite Valley was unquestioned.

Hutchings assumed guardianship on October 1, 1880,[18] and took up residence in his former cabin home on the sunny north side of the Merced River, which lessee John Barnard "with considerate and large-hearted kindness" agreed to let him use. Although he performed his duties with resolution and accomplished a number of improvements within the grant, his tenure lasted only four years. In large measure, Hutchings' removal resulted from his tactless, imperious attitude, which irritated residents and commissioners alike. "He was not a generally popular man," wrote Pinkie Ross, a frequent Yosemite visitor. "Perhaps his being an Englishman may have accounted for it. Among many, however, I was always fond of him and found him most considerate." On October 1, 1884, Hutchings was replaced as guardian by Walter E. Dennison.[19]

Dennison, a native of Illinois,[20] arrived in California in 1880 and

This picture of Walter E. Dennison was taken on October 6, 1884, in Yosemite Valley, a week after he replaced James Hutchings as guardian. Dennison is best remembered in Yosemite history for naming "Happy Isles."

Guardian Walter Dennison sits with his family in front of the former Cosmopolitan saloon in 1887, three years after the state took over the building. (I. W. Taber)

Mark McCord's ineffective term as guardian lasted only twenty-one months.

became an agent for the Continental Oil and Transportation Company, working variously at company offices in Stockton, Sacramento, and San Francisco. Soon after being named guardian, Dennison, a married man with children, established an office and expansive living quarters in the Cosmopolitan building, which the state had acquired at the close of the 1884 season.

Dennison's management of the Yosemite Grant turned out to be a disaster. Residents resented his taking over the popular Cosmopolitan saloon and bathhouse for his own use. Valley businessmen were alienated by steep increases in their annual fees, some to twice the previous amount. And nearly everyone objected to Dennison's policy of allowing overgrazing and ploughing in the meadows, which soon became little more than dusty stubble.

"His petty tyranny and individual persecution were a matter of county scandal," said one critic. "A state senator was elected from Mariposa County under a pledge to remove Dennison within ninety days." The widespread dissatisfaction with Dennison's administration ultimately forced him to resign in August, 1887, to be succeeded by Mark L. McCord, an employee of the Southern Pacific Company and a friend of several of the commissioners.

McCord had never even seen Yosemite Valley before taking office on August 28, 1887. His brief regime was filled with controversy, highlighted by an investigation by the California legislature in February, 1889, into the management of the Yosemite Grant. On June 6, 1889, the commissioners fired McCord and restored Galen Clark, age seventy-five, to his old position as guardian by a vote of six to one.

INVESTIGATION OF THE YOSEMITE COMMISSIONERS

From time to time over the years, various complaints were raised against the Yosemite Board of Commissioners, but most of these were dismissed as coming from disgruntled bidders for Valley privileges. In the late 1880s, however, one particularly vocal critic aired his views in the San Francisco press and eventually caused an investigation of the commission's affairs by the state legislature. His name was Charles Dorman Robinson (1847–1933), a close ally of Hutchings and a self-styled "crank" who spent part of each year between 1880 and 1890 in Yosemite Valley. An artist of considerable talent, Robinson painted more than ninety scenic canvases of Yosemite during his seasonal residence there, many of which he sold to visiting Englishmen (one now hangs in Buckingham Palace).

In 1885 the commissioners leased studio space to Robinson adjoining the guardian's office in the old Cosmopolitan building. After two summers there (1885–86), his lease was canceled and—according to Robinson—his studio forcibly entered and taken over by Guardian Walter Dennison. During the spring of 1887, Dennison moved the post office and Wells Fargo office from Folsom's hall to Robinson's former quarters.

His wrath thoroughly aroused, Robinson brought twenty-two charges of misconduct against the commissioners, ranging from "forcibly breaking and entering private property" to "general failure and incompetence." The accusations were printed throughout the summer of 1888 by the *San Francisco Examiner* in a series of articles and editorials derogatory to the commission and its policies. The *Examiner's* muckraking zeal stemmed largely from publisher William Randolph Hearst's unrelenting hatred of the Southern Pacific Railroad, which held effective control of the state legislature and, indirectly, the Yosemite commission.

Soon after the Twenty-eighth Session of the California legislature opened in January, 1889, Assemblyman E. C. Tully of San Benito County introduced Robinson's twenty-two sworn charges against the commissioners. Both the senate and the assembly appointed committees to investigate the matter with the stipulation that they report back to the legislature before the end of the session. Testimony began on February 4, 1889.

The senate committee could "find nothing more than a difference of opinion between some witnesses and the Yosemite Commissioners as to the best method of management of the affairs of the valley." The assembly investigating team, which conducted a much more thorough examination, submitted majority and minority reports to the legislature. The majority report absolved the commissioners of most of Robinson's charges, called specific attention to several others, and suggested a number of changes in the management of the Yosemite Grant, none of which were ever implemented. In effect, the state investigation of 1889 generally vindicated the Yosemite commissioners, a conclusion the *Examiner* labeled a "whitewash."[21]

DEVELOPMENT IN THE YOSEMITE GRANT

Until 1888, community activities in Yosemite Valley were split between the Upper and Lower Villages, located about three-quarters of a mile apart, a situation created when the Valley's original two hotels were established in the late 1850s. In 1884, at the peak of its three-decade existence, the Lower Village contained about a dozen buildings clustered in two groups around Cook's and Leidig's Hotels. These included (see map):

Folsom's Hall, which Ira B. Folsom had essentially completed in late 1874 to be opened the following summer as a saloon, dance hall, and store. The property was acquired by the state in the 1874 indemnification of all Valley claims. On January 23, 1875, the commissioners denied Folsom's application for a lease on his former building for unstated reasons. After James Hutchings' ill-starred attempt to operate an illegal hotel on the premises during the summer of 1875, the commissioners utilized various rooms in the one-story structure for the Valley post office and Wells Fargo office, a bar run in conjunction with Black's Hotel (later Cook's), and (in 1877) M. M. Hazeltine's photography shop. The building was torn down in 1888 along with Cook's and Leidig's Hotels.

Henry Stegman, who came to Yosemite about 1874 and briefly ran a business collecting and selling sequoia seeds, was the Valley postmaster and Wells Fargo agent in Folsom's building from 1879 through 1886, after which both offices were moved to the Upper Village by the guardian. Stegman also operated a livery business in Bridalveil Meadow from about 1875 to 1889 under an annual lease of $150 from the state.

Westfall's Butcher Shop stood on the south side of the Valley road opposite Galen Clark's house from about 1874 until removed by the

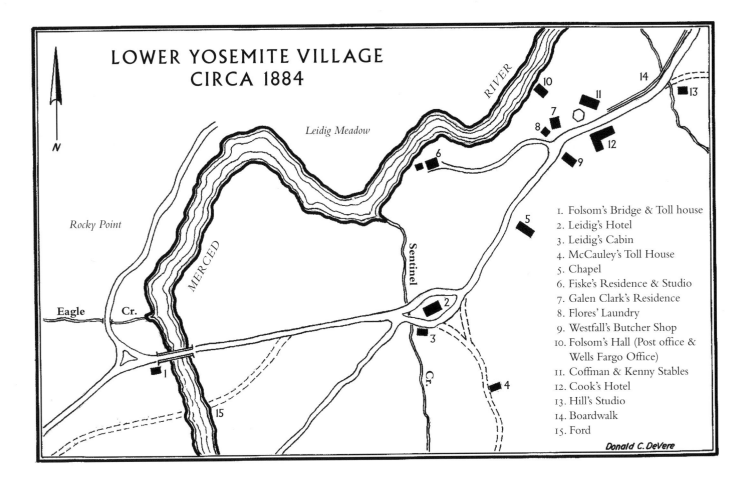

LOWER YOSEMITE VILLAGE
CIRCA 1884

Leidig Meadow

Rocky Point

MERCED

Eagle Cr.

Sentinel

N

RIVER

1. Folsom's Bridge & Toll house
2. Leidig's Hotel
3. Leidig's Cabin
4. McCauley's Toll House
5. Chapel
6. Fiske's Residence & Studio
7. Galen Clark's Residence
8. Flores' Laundry
9. Westfall's Butcher Shop
10. Folsom's Hall (Post office & Wells Fargo Office)
11. Coffman & Kenny Stables
12. Cook's Hotel
13. Hill's Studio
14. Boardwalk
15. Ford

Donald C. DeVere

commissioners in the fall of 1892. It was operated by Joel J. Westfall in conjunction with the Valley slaughterhouse, which was located in a meadow (Slaughterhouse Meadow) on the north side of the Merced River near the foot of El Capitan about a mile southwest. Incomplete records indicate that, over the years, the slaughterhouse and accompanying cattle were kept variously by Westfall, Colwell Drew, who had a state permit in 1880, and an unnamed Spaniard. The slaughterhouse buildings were ordered razed by the commissioners at their meeting on July 27, 1892.

Joel Westfall was born in Virginia in 1819 and came to Mariposa County in 1854. In the 1860s he claimed 160 acres on the old trail between Wawona and the Valley and ran cattle on the property in the summer. He is listed on the 1872 Mariposa County assessment role as having 160 acres near Peregoy's, now called Westfall Meadows, with improvements thereon valued at twenty dollars. Westfall, who served as a county supervisor for many years, first received a permit for his meat market at an annual rent of fifty dollars from the commissioners in 1874. He ran his store in the Lower Village until 1889 when he moved to the south side of the road at the west end of the Upper Village. He is last listed on the commissioners' lease records in 1891. John Peter Mieson and George Meyer, who had a ranch at Big Meadow near present Foresta, received a contract to supply fresh meat to the Valley in 1892.

Manuel Flores worked as a packer and guide before stage roads reached the Valley in 1874 (Laurence Degnan said that Flores packed in Galen Clark's wagon in 1870). In July, 1874, Flores obtained a permit from the commissioners to open a laundry in the Lower Village just west of Galen Clark's residence. Little more has been recorded about

either Flores or his business except for occasional references to "a Mexican family that took in washing." When Flores departed the Valley is uncertain. His last lease for an unspecified period of time was granted in 1880.

George Fiske (1835–1918), a portly, bewhiskered protégé of photographer Carleton Watkins, visited Yosemite in 1872 and 1875. In 1879–80 he and his wife Mira spent the winter at Leidig's Hotel. His photographs of snow-covered landscapes taken in the Valley that season were so well received that he asked the commissioners for a permit to open a photography business in Yosemite. Granted the privilege in the summer of 1880 at an annual fee of twenty dollars, Fiske and his wife soon moved permanently into a small frame house originally occupied by one Charles Staples. (Also a photographer, Staples had worked with Fiske at Watkins' San Francisco studio in the mid-1870s. His brief connection with Yosemite is not clear from the commissioners' lease records, which state only that "Fiske is given permission to occupy the former Charles Staples house.")

The building was situated at the end of a road near the Merced River a short distance west of Flores' laundry. In 1883 Fiske erected a rather quaint one-and-a-half-story clapboard studio close by his residence. Fiske sold his photographs, principally winter scenes, at this site until the commissioners moved the building to the Upper Village in 1899 for use as the guardian's office and residence. Fiske, who had been requesting

THE YOSEMITE GRANT: 1864–1906

another location nearer the route of travel for some time, transferred his studio to a structure along the road near the Yosemite Chapel in the Lower Village in 1898. He operated in this location until fire destroyed the building in May, 1904.

The Yosemite Chapel is the oldest structure in Yosemite Valley although it no longer stands in its original place. On May 2, 1878, the Yosemite commissioners granted members of the California State Sunday School Association permission to build a chapel in the Valley to be used for undenominational services. On May 14 the Yosemite Union Chapel Association was incorporated for that purpose and a fund-raising campaign begun. Children were asked to contribute small coins at Sunday school services. Larger sums were solicited from prominent members of the association. By the summer of 1879, using plans donated by a leading San Francisco architect, a twenty-six-by-fifty-foot wood-frame building had been erected at "a cost between three and four thousand dollars" on a rise of ground along the south side of the road near the base of the Four Mile Trail in the Lower Village.

The chapel was formally dedicated on June 9, 1879, according to the *Mariposa Gazette,* when "an eloquent sermon was given by Dr. Guard to delegates attending a National Sunday School Convention in Yosemite." From that time on, the dark-painted, white-trimmed church remained continuously open for the free use of worshippers of every denomination, even though it had no resident pastor. Whenever an accommodating minister visited the Valley on a Sunday, the church bell's peal apprised the faithful that formal services would soon be forthcoming.

The first of what has since become thousands of chapel weddings took place on October 24, 1884, when Abbie Crippen, eldest step-daughter of hotel proprietor John Barnard, and Harry L. Childs, a Bodie mining engineer who constructed a telephone line from Bodie to the Valley in 1882, culminated their Yosemite romance in marriage. The reed organ that sounded the bridal march was a gift from an Eastern woman in memory of Florence Hutchings, the first white child born in the Valley, who died in a hiking accident in 1881 at the age of seventeen (see note 18).

Because the Lower Village essentially ceased to exist in the 1890s, the commissioners moved the chapel to its present location in the then-thriving Upper Village in the fall of 1901 at a cost of $350 and rebuilt it exactly as it had previously stood. The building came into National Park Service ownership in 1927 and has since been added to, stabilized, and rehabilitated over the years. On November 12, 1973, the chapel became the first structure in Yosemite National Park to be entered in the National Register of Historic Places.

Coffman and Kenney formed a partnership in 1884 to operate the Valley stables across the road from Cook's Hotel in the Lower Village. William F. Coffman was briefly associated with Henry Washburn in the construction of the Wawona Road and served for a time as county assessor. George W. Kenney, who reportedly

George Fiske, a native of Amherst, New Hampshire, spent nearly forty years as a resident photographer in Yosemite Valley.

The first of Fiske's three Valley studios stood directly in front of his residence at the end of a side road near the Merced River in the Lower Village. The building was moved to the Upper Village in 1899 by the commissioners and became the guardian's office and residence.

The Yosemite Chapel, shown here before window glass was installed, comprised a single room containing benches, an altar, coal-oil lamp fixtures, and exposed studs and rafters. Note the outhouse at the right rear.

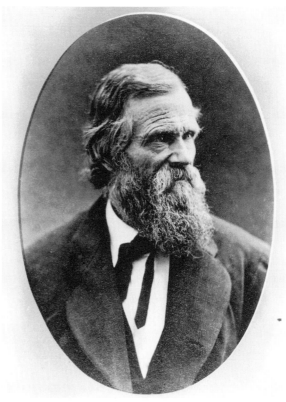

Carleton Watkins took this formal photograph of Guardian Galen Clark in the mid-1870s.

Galen Clark moved into this small house in the Lower Village early in 1875 after losing his Wawona property. Clark's carriage, which was packed into the Valley by mules in 1870, can be seen at the right of the large cedar tree.

"had a way with horses," came to Yosemite from Sonora at age sixteen to work for James Hutchings as a guide and hostler.

Hutchings described the livery in his book, *In the Heart of the Sierras* (1886), as follows: "The livery stables, carriages, and saddle horses are kept by Messrs. Wm. F. Coffman and Geo. Kenney, two wide-awake, square men, who wait upon guests at the hotel every evening to learn their wishes concerning the rides around the Valley in carriages or up the mountains on horses, for the next day. When they present themselves, it will be well for visitors to have considered their plans for the morrow, and give to them their order accordingly; as, by so doing, all delays, and many annoyances, are avoided in the morning."

In the summer of 1888, Coffman and Kenney moved their stables to James Lamon's former Royal Arch farm, the site of the present Ahwahnee Hotel, where the state leased them commodious new quarters.

Galen Clark took up residency in a small house on the north side of the road in the Lower Village after losing his South Fork property to creditors in December, 1874. The rustic ten-by-thirty-foot structure functioned both as Clark's home and the guardian's office until Clark was removed from that position in 1880. The commissioners continued to lease the building to Clark as a residence for a token one dollar a year "in consideration of his long service" until his death on March 24, 1910, four days short of his ninety-sixth birthday.

Thomas Hill (1829–1908), a noted English landscape painter, made the first of several trips to Yosemite in 1862. In 1882 the commissioners granted him the right to erect a studio "at a site to be selected." The following year Hill built and seasonally occupied a small studio at the east end of the Lower Village where he displayed and sold his Yosemite paintings. In 1886, after his daughter married John Washburn, one of

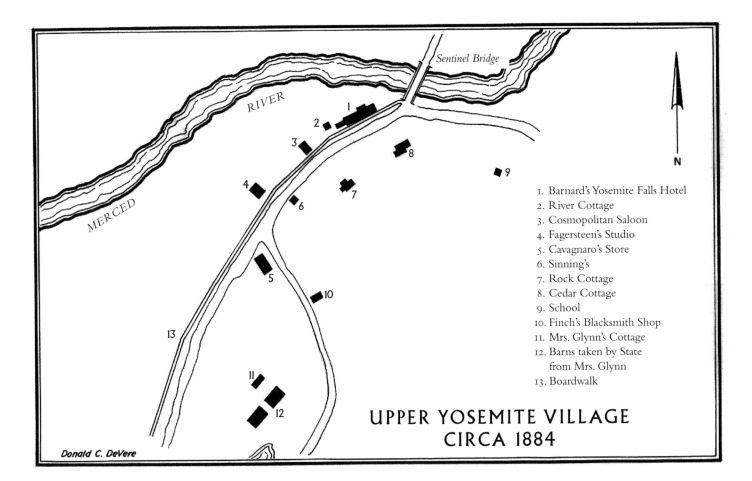

Sentinel Bridge

RIVER

MERCED

N

1. Barnard's Yosemite Falls Hotel
2. River Cottage
3. Cosmopolitan Saloon
4. Fagersteen's Studio
5. Cavagnaro's Store
6. Sinning's
7. Rock Cottage
8. Cedar Cottage
9. School
10. Finch's Blacksmith Shop
11. Mrs. Glynn's Cottage
12. Barns taken by State
    from Mrs. Glynn
13. Boardwalk

**UPPER YOSEMITE VILLAGE
CIRCA 1884**

Donald C. DeVere

Henry's brothers, Hill opened a larger studio at Wawona and took up summer residence at the Wawona Hotel. He spent the winters in nearby Raymond. Hill continued to show his paintings at the Valley studio for several years after moving to Wawona. His name appears on state lease records as late as 1888. On July 14, 1891, the commissioners ordered that "the building known as Hill's Studio be removed."

The Upper Village in 1884 consisted of Barnard's Yosemite Falls Hotel group, the Cosmopolitan saloon and bathhouse, Fagersteen's photography studio, Sinning's cabinet shop, Finch's blacksmith shop, the Yosemite school, Cavagnaro's store, Mrs. Glynn's boardinghouse, and an assortment of small shacks and tents used as residences by workers and guides.

Gustavus Fagersteen was active in the Yosemite region from 1876 through 1890, part of that time in a loose partnership with S. C. Walker, a Stockton photographer. In 1880 Fagersteen received a permit from the commissioners to open a photography studio in the Upper Village west of the Cosmopolitan saloon at an annual rent of ten dollars (later raised to forty dollars). Although a respected member of the Valley community (Hutchings called him "one of the best residents of Yo Semite"), Fagersteen was not a great photographic artist. His main output consisted of taking posed pictures of tourists with Yosemite Falls as a backdrop.

Fagersteen evidently died rather suddenly about 1890, after which his personal property was sold at auction. Only a pile of glass negatives remained in the abandoned studio. These were eventually scattered over the floor and gradually crushed under the feet of playing children.[22]

Adolph Sinning (1813–1889), a creative and talented German woodworker, leased a small frame building for fifty dollars a year in the Upper Village in 1877 for use as a cabinet shop and residence. Built before

Adolph Sinning, "Art Worker in All Fine Yosemite Woods," stands in front of his shop and residence in the Upper Village.

1874, the structure, probably Henry Stegman's old seed store, stood across the road from the Cosmopolitan. A tourist in 1878 wrote that "Sinning did an active trade in samples of the woods found in and about the valley, which were made into little boxes and various ornaments, beautifully polished. The little ornaments are made for the most part of manzanita, madrone, and a species of laurel, all of which are exceedingly beautiful. The manzanita cuff buttons are very pretty."[23]

Hutchings described Sinning as "having the rare gift of uniting the taste of the artist with the skill of the workman. His choice specimens of various woods, found in this vicinity, most admirably joined and beautifully polished, are so arranged that one colored wood is made complementary to that of the other adjoining it. They are simply perfect, both in arrangement and mechanical execution. Then, it gives him such real pleasure to show you, and explain all about his work, that his eyes, seen through a single pair of glasses, actually double in brightness when you admire it. Nor need you be afraid of offending him if you do not purchase, as he readily sells all that he can make, notwithstanding he is at his bench on every working day, both winter and summer, making and finishing the most beautiful of ladies' cabinets, glove-boxes, etc."[24]

In 1878, Sinning, a music lover who had been a widower for twenty-eight years, married Elizabeth King, a pianist. Galen Clark wrote in the *California Farmer* of October 14, 1878, that "Sinning decided it would not be good to be alone in his declining years and chose that the sunset of his life should be cheered and brightened by the company and smiles of a loving wife." Sinning had less than a dozen years to enjoy his new companionship. He died on June 20, 1889, after which the state used his cottage for other purposes. His heir, Julius Starke of Santa Barbara, succeeded Sinning in the woodworking business at another location in the

Upper Village. Roland B. Dexter took over Starke's operation in 1903.

Johnny Finch ran the Valley blacksmith shop across the road from the present chapel location from 1876 until the early 1890s. He is last shown on the commissioners' lease records at twenty dollars a year in 1892.

The Yosemite School district was formed in May, 1875, to satisfy a request from a group of Valley families with school-age children. The *Mariposa Gazette* said on August 5, 1876, that "J. A. Chestnutwood on July 6, 1875, organized and taught school for a week under a large oak tree about one mile distant from Yosemite Falls [probably at the foot of Indian Canyon near Indian Creek]. Children sat on a prostrate log and on boxes. A dry goods box was used as a blackboard by the teacher, as there were no books in a class of seven beginners. During the first week, George Anderson [pioneer trail builder and the first to climb Half Dome] built a cloth structure, twelve by sixteen feet, with upright posts hewn out of a fallen cedar."[25]

A permanent school building soon followed, most likely in the summer

The first Yosemite school building was a rough, unpainted shack. Teacher Mary Adair and her students posed for this picture in 1882.

of 1875 when a rough, unpainted one-room shack, twenty-four feet long by sixteen feet wide, was erected at the edge of a small meadow about 250 yards southeast of Barnard's Hotel. The walls were a single thickness of vertical boards and battens, which directly supported the wall plate and shake roof without benefit of studding. The interior contained long benches with small tables for desks, later replaced by factory-made school desks. Furnishings included a dictionary, abacus, maps and globes, a wall blackboard, a mannequin of the human body, and a tiny library. Pupils ranging in age from five to sixteen received their primary education in the flimsy building, which withstood the Valley's winds and storms for more than twenty years. In 1897 the school was moved to a former stage office near the present LeConte Memorial Lodge farther up the river.

Angelo Cavagnaro became associated with Aaron Harris in 1876 in the operation of the Valley general store situated just northeast of the present chapel site in the triangle formed by the roads. Harris had come from Sonora in 1874 and was issued a permit at an annual rent of sixty dollars to open a store. After Harris began the Valley's first public campground in 1878, Cavagnaro ran the store himself, and in 1881 bought out Harris' interest. The store stocked a diversified inventory ranging from a "box of paper collars to a side of bacon," but the busiest part of the establishment was the saloon, which occupied the westerly half of the store building. Angelo's uncle, G. B. Cavagnaro, assisted his nephew in the business until his death from unknown causes on September 9, 1885. He was interred in the Yosemite cemetery.

Cavagnaro had another store in Fresno Flats (now Oakhurst) and spent the winters there in later years. He was shot and killed at that store in 1895 by an Indian, one Abraham Lincoln Speckerman, following a quarrel between the two men.[26] His widow continued to operate the Yosemite store until 1898 when the commissioners refused her a new lease. The following year the state built a twenty-five-by-forty-foot, two-story frame building across the road and leased it to another Italian named John Garibaldi (called "Garibaldi's New Store"). Nelson L. Salter took over the premises about 1903.

Elizabeth Glynn (1819–1904) lived full time in the Valley after she and her husband Thomas were displaced as managers of the Glacier Point Mountain House by James McCauley at the end of the 1879 season. Thomas Glynn, a veteran of the Mexican War, died on December 19, 1881. Galen Clark presided at his burial in the Yosemite cemetery. About this time, the gullible Mrs. Glynn paid $780 to Henry Hedges for a frame house and two small barns that really belonged to the state. She had no sooner moved in than the guardian ordered her out. Pleading poor health and indigence, Mrs. Glynn eventually persuaded the commissioners to lease her the place, which stood just west of the present chapel, for a token one dollar a year.

For more than two decades, Mrs. Glynn eked out a meager living by taking in washing, selling baked goods, and keeping two or three boarders. In her yard, an assortment of chickens and turkeys noisily coexisted with more than a dozen cats. Despite her peculiarities, she was well-liked by her Valley neighbors. In 1903 Mrs. Glynn was removed to the Mariposa County Hospital by the guardian after suffering a serious leg ailment that confined her to bed. She died the following February.

THE HARRIS CAMPGROUND (1878-1887)

During the early years of Yosemite visitation, campers were not a significant problem in the Valley. The vast majority of tourists traveled via guided saddle-trains and obtained their meals and lodging at the various hotels. After the completion of stage roads in 1874–75, however, campers began driving their own conveyances to Yosemite, carrying their equipment and supplies with them. Tents were set up wherever convenient, and horses turned out to forage in the meadows without regard for environmental damage.

In 1876 the board of commissioners determined that a prescribed camping location offering supplies and supervision had become a necessity in the Valley. At a meeting held December 19, 1876, the board awarded storekeeper Aaron Harris a ten-year lease at an annual fee of $450 on a portion of James Lamon's former property in the vicinity of the present Ahwahnee Hotel for that purpose.[27] The premises, known as the Royal Arch Farm, consisted of forty-five acres of land, Lamon's northern orchard and vegetable garden, and the substantial two-story cabin and outbuildings Lamon had erected in 1869. Harris subsequently

laid up thirty tons of hay and three tons of barley, brought in cows and chickens, and stocked a store. According to the Harris Camping Register, now in the Yosemite Museum, the campground opened for business on June 19, 1878.

Kenneyville grew into a bustling complex during the days of animal transportation.

James Hutchings wrote about Harris' operation in 1886: "As Mr. A. Harris grows and keeps an abundant supply of fodder, besides stabling for animals, his place is deservedly popular with camping parties. Milk, eggs, and other farm products are obtainable here; and should the bread burn at the campfire, and the yeast become sour, Mrs. Harris has always the remedy on hand to help strangers out of their difficulty, and that most cheerfully."[28]

Harris ran his popular campground for ten seasons, serving the last of thousands of customers on September 16, 1887. Soon after he had departed the Valley for the winter that fall, a fire, probably caused by sparks from a log left smoldering in the fireplace, burned Harris' buildings to the ground. When the state refused to replace the structures, Harris, whose lease had recently expired, gave up his enterprise and departed the Valley for good.

KENNEYVILLE

In the summer of 1888, the commissioners erected expanded new facilities on the Royal Arch Farm site and moved the Valley stables to the property. The buildings comprised a barn, fifty-two by one hundred feet, for fifty-two horses and provender; a carriage shed, sixteen by sixty feet; men's quarters and office, sixteen by sixty feet; a residence, twenty-four by sixty feet, with verandas on two sides; and a large corral. Ninety percent of the lumber used in construction came from the removal of Black's and Leidig's Hotels and Folsom's hall from the Lower Village earlier in the year. In July, 1888, Coffman and Kenney received a lease to the premises at an annual rent of twelve hundred dollars, and opened for

Chapman Avenue, Kenneyville's main street, was named for Commissioner Emery W. Chapman, who supervised construction of the stable area. (Author's collection)

business at the new location the following month.

During the ensuing years, "Kenneyville"—named after managing partner George W. Kenney—became a thriving village replete with all the people, structures, and paraphernalia necessary to sustain a large stable complex. Besides the main barns, this included blacksmith, saddle, harness, and wagon shops; storerooms, sheds, corrals, and office; dormitory accommodations for a small army of guides, drivers, hostlers, and other employees; and a scattering of houses for families (Kenney himself had eight children). Most of the rustic, wood-framed buildings fronted dusty, tree-lined Chapman Avenue,[29] Kenneyville's main street, which took on the appearance of an Old West frontier town.

All through the busy summer months, Coffman and Kenney supplied carriages and drivers to transport sightseers to various viewpoints on the Valley floor. For the more adventurous, guides, saddle horses, and pack animals provided access to the Yosemite backcountry.[30] The assortment of wagons, stages, buggies, and more than a hundred horses involved in the complicated operation represented a considerable investment. In the winter, the proprietors locked up their vehicles and equipment in the buildings, guarded by a caretaker, and moved their families and livestock to the foothills.

Later History: William F. Coffman died in 1898, but his heir, John W. Coffman, Jr., continued in partnership with Kenney until January 23, 1911, when Anna M. Kenney, George's widow, sold her interest to Coffman for ten thousand dollars. On May 9, 1916, Coffman sold the business to the Desmond Park Service Company, then the principal Yosemite concessionaire. By this time, motor stages and automobiles had replaced horse-drawn conveyances as the preferred method of transportation on Yosemite roads. Only riding stock and pack animals were needed to serve visitors.

Kenneyville continued to function on a reduced basis until 1926, when the buildings were leveled to provide space for the construction of The Ahwahnee (opened July 14, 1927). A smaller Valley stable was erected at its present location near Lamon's first orchard.

THE YOSEMITE CEMETERY

Yosemite's cemetery, across the street and to the west of the National Park Service Administrative Offices, was established in the 1870s (at least as early as 1875). A few Native Americans and pioneer settlers had previously been buried at other places in the Valley. Later, their remains were transferred to this location. Some of the people interred in this diminutive graveyard played important roles in the growth and development of what is now Yosemite National Park. Others were only casual visitors. Some, like Galen Clark, lived rich, full lives. Others hardly began theirs. Of the forty-seven people buried there, eleven are Native Americans. The last burial occurred in 1956, when the cemetery was closed to further interments.[31]

STEREOGRAPHY IN THE YOSEMITE GRANT

Stereography is the technique of pairing two photographs, taken at slightly different angles, then viewing them through an instrument that brings them together as a single image to create a three-dimensional effect. The principle of stereography was discovered in the late 1830s, but no practical method of mass production was available until the 1850s when the development of the wet-plate process made it possible to turn out glass transparencies and paper prints of high quality quickly and inexpensively. The prints, mounted in paired sets on stout cardboard and stored in light-proof boxes, survived in good condition for many years. The innovative system was immediately popular, and photographers traveled far and wide gathering stereographs of well-known scenes to meet the demand.

Yosemite provided a perfect subject for three-dimensional pictures. Charles Weed and Carleton Watkins carried double-lensed stereo instruments along with their bulky view cameras on their pioneering photographic excursions to Yosemite. Englishman Eadweard Muybridge (1830–1904), who first photographed the Valley in 1867, published hundreds of stereographs in addition to his spectacular mammoth-plate prints.

During the 1870s, stereographs of famous Yosemite landmarks became almost a requirement in publishers' catalogs, and dozens of photographers journeyed from the East to take pictures of the Valley scenery. Among the more prominent were Charles Bierstadt, who came west with his brother Albert, the noted artist; Charles L. Pond from Buffalo; Thomas C. Roche from New York; and John C. Soulé from Boston. Sometimes they sold their views under their own names; other times they marketed them through publishing houses like Lawrence and Houseworth of New York and San Francisco, or the Anthony Brothers of New York.

By the summer of 1876, so many photographers were active in Yosemite that the board of commissioners at their annual meeting on

June 16 voted that "photographers plying their vocations of taking and selling photographs in the valley shall pay in advance an annual license of $10 and must obtain a permit from the Secretary of the Board before proceeding."

The first photographer to establish a studio in the Valley was John James Reilly (1838–1894), who arrived in Yosemite on May 22, 1870, and subsequently erected a spacious white tent in a meadow near Hutchings' hotel. A banner running the length of the tent proclaimed in large letters: "J. J. REILLY'S STEREOSCOPIC VIEW MANUFAC-TORY ★ GROUPS TAKEN." Reilly was a Scottish emigrant who moved to California from Niagara Falls, New York, in search of a new life. After serving as a volunteer in the Union Army, he became a naturalized American citizen in 1866 and took up photography as a vocation. Reilly, who wintered in Stockton, operated his Yosemite tent studio for seven seasons (1870–76) and produced hundreds of stereographs of both Valley and High Sierra scenes. His assistant on one of his several trips into the high country was John Muir. Their names appear together in Snow's La Casa Nevada register in 1873.

A first-rate landscape photographer, Reilly deplored the fact he could get no better prices for his best work than that received by slipshod cameramen. In an undated flyer describing his business (copy in the Yosemite Museum), Reilly said: "The trip to Yo-Semite Valley and Big Trees is never complete unless you carry home some of those stereoscopic views manufactured and for sale by J. J. Reilly, in Yosemite Valley, to show those at home that you have seen the wonders of nature. . . All publications on photography say these are the best."

Reilly left the Valley permanently in the fall of 1876. He later worked in the photography business in San Francisco, Marysville, and Eureka. Serious financial problems and two failed marriages may have caused his suicide in San Francisco in 1894.

Reilly's successor in Yosemite was Martin Mason Hazeltine (1827–1903), an itinerant photographer who passed through the Valley five times between 1867 and 1877. At different periods he was variously a competitor and a partner of Reilly's. In 1877 Hazeltine received a permit from the commissioners to open a photography studio in a portion of Folsom's former building in the Lower Village, which also housed the post office, Wells Fargo office, and a bar. Hazeltine printed a trade card that summer advertising "Photographs of the Yosemite Valley, mammoth trees, and Pacific Coast. . . Rooms next door to the Post Office, Yosemite Valley. M. M. Hazeltine, Photographer."

For unrecorded reasons, Hazeltine operated his business for only one summer in Yosemite Valley. His position as resident photographer was very shortly taken over by Gustavus Fagersteen in the Upper Village, and George Fiske in the Lower Village. By the time their studios were established in the early 1880s, the popularity of the stereograph had begun to wane in favor of eight-by-ten-inch and smaller prints for albums.

Itinerant photographers like this one at the Mariposa Grove often passed through the Yosemite Grant during the summer, taking and selling pictures. (Author's collection)

THE ASCENT OF HALF DOME

Scotsman and ex-sailor George G. Anderson worked as a guide, laborer, and trail builder in Yosemite Valley from about 1870 until his death from pneumonia on May 8, 1884. Anderson, a "brawny, powerful Viking of a man," was known for his amazing strength. The story was told for years that when the state was building the lower iron bridge across the Merced River in the fall of 1878, Anderson carried one of the sections of the bridge in his hands, laid it on the ground, and put it into place by himself. The piece weighed 525 pounds!

Anderson engineered and constructed the substantial trail along the north side of the Merced River from Happy Isles almost to the base of Vernal Fall in 1882–83 under contract with the state, but he is best remembered in Yosemite history as the first person to climb 8,836-foot-high Half Dome. In Anderson's time the summit of Half Dome was considered beyond man's reach. ("Never has been, and never will be trodden by human foot," State Geologist Josiah D. Whitney proclaimed in 1868 in *The Yosemite Book.*)

James Hutchings made the first documented attempt to climb Half Dome in 1859. He wrote about his unsuccessful effort in his book, *In the Heart of the Sierras,* 456–57, although he gives the wrong date. During the next fifteen years, other daring adventurers, including Anderson himself, tried vainly to reach the top. In October, 1875, however, the

John James Reilly, Yosemite's first resident photographer, ran a tent studio in the Valley for seven seasons. Here Reilly stands beside a row of slanted boxes in front of his tent. According to photographic historian Ted Orland, these were printing frames used for making contact prints by exposing negative and paper, clamped tightly together under glass, to sunlight for several minutes. (Author's collection)

The first tourist ascent of Half Dome was made on October 16, 1875, by a party of Englishmen and Americans guided by George Anderson, four days after Anderson scaled the summit. Two of the six men in the group, shown here with Anderson (at left), made it only part way up the rope, but the other four reached the top. The tourists arrived at Snow's Hotel on October 9 and had been exploring the area before meeting Anderson and arranging for the climb. They wrote about their experience in Snow's register on October 16. (Carleton Watkins)

Even today it requires considerable effort to ascend the two steel cables to the top of Half Dome. (Bill Johnston)

intrepid young Scotsman devised a new method for making the ascent. Hutchings described what went on: "Mortified by the failure of all his plans hitherto, yet in no way discouraged, Anderson procured drills and a hammer, with some iron eyebolts, and drilled a hole in the solid rock; into this he drove a wooden pin, and then an eyebolt; and, after fastening a rope to the bolt, pulled himself up until he could stand upon it; and thence continued that process until he had finally gained the top— a distance of nine hundred and seventy-five feet. . . This was accomplished at 3 o'clock P. M. of October 12, 1875."[32]

Anderson then returned to the Valley to put together a more substantial rope to allow tourists to make the climb. Cosie Hutchings remembered his preparations: "Along the old plank walk between Hutchings' old corral to Sentinel Bridge, Anderson stretched five separate strands of baling rope [a soft, loose-fiber rope about the thickness of a lead pencil, but strong and easy to use]. With another strand he went along the 975-foot length knotting the five strands together with a sixth strand and a good sailor's knot a foot apart—a convenient space for climbers to grasp as they made the ascent. The knotted rope was coiled, tied together, put on a pack mule, and carried to the shoulder of the Dome. Here Anderson shouldered it himself, packed it to the top of the Dome, unloosed it, fastened one end to an iron pin in rock on the summit, slid it down, uncoiling and fastening it in other iron-pin eyebolts he had placed on his first ascent as he went."[33]

Within days, others, including one woman and sixty-one-year-old Galen Clark, pulled themselves up Anderson's ropeway—forerunner of today's steel cables—to see the panoramic view. In November, John Muir became the ninth person to make the intimidating climb.

Anderson hoped to replace the rope with a wooden staircase, but he died without realizing his goal. In its *Biennial Report* for 1882, the board of commissioners said: "South Dome should be made accessible by better means than a rope attached to iron keys. Two thousand dollars would put a substantial and safe flight of steps up the rock, with balusters on the sides and fenders to protect the structure against danger from snowslides in winter. Thousands of people would stand on this commanding summit nine thousand feet above the sea, and dangle their feet over a precipice a little less than a mile high, if safe and comparatively easy means of ascent were provided. (The exercise of 'dangling' is optional.)"

Not only was no staircase ever built, but Anderson's ropeway broke from sliding ice and snow, which also ripped out some of the eyebolts, in 1883–84. It was replaced by two young daredevils, who duplicated Anderson's original climb in the summer of 1884.[34] The ropeway had to be at least partially replaced again in 1895, 1901, and 1908. In 1919 the Sierra Club installed two steel cables, raised on pipe supports with footrests every ten feet, to make a safer climb. The supports and footrests are put up and taken down annually, and the oft-repaired cableway is still in use.

Artist's sketch of one of the "two young daredevils" replacing Anderson's broken ropeway to the top of Half Dome in the summer of 1884. (Author's collection)

A stage owned by David Lumsden prepares to depart Chinese Camp for Yosemite with a group of tourists recently arrived via the Sierra Railroad. (Tuolumne County Historical Society collection)

STAGING TO YOSEMITE VALLEY

The colorful era of horse-stage travel to Yosemite Valley began with the completion of three private toll roads in 1874–75 and ended when motor vehicles took over in 1915. At various times during this forty-year period, eight different routes, served by a number of stage lines, competed vigorously for tourist business. All originated at some point on the Southern Pacific or connecting railroads. Each had its advantages and liabilities. In the following brief descriptions of the routes, the mileages given are from San Francisco to Barnard's Hotel.

(1) The Milton and Calaveras Big Tree Route: By rail from San Francisco to Milton at the end of the Stockton and Copperopolis Railroad. Then by stage via the Calaveras Grove of Big Trees, Chinese Camp, and the Big Oak Flat Road to the Valley. Rail: 133 miles. Stage: 153 miles. Total: 286 miles

(2) The Big Oak Flat Route: By rail to Milton. Then by stage via Copperopolis, Chinese Camp, and the Big Oak Flat Road to the Valley. Rail: 133 miles. Stage: 91 miles. Total: 224 miles.

(3) The Merced-Coulterville Route: By rail to Merced. Then by stage via Snelling, Merced Falls, Coulterville, Merced Grove of Big Trees, and the Coulterville Road to the Valley. Rail: 152 miles. Stage: 94 miles. Total: 246 miles.

(4) The Modesto-Coulterville Route: By rail to Modesto. Then by stage via La Grange, Coulterville, Merced Grove of Big Trees, and the Coulterville Road to the Valley. Rail: 114 miles. Stage: 99 miles. Total: 213 miles.

(5) The Sierra Railway-Chinese Camp Route: By rail to Chinese Station on the Sierra Railroad.[35] Then by stage via Chinese Camp and the Big Oak Flat Road to the Valley. Rail: 172 miles. Stage: 64 miles. Total: 236 miles.

(6) The Berenda-Raymond Route: By rail to Raymond at the end of the Southern Pacific's Yosemite branch via Berenda.[36] Then by stage via Grant's Sulphur Springs, Chowchilla Mountain, Wawona, and the Wawona Road to the Valley. Rail: 200 miles. Stage: 61 miles. Total: 261 miles. ★

(7) The Madera Route: By rail to Madera. Then by stage via Fresno Flats, Fish Springs, Wawona, and the Wawona Road to the Valley. Rail: 185 miles. Stage: 95 miles. Total: 280 miles.★

(8) The Mariposa Route: By rail to Merced. Then by stage via Hornitos, Mariposa, Wawona, and the Wawona Road to the Valley. Rail: 152 miles. Stage: 94 miles. Total: 246 miles.★

★*Optional side trip to Mariposa Big Tree Grove and return: Additional 17 miles by stage.*

Although far less arduous than clinging precariously to a saddle, a journey by stage to Yosemite over any of the three toll roads was an experience not soon forgotten. Ruts, sharp curves, and sheer drop-offs predominated along the narrow rights-of-way across the mountains. And always there was dust, ever-present, enshrouding clouds of dust, which left Yosemite passengers so begrimed upon their arrival that even their closest friends would have had difficulty making identification. At Valley hotels, stages were met by porters brandishing great feather dusters, which they immediately put to good use. This served two purposes: the cleanliness of the hotel and the comfort of the guests.

But dust and rough roads were not the only hazards facing Yosemite-bound travelers. Besides the occasional runaway team, there was always the chance of a holdup. Stage robberies were commonplace in California's Mother Lode country from the days of the '49ers until well into the twentieth century. At least sixteen holdups of horse-drawn or motor-driven stages occurred on the foothill sections of the Yosemite roads between 1883 and 1920.

Two were more unusual than the rest. The first, which took place near present Oakhurst on June 2, 1900, was committed by a lone bandit who boldly intercepted three stages and two private wagons in succession, waiting for each to round a turn in the road, then politely but

This map delineates the principal rail-and-stage routes to Yosemite Valley before 1907, when the Yosemite Valley Railroad was completed. (Author's collection)

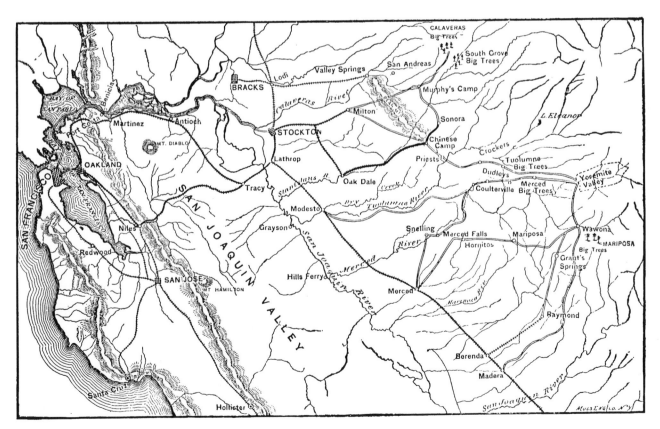

firmly motioning with his rifle for the driver to stop and fall into place behind the others. Ultimately, thirty-four men and five women were assembled alongside the road after depositing their money in a hat passed down the line for that purpose. Despite the sudden arrival of the United States Cavalry, which was en route to Yosemite for summer duty, the daring road agent escaped into the surrounding brush and was never apprehended.

The second holdup, on August 15, 1905, was unique in that the bandit permitted one of the passengers to snap two pictures of the robbery in progress. Only one came out, but that print exists today as perhaps the only authentic photograph of a real stagecoach holdup ever taken.[37]

TUNNEL TREES

In the summer of 1878, as an inducement for tourists to travel the Big Oak Flat Road to Yosemite, the owners of the route hired brothers David and James Lumsden of Groveland to cut a tunnel through the burned-out base of the "Dead Giant" in the Tuolumne Grove. The agreement specified that blasting could not be employed, and that the opening be large enough to accommodate a fully-loaded stage. On July 13, 1878, the *Sonora Union Democrat* reported: "The tree tunnel has been completed. In height it measures 12 feet, and it is 10 feet wide at the top." From this time on, stages passed through the tunnel—an experience eagerly anticipated by travelers—both going and coming from Yosemite.[38]

Not to be outdone, Henry Washburn received permission from the commissioners in 1881 to enlarge a natural cavity in a giant sequoia tree, 227 feet high, which blocked a new road he was building from the Lower Mariposa Grove to the upper one under state contract. Brothers Otis, Ben, and Lyman Scribner were paid seventy-five dollars to cut a tunnel ten feet high by nine and one-half feet wide at the bottom, tapering to six and one-half feet wide at the top. Total length was twenty-six feet. The project was completed in early August, 1881, and soon after, a party of Knights Templar from Philadelphia arrived. The stage was held up until the workmen removed the blocks of freshly chopped heartwood from the roadway so this stage might be the first vehicle to pass through the new "living tunnel."

Later History: As time went on, the Wawona Tunnel Tree became a tourist mecca visited annually by thousands of people who came on foot, horseback, by stage, and eventually, automobile. A good many stopped to have their passage immortalized in photograph to show the folks back home. Before the development of the snapshot camera, a man made a decent living doing nothing but taking photographs of persons and vehicles as they emerged from the tunnel, which he later sold to the delighted subjects. The Wawona Tree was the most photographed tree in the world when it fell during the heavy winter of 1968-69.

Washburn also cut a tunnel through the lesser-known California Tree in the Lower Mariposa Grove in 1895. When winter snow blocked the

Passenger Anton Veith's snapshot of an actual robbery of a Yosemite-bound stage in progress. The bandit, whose take amounted to about one hundred dollars, stands in the white duster and hat near the center of the picture. He was never apprehended.

road to the upper grove where the Wawona Tree was situated, enterpris-
ing stage drivers sometimes placed the Wawona Tree sign at the
California Tree, and few tourists knew the difference. The California
Tree still stands, but the road was rerouted around it in 1932.

PURCHASE OF ROADS AND TRAILS

During the first sixteen years of state ownership of the Yosemite Grant,
the commissioners were obliged to offer leases to private parties to build
needed roads and trails because of the legislature's insufficient appropriations. When the replacement board appointed by Governor George C.
Perkins took office in 1880, one of its first acts was to unanimously recommend that the state immediately purchase all roads and trails within
the grant and make them free to the public. "The collection of tolls [on
private roads and trails] is one of the most annoying experiences of visitors," Guardian James Hutchings said in his 1880 report. "It creates
more complaining and dissatisfaction than any, if not all, other causes put
together."

Responding to the board's request, the state legislature appropriated
$25,000 for that purpose during its 1880 session. The commissioners
then began construction of the Grand Carriage Drive around the Valley
floor, on which they continued work until the funds were exhausted.
Two years later the commissioners asked the legislature for another
$25,000 with which to complete the project. After some delay, the new
appropriation was finally approved, effective March 3, 1885.

The act specifically allocated $10,000 of the total for purchasing the

*The tunnel through the "Dead Giant"
in the Tuolumne Grove of Big Trees
was cut in 1878 to entice tourists like
these two intrepid women to travel the
Big Oak Flat Road to Yosemite.*

This early photograph of the Wawona Tunnel Tree may have been taken shortly after the opening was completed in August, 1881. The identities of the three men are unknown.

four-mile section of the Coulterville and Yosemite Turnpike Company's road extending from the lower iron bridge down the Merced Canyon to the grant line just east of the Cascades. It also allotted $3,500 to acquire the 4.37-mile section of the Big Oak Flat Road running from the grant line below Gentry's to the Valley floor. On April 2, 1885, the Coulterville company, in return for $10,000, executed a deed to the state for the piece in question, which had cost Dr. John McLean $12,000 to construct. The following year the mountainside stretch of the Big Oak Flat Road was sold to the state for $3,500. It had cost the Yosemite Turnpike Road Company more than $16,000 to build the zigzag route down the cliffs. Perhaps the disparity in the purchase prices was the commissioners' way of making up for some of the injustice done by the legislature to Dr. McLean over the years.

In 1888 the legislature appropriated $8,000 to buy the seven-mile section of the Wawona Road lying between the grant line near Fort Monroe and Lower Yosemite Village, which had cost the Yosemite Stage & Turnpike Company $16,000 to build thirteen years earlier. With this purchase, consummated June 6, 1888,[39] all roads within the Yosemite Grant were the property of the state.[40]

The Legislative Act of March 3, 1885, also provided $1,500 to buy John Conway's Eagle Point Trail to the top of Yosemite Falls and beyond, the only toll trail still remaining in the grant. The commissioners had previously acquired the others by purchase or expiration of the lease.

EVENTS LEADING TO THE ESTABLISHMENT
OF YOSEMITE NATIONAL PARK

Efforts to enlarge the Yosemite Grant began as early as March 22, 1881, when the commissioners unanimously adopted a resolution asking the federal government for an extension of the Yosemite Valley and Mariposa Big Tree Grants. "The control of the watershed that discharges into Yosemite Valley," the board said, "and its preservation in its natural state, is vital to the future existence of the valley. . . In our judgment the territory embraced in the watershed of the valley proper, or in other words the entire basin of every stream leading into the valley should be under the control of the Commissioners to the end that the timber, shrubbery, and grasses thereon may be preserved to retain the snow and rain upon which the grandeur and beauty of all Yosemite streams depend."

The commissioners instructed Secretary M. C. Briggs to procure signatures from influential citizens favorable to enlargement. In June, 1881, this petition was left at the Capitol in Washington by Briggs following his interview on the subject with President James Garfield just three days before Garfield's assassination. In their *Biennial Report*s of 1882 through 1888 the commissioners reiterated their desire for an extension of the grant[41] and asked the state legislature to petition Congress on the matter by resolution, which it did in 1889.

When Congress acted the following year, however, it was not in the form envisioned by either the commissioners or the legislature. On March 18, 1890, Representative William Vandever of Ventura County, California, introduced a bill (H.R. 8350) asking Congress to establish a *federal* reserve consisting of a block of eight townships surrounding and including the state-controlled Yosemite Valley Grant, an area of approximately 288 square miles, "for the purpose of preserving the forest, and as a recreation ground for the people as a public park."

The Yosemite Board of Commissioners said in their 1885–86 Biennial Report that "a comfortable and artistic log cabin has been erected at a central point in the Mariposa Grove for the shelter and convenience of visitors, ornamented by a shapely massive chimney of stone, with commodious fireplace graced by traditional crane and pendent kettle." The cabin was enlarged in 1902 and replaced in 1930.

As Vandever's bill slowly worked its way through committee, support began to grow to set aside a much larger reserved area that would include important sections of the High Sierra such as Tuolumne Meadows, Hetch Hetchy Valley, the Tuolumne Canyon, Tenaya Lake, and the Ritter Range. One of the most persuasive advocates for incorporating these vital areas into a great national park was John Muir, James Hutchings' former sawyer, who had since gained a national reputation in the scientific and literary world through his influential writings.[42]

In 1889 Muir joined forces with Robert Underwood Johnson, editor of the *Century Magazine*. In two articles written for that publication in August and September, 1890, about the "proposed Yosemite National Park," Muir eloquently described the beauties of the region, identified

A noted conservationist and author by 1890, John Muir played an important role in the creation of the Yosemite Forest Reservation, soon to be known as Yosemite National Park.

the forces at work in their destruction, and strongly urged adoption of a comprehensive park bill. In Washington, Johnson presented letters from Muir to the House Committee on Public Lands asking its members to extend the limits of the Vandever bill to include the Tuolumne River watershed and the Ritter Range on the east. Other supporters of the proposal soon came forth, ranging from the powerful Southern Pacific Railroad, which foresaw the potential of increased tourist traffic, to Secretary of the Interior John Noble and President Benjamin Harrison.

The widespread pressure resulted in a second Yosemite bill (H.R. 12187), also sponsored by Vandever, being substituted for the previous one. The revised bill provided for a reserved area that was almost township for township like the one Muir had sketched in his *Century Magazine* articles. The new bill cleared both houses of Congress on September 30, 1890, without the customary bill printing, and was signed into law by President Benjamin Harrison on October 1, a legislative feat rarely accomplished in so short a time.[43]

Curiously, H.R. 12187 used the phrase "Yosemite forest reservation" rather than "Yosemite National Park," as did Vandever's original bill. The lands were "withdrawn from settlement, occupancy, or sale" and placed under the control of the secretary of the interior. The act explicitly provided that nothing in it "should be construed as in anywise affecting the grant of lands made to the State of California," over which the secretary had no authority or control.

The rectangular reserved area was huge—about forty-two townships, or nearly 1,513 square miles in all, including the 56.4 square miles of the Yosemite Valley Grant. After deducting the state-owned portion, the new federal reserve encompassed 932,600 acres, or approximately 1,457 square miles (the Mariposa Big Tree Grant was outside the southern boundary and remained under state jurisdiction).

Thus began a unique seventeen-year period (1890–1906) of dual administration, literally a park within a park: the centerpiece, Yosemite Valley, still administered by the state of California; the much larger surrounding territory managed by the federal government.

NOTES AND REFERENCES

1. The commissioners tried to avoid any semblance of favoritism by stating in their report of the lease to Coulter and Murphy that "had there been two applications from parties equally desirable, as a matter of taste, the Commissioners would have declined to entertain propositions involving business relations from any one of their own number." Coulter was replaced on the board by P. D. Wigginton of Merced, who served only a year before being elected to Congress in 1876. He was succeeded by Thomas P. Madden of San Francisco. The bridge mentioned in the agreement was the finished timber span with superstructure that Hutchings erected in 1868 to replace Hite's original log bridge, which washed away during the high water of December, 1867.

2. In a letter to the *San Francisco Bulletin* in 1875, Ashburner described the controversy from the viewpoint of the commissioners, saying that Hutchings was defeated in the courts, had refused to bid for the hotel concession, and had refused to leave when the lease was awarded to another party. "Mr. Hutchings," Ashburner wrote, "by his writings, his talk, his lectures, his persistent abuse of the Commissioners, his claims to persecution and martyrdom, has succeeded in

manufacturing a large amount of public sympathy, which seems to display itself whenever an occasion suitable or otherwise offered itself." Ashburner denied that the commissioners took part in the "firing of guns or other powder preparations" in celebration of Hutchings' departure from the Valley, but admitted that guns were fired by others upon the "vindication of the law which Mr. Hutchings himself most defiantly outraged."

3. Effie Maud Crippen, Joshua and Adelaide's youngest daughter, died on August 31, 1881, at age fourteen and was buried in the Yosemite cemetery. Effie stepped on a broken wine bottle while wading in Mirror Lake and severed an artery in her foot. Three miles from home, with no doctor available, she lost too much blood to be saved.

4. Constance Frederica Gordon-Cumming, *Granite Crags of California* (Edinburgh and London: William Blackwood and Sons, 1884), 126–28. Fannie Crippen Jones, one of John Barnard's four stepdaughters, said some years later that "many times guests would sit around the fire in the Big Tree Room, listening to the experience of one another in other climes. Mr. Hutchings was always ready to tell his experiences of conquering the wilderness [this obviously occurred during Hutchings' term as guardian between 1880 and 1884]. It was a 12 o'clock midnight story. It was interesting the first time, or the 101st, but oh, the 1,000,001th. Goodnight! Hutchings had a false four-teeth upper set. About 10:30 p.m. he would commence to drop them and catch them with a clack. If I told you the number of times he clicked them between 10:30 and midnight, I'm afraid you'd cut my acquaintance!" Letter from Fannie Crippen Jones to Dr. Carl Russell, December 11, 1924, in the Yosemite Research Library.

5. The windmill was dismantled after water was piped to Barnard's Hotel in 1890 from the excellent Glacier Point spring.

6. On April 28, 1893, the *San Francisco Call* reported: "John K. Barnard, the Yosemite Valley hotelkeeper, must gather together his effects and leave his mountain home. So says the Supreme Court in a decision filed yesterday. In probable anticipation of this decision, Barnard has not opened his hotel this season, although tourists commenced to flock into the valley nearly three weeks ago. The old hotel, with its picturesque cottages and 'Big Tree Room,' has remained deserted and will so remain until the new tenant begins competition with the Stoneman House, the only other hotel in the valley. Barnard first came to the valley in the seventies. He held a lease of the premises known as the Barnard's Hotel, also the old Hutchings' Hotel, which did not expire until January 1, 1885. In January, 1882, however, the commissioners gave him another lease running to January, 1892, a period of ten years. He was to pay for his privileges partly in rent and partly in repairs. During the last few years Barnard stopped paying rent altogether, claiming he made certain improvements upon the property which offset the rent due. The commissioners asserted that his claim was absurd and that he had no possible excuse for his failure to pay.

"Barnard defied them, however, and in the meantime kept his hotel going full speed, pocketing the profits and securing, as it is currently rumored in the valley, all attachable property. When his lease expired, he still refused to vacate, claiming that the instrument should read 1885 instead of 1882, and that the mistake was caused by inadvertence in copying. The commissioners immediately brought suit in the Superior Court of Mariposa County and obtained judgment. Although he apparently had no case, Barnard appealed to the State Supreme Court and during last year continued to operate the hotel. After deducting the expense of appeal from his profits, there probably remains a good round sum to reward him for his defiance of the commissioners.

"The only person who suffers from the transaction besides the public is Glasscock, the Raymond hotel man, to whom the commissioners leased the hotel in August, 1891, expecting to give Glasscock possession the following January when it was optimistically believed that Barnard would yield possession. Glasscock sold out his hotel in Raymond, purchased some $500 worth of furniture, and had it shipped to the valley where it was stored for the winter. Barnard refused to budge and poor Glasscock's furniture has been gathering dust ever since. Barnard will now be promptly ejected, and Glasscock will probably get the hotel." (Glasscock's subsequent activities are described in Chapter VII.)

7. After the Leidig family departed in 1888, no winter accommodations were available in Yosemite Valley until 1907–08, when the Sentinel Hotel began year-round operations following completion of the Yosemite Valley Railroad.

8. James Hutchings, *In the Heart of the Sierras* (Oakland and Yosemite: Pacific Press Publishing House, 1886), 447.

9. Pinkie P. Ross, "Biographical Sketches," n.d., handwritten manuscript in the Yosemite Research Library.

10. "John Baptiste" may have been John Baptiste Lembert who homesteaded at Tuolumne Meadows from 1885 until he was murdered in the late 1890s. Snow's three-volume guest register is now preserved in the Yosemite Museum.

11. The meadow and stone bridge in the area are also named for Stoneman. At their annual meeting, held June 2, 1886, the commissioners voted five to two to build the Stoneman House "near the Glacier Wall" rather than between Yosemite Falls and the Merced River. The board felt the latter location "as too dangerous to be thought of—contiguous to threatened overflows in front, and to the titanic hurling of bowlders of all denominations of weight from the rear. . . Nineteen out of every twenty persons concede that its location—all things considered—is the best that could have been made."

12. The Firefall was continued intermittently by others after McCauley left his Glacier Point hotel in 1897. David Curry, founder of Camp Curry near the base of Glacier Point in 1899, put the Firefall on a nightly basis about 1900. The Firefall was discontinued permanently after January 25, 1968, on orders from the Director of the National Park Service, who considered it a man-made attraction that caused congestion and reduced the supply of red fir bark on dead trees.

13. Fred McCauley, "The Life of James McCauley," handwritten manuscript dated February 23, 1930, in the Yosemite Research Library.

14. Whorton, at one time an important figure in the Yosemite area, was justice of the peace, grand marshal of parades, and a cattle rancher near El Portal. On April 4, 1887, Whorton was shot to death at the Cascades by Abel Mann. Several factors played a part in the killing, including rivalry over a woman and continued ill feelings about the Civil War (Whorton was from Alabama; Mann from Rhode Island). Mann was tried for murder in the Mariposa County Superior Court, but was acquitted. Some years afterward, Mann tried unsuccessfully to kill his wife by slitting her throat at their Raymond home. He was believed to have committed suicide when surrounded by a sheriff's posse.

15. Mirror Lake was a much larger body of water in those days than now. The National Park Service has discontinued the practice of periodically damming and dredging the lake to remove the detritus brought down Tenaya Creek, believing that nature should be allowed to take its course. As a result, Mirror Lake is slowly filling in and will eventually disappear. In 1884 Guardian James

Hutchings reported that he had "moved several large blocks of granite—some weighing ten to fifteen tons each—from the adjacent banks into the narrowest neck of the channel of exit of Tenaya Creek, thereby treasuring up the waters of Mirror Lake and at the same time increasing the area of the lake nearly six times."

16. The *Act to provide for the management of the Yosemite Valley and the Mariposa Big Tree Grove* contained six sections. Principal among them was the stipulation that the commissioners, who had previously been appointed more or less for life, were now limited to four-year terms, although they could be reappointed. Terms were staggered so that half the board was appointed every two years. The act also specified that the guardian could not be a member of the commission.

17. The Supreme Court's ruling, *Ashburner v. California,* 103 U.S. 575–579 (1881), which also ordered Ashburner to turn over the books of the commission, subjected all future appointees to the Yosemite board to the political whims of any governor who chose to exercise the spoils of his office.

18. After being ousted from the Valley in 1875, Hutchings moved back to San Francisco with his wife Elvira and their three children. He opened a tourist agency, gave illustrated lectures on Yosemite, and escorted private tours to the Valley and surrounding high country in the summer. He also resumed his writing and publishing work with a final printing of *Scenes of Wonder and Curiosity in California* (1876), and the issuance of a new book called *Hutchings' Tourists Guide to the Yo Semite Valley and the Big Tree Groves for the Spring and Summer of 1877* (San Francisco: A. Roman & Co., 1877). Moody, wistful Elvira eventually left him and divorce ensued. It was an unusual breakup in that Hutchings and his three children continued to live with Elvira's mother, Florantha Sproat. In 1879 Hutchings married a recent widow named Augusta Ladd Sweetland.

The following year the family, including Mrs. Sproat, returned joyfully to their beloved Yosemite after Hutchings' appointment as guardian. His elation at being back in the Valley turned to sorrow on September 20, 1881, when popular, tomboyish Floy, barely seventeen, was killed in an unfortunate accident. According to sister Cosie, Floy and a party of friends were climbing the Ledge Trail to Glacier Point when someone hiking above inadvertently loosened a large rock, which rolled down and struck Floy. Badly injured, she died the following day. Mount Florence, a 12,567-foot Yosemite peak, is named in her honor. Six weeks later, tragedy again struck the Hutchings household when second wife Augusta Hutchings died suddenly from a lung hemorrhage after an illness of only a few hours. She had probably contracted tuberculosis from her deceased first husband.

In 1884 Hutchings returned to San Francisco with his two remaining children and resumed his tour business. In 1886 he published his most famous book, *In the Heart of the Sierras.* About 1892 he married his third wife, an attractive English woman named Emily Ann Edmunds, who joined her husband in leading summer tourist parties to the Sierra. In the summer of 1899, at the age of seventy-five, Hutchings took over management of the Calaveras Big Tree Grove Hotel, situated above Murphy's Camp northwest of Yosemite.

19. In testimony before the Investigative Committee of the state assembly in 1889, Hutchings said that he was not re-elected guardian because he had fired the "lazy, impertinent sons of one of the Yosemite Commissioners." No corroboration of this allegation has been found.

20. Walter E. Dennison was born in Kankakee County, Illinois, on August 17, 1856; graduated from Ohio Wesleyan University in 1877; was a school principal at Upper Sandusky, Ohio, 1877–78; and attended Cincinnati Law School,

1879–80. He married Isabella Richardson on November 2, 1882, and the couple had five children, one of whom, Leonidas Richardson Dennison, was born in Yosemite Valley on February 3, 1885. After his term as guardian, Dennison engaged in a variety of business enterprises in California, including mining, civic improvement projects, and a pottery works in San Francisco. He died at Alameda on September 6, 1929.

Dennison's principal contribution to Yosemite history was to bestow the name "Happy Isles" to three islets in the Merced River just above the bridge at the east end of Yosemite Valley in 1885: "Commemorative of the emotions which I enjoyed while exploring them, I have named them the *Happy Isles,* for no one can visit them without for the while forgetting the grinding strife of his world and being happy." Letter from W. E. Dennison, guardian of Yosemite Valley, October 25, 1885, copy in the Yosemite Research Library. In the early 1930s, Dennison's daughter Isabel and her son Walter E. Simmonds scattered both Dennison's and his wife's ashes around Happy Isles as they had requested. Letter from Walter Simmonds to Shirley Sargent, September 1, 1993, in the Yosemite Research Library.

21. In 1892 C. D. Robinson gathered together a "company of gentlemen" willing to back him in a huge cyclorama of Yosemite. In a building in San Francisco, Robinson set up scaffolding to support a circular canvas, 50 feet high by 380 feet long, depicting the Valley from the south wall near Inspiration Point. He laid railroad tracks on the ground and built three towers that artists could ascend in order to reach the canvas. As one section was finished, the towers were rolled along the tracks to the next section. The two tons of canvas sagged so badly under the weight of three tons of paint that he twice had to raise the top edge to keep the painting off the floor.

Robinson wanted the panorama to be so realistic the viewers would have the illusion of actually standing on Yosemite's rim gazing at the magnificent scene before them. To enhance the effect, he covered the viewing platform with real Yosemite rocks and also planted shrubbery of the actual species found in the area. Finished in 1893, the panorama was a financial failure in San Francisco. Robinson then took it to the Paris Exposition in 1900, but was unable to have it displayed. He eventually cut it up into marketable sizes and sold enough pieces to earn passage back to the states. Robinson's illustrated account of the creation of his ill-fated work appeared in his "Painting a Yosemite Panorama," *Overland Monthly* 22 (September, 1893): 243–56.

22. Letter from Laurence V. Degnan to Ralph Anderson, February 3, 1952, copy in the Yosemite Research Library. Degnan lived across the road from Fagersteen's Studio as a child.

23. Dio Lewis, *Gypsies, or Why We Went Gypsying in the Sierras* (Boston: Eastern Book Company, 1881), 180.

24. Hutchings, *In the Heart,* 350.

25. There are several conflicting accounts of the location of temporary schools in Yosemite Valley used prior to the first permanent building. For other versions, see Linda Wedel Greene, *Historic Resource Study: Yosemite,* 3 vols. (Washington, D. C.: U. S. Department of the Interior, National Park Service, 1987), p. 163.

26. Letter from Laurence V. Degnan to Douglass Hubbard, October 13, 1958, in "Yosemite Cemetery" file at the Yosemite Association.

27. The commissioners first leased the Lamon property to Fred Brightman and George W. Kenney in 1875. The partners borrowed $2,100 from storekeeper

Harris to finance their enterprise, which apparently was to consist of a farm and stables. When they were unable to make any payments on the loan, Brightman and Kenney, with the approval of the commissioners, assigned their lease to Harris in December, 1876, as security for money advanced.

28. Hutchings, *In the Heart,* 355.

29. Emery "Wash" Chapman, a pioneer Madera businessman, engineer, and surveyor, had been a partner with William Coffman and Henry Washburn in the building of the toll road from the South Fork to the Valley in 1875. While serving as a Yosemite commissioner in 1888, he worked for a number of weeks without charge supervising the construction of the new buildings on the former Lamon farm. Chapman Avenue was named by the commissioners in appreciation of his efforts.

30. In their *Biennial Report* for 1894, the commissioners complained that "campers insist upon going on the trails with their road horses, animals entirely unfit for such service. They take the trails without guides and without regard to the perils of passing parties that may be met mounted on the regular trail animals, and without thought of the consequences fatal to themselves and others that may result from their own lack of judgment and the inexperience of their animals. During the last season the committee has to report two accidents on the Glacier Point trail from these causes. In one, a road horse, ridden by a lady, went over the cliff, carrying with it the rider, who, fortunately, was caught by a tree top and saved from death. In the other, a horse unaccustomed to packing, but used to carrying a camper's lunch up the same trail, went over and was never seen nor heard of afterward. Your committee need not dwell upon the melancholy consequences, if at the occurrence of either accident, when the bodies of the animals went rolling and bouncing down the cliff, loosening stones and dirt, there had been a mounted party below, with the resulting scare and stampede which such a sight would cause even amongst the regular trail animals."

31. For further information about the cemetery, see Hank Johnston, *Guide to the Yosemite Cemetery* (Yosemite: Yosemite Association, 1995).

32. Hutchings, *In the Heart,* 457–58.

33. Letter from Cosie Hutchings Mills to Mrs. Gregory (Elizabeth H. Godfrey), October 15, 1941, in the Yosemite Research Library.

34. Two fascinating accounts of the ascent by the "two young daredevils," A. Phimister Proctor of Colorado and Alden Sampson of New York City, are given in Hutchings, *In the Heart,* 460–63; and A. Phimister Proctor, *An Ascent of Half Dome* (San Francisco: Grabhorn Press, 1945).

35. In 1897 the Sierra Railway built a new line from Oakdale on the Southern Pacific to Jamestown, Sonora, and other points in the foothills. When the rails reached Chinese Station at milepost 35, D. A. Lumsden & Co. (the same Lumsden who tunneled out the "Dead Giant" in the Tuolumne Grove) began regular stage service over the Big Oak Flat Road from Chinese Station, about two miles north of Chinese Camp, to Yosemite Valley. This reduced the dusty carriage ride to only sixty-four miles. Yosemite-bound travelers no longer used the Stockton and Copperopolis Railroad to Milton unless they also intended to visit the Calaveras Grove of Big Trees. The Chinese Camp to Yosemite stage line ceased operations in 1915.

36. The San Joaquin Valley & Yosemite Railroad, known as the "Raymond Branch," was incorporated on February 15, 1886, by the Southern Pacific

Company to supply an easier, shorter route to Yosemite. A twenty-two mile railroad was constructed from Berenda (thirty miles north of Fresno) to the new town of Raymond, named in honor of Walter Raymond of the popular Raymond-Whitcomb tours. The Yosemite Stage & Turnpike Company built corrals, barns, cottages, and a large hotel there (A. B. Glasscock was the first manager) for its staging operations.

The first train arrived on May 14, 1886. Daily trains, one from Los Angeles and the other from San Francisco, brought passengers to Raymond where they spent the night. The next morning, fifty or sixty tourists boarded stages for the sixty-one-mile journey to Yosemite Valley over Chowchilla Mountain. In 1890 a new road was built bypassing Chowchilla Mountain via Miami Lodge, which added six miles to the route.

The Cannonball Stage was inaugurated in June, 1901, so-called because it would "shoot you through in one day." The Cannonball traversed the sixty-seven bone-shaking miles from Raymond to Yosemite Valley in twelve hours. Four-horse teams, changed every seven or eight miles, traveled at a trot, uphill and down. One stage left from Raymond each morning, another from the Valley, with a quick stop for lunch at the Wawona Hotel. Seats on the Cannonball were in such demand that reservations had to be booked months in advance.

The opening of the Yosemite Valley Railroad in May, 1907, caused the demise of the Raymond Branch as an important Yosemite route although service remained available for some years thereafter to serve Wawona and the Knowles quarry. Trackage east of Daulton was abandoned in 1942; the balance of the line was removed in 1956.

37. A comprehensive account of the various holdups on the Yosemite roads is contained in Hank Johnston, *Yosemite's Yesterdays* (Yosemite: Flying Spur Press, 1989), 20–35.

38. As of this writing, automobiles may still be driven through the tunnel in the "Dead Giant" via the one-way section of the old Big Oak Flat Road running from Crane Flat to Hodgdon's Meadow.

39. The state controller refused to draw the warrant, saying that the road had become state property upon expiration of the original ten-year franchise agreement in 1885. He denied the commissioners' right to renew the lease, which they had done in due time. The stage company took the matter to superior court, and on February 28, 1890, the court ordered the controller to issue the warrant.

40. The acquisition of the toll roads within the Yosemite Grant had little real effect on the three road companies except to relieve them of considerable maintenance because tolls had always been collected outside the grant boundaries by state order. Although commendable from the standpoint of reducing private claims in the Valley, the taking over of the roads added considerably to the cost of Valley maintenance without compensatory appropriations from the legislature, a situation the commissioners complained about in their *Biennial Report* for 1890.

41. The commissioners never had sufficient funds or authority to enter into long-range planning for the future of the Yosemite Grant and its surrounding territory. Aside from Frederick Law Olmsted's suppressed treatise of 1865, the only time the board really looked into planning was in 1881, when the commissioners asked William Hammond Hall, the state engineer, to conduct a survey of the grant and advocate policies to guide future actions. Hall submitted his report, "To Preserve from Defacement and Promote the Use of the Yosemite Valley," to the board on May 20, 1882. It was printed as an appendix

to the commissioners' 1885–86 *Biennial Report*. One of Hall's principal proposals was that the limits of the Yosemite Grant be expanded to include the entire watershed of the Merced River, an area of about 358 square miles. The commissioners used Hall's recommendation to strengthen their petition for enlargement. They also took some guidance from his report in general matters, and employed it to back up funding requests to the legislature, the majority of which went unfulfilled.

42. After Muir's five-year residency in Yosemite (1869–73), he traveled extensively and continued to write about the wonders of the Sierra Nevada in journals and periodicals. His reputation grew, and his persuasive arguments for glaciation as the origin of Yosemite Valley gained him both supporters and antagonists—notably Josiah D. Whitney, the California state geologist, who was convinced that subsidence had been the principal cause. In 1880 Muir married Louisa Strentzel, and for nearly a decade occupied himself managing her father's extensive orchards and vineyards in Martinez, California. Ultimately, much of the acreage was sold or leased out, and Muir had more time for writing and exploring. He published his first book, *The Mountains of California,* in 1894 and spent the rest of his life working diligently for preservation of the natural resources. He died on Christmas Eve, 1914.

43. A further account of the Yosemite legislation appears in Holway Jones, *John Muir and the Sierra Club: The Battle for Yosemite* (San Francisco: Sierra Club, 1965), 35–47.

CHAPTER VII

Countdown to Re-cession
(1890–1906)

ARMY ADMINISTRATION OF YOSEMITE NATIONAL PARK

In conjunction with the Yosemite Act of October 1, 1890, Congress also set aside two separate tracts of timberland in Tulare County embracing the Big Trees of Giant Forest and the General Grant Grove.[1] The statutes establishing the three reservations required the secretary of the interior to make and publish rules "for the preservation from injury of all timber, mineral deposits, natural curiosities, or wonders, and their retention in their natural condition." Furthermore, he was to "provide against the wanton destruction of the fish and game and their capture or destruction for purposes of merchandise or profit," and to "cause all persons trespassing to be removed."

Unfortunately, Congress failed to make any appropriations to carry out the regulations, and no penalties were designated for the offenses named. Moreover, a considerable amount of patented land lay within the boundaries of the reserved areas, but the rights of the property owners were not defined.

Secretary of the Interior John Noble, to whom the administration of the three reserved areas was entrusted, did the best he could under the circumstances. To begin with, he gave names to the preserves: Sequoia National Park (suggested by George W. Stewart, editor of the *Visalia Delta* and a vigorous campaigner for the Tulare County reservations); General Grant National Park (for the General Grant Tree, which had been so designated in 1867); and Yosemite National Park (proposed by John Muir and Robert Underwood Johnson).[2]

Following the precedent established five years earlier in Yellowstone National Park, United States cavalry troops were assigned by the War Department, approved January 13, 1891, upon the request of Secretary Noble, to patrol both Yosemite and Sequoia parks and take general charge during the summer.[3]

One of the advantages of military guardianship of the several parks was that the use of soldiers entailed little or no appropriation of money beyond what was normally spent to sustain the troops. The Adjutant General's office estimated that the additional cost to the federal government averaged only $7,557 a year, a figure far less than that required to subsidize an equal civilian protective force. In addition, the summer assignment provided six months of intensive field training for the soldiers rather than the monotony of parade ground exercises.

Early in May, 1891, Troops "I" and "K" of the Fourth U.S. Cavalry, accompanied by several supply wagons and a long string of pack mules, left the Presidio in San Francisco and began a two-week march of more than 250 miles to their new duties in the Sierra parks. After passing through Pacheco Pass, the troops headed down the hot, dusty San Joaquin Valley, which took five days to traverse. At Madera, the two forces split: Troop "K" continued on to Giant Forest and Grant Grove; Troop "I" under the command of Captain Abram Epperson Wood proceeded northeast up the road through Coarse Gold Gulch and Fresno Flats to Wawona. Arriving on May 17, Troop "I" established a headquarters camp, later known as Camp A. E. Wood,[4] on a flat along the Merced South Fork about a mile north of the Wawona Hotel. Today a public campground marks the site. Wood said he chose the location because the climate was pleasant, fresh beef could be procured, and other necessary supplies were available for delivery at reasonable rates. It also placed the troops on the main tourist route to Yosemite Valley. The soldiers remained in the park until November when they decamped and retraced their route back to the Presidio for the winter.[5]

Captain Wood and his men faced five major problems in protecting the new reservation: miners, hunters, campers, ranchmen, and sheepherders. Miners caused the least trouble, mainly trespassing to locate new mines to which they could never get title, and the occasional killing of deer or bear. Hunters committed great depredations on game, especially during winter when the troops were absent. Campers started fires through carelessness, and defaced many natural objects. Cattlemen, mostly settlers who had taken up land before the park was formed, illegally grazed stock on reserved acreage adjoining their claims.

The worst offenders were the sheepmen, who took over the Sierra as their private grazing ground after the drought of 1864 forced them into the high country to obtain feed and water for their animals. The shepherds, who by 1890 were largely of Portuguese and Basque descent, ignored the army's warnings to desist from grazing their flocks in the park once they discovered they could not be penalized.

During the first four summers of army administration, soldiers spent far more time learning the territory than chasing sheepherders. Because the area was largely unmapped except for the most prominent features, park boundaries were uncertain, and only meager information was available concerning the outlying regions. The sheepmen, on the other hand, knew the country thoroughly. "They band together and hire men who act as scouts," one officer wrote in his report. "They watch the trails from commanding points and give warning when troops are seen."

Eventually the soldiers learned the topography, blazed trails, and made the first detailed maps of the reservation. Many of the place names in Yosemite National Park today—Benson, McClure, Smedberg, Rodgers, Young, Fernandez, Arndt, Foerster, Isberg, and Bigelow, among others— were bestowed by army officers, sometimes in recognition of meritorious service by their men or commanders, in other instances merely to get rid of the sheepherders' designations.

In 1895 Troop "K" of the Fourth Cavalry under the command of Captain Alexander Rodgers took charge of the park and a new era began. Although still constrained by lack of any penalty for wrongdoing except expulsion, Rodgers instituted an inspired plan that soon turned the tide of battle with the sheepmen. When troopers captured shepherds

87406

*Yours Truly
A E Wood.
Capt 1st 4" Cav...*

The Mariposa Gazette *called Captain Abram Epperson Wood, the first acting superintendent of Yosemite National Park, a* "genial gentleman who has endeared himself to the people around Wawona during the time he has spent there."

anywhere in the park, their sheep were gathered together, mixing the brands, and then driven out of the reserved area over the nearest boundary. Meanwhile, the herders themselves were escorted on a fatiguing journey of several days across the most mountainous regions of the park and ejected at a far distant point. By the time the herders got back to their widely scattered flocks, the season's profits were gone.

Pressure on the sheepmen grew even greater the following year when the War Department doubled the number of soldiers in the Sierra parks. On April 4, 1896, the *Mariposa Gazette* reported: "Four companies are to be sent to Yosemite and Sequoia Parks this summer instead of two as before. The two companies have complained of overwork. Companies 'B' and 'K' under Lt. Col. S. B. M. Young will go to Yosemite. The force consists of six officers and 106 rank and file in two companies, fully equipped with wagons and pack mules." One of the units, Troop "K," had been in Yosemite the previous year and knew the country thoroughly.

Colonel Young established sub-posts on the Big Oak Flat Road and in several strategic backcountry locations. In previous years, the smallness of the force did not permit this disposition. Most of the work was accomplished by patrols of five to ten men, sometimes under an officer but not always. Orders were to drive out and scatter all sheep, arrest all herders, disarm all campers and tourists, and see that ranchmen kept their stock within fences on their own property.

As time went on, attempts to graze sheep and cattle became less and less of a problem in the park, although there were occasional complaints as late as 1910. Instead of arduous patrols over rough country, soldiers spent their time collecting tolls, searching for lost parties, planting fish, guiding tourists, and fighting forest fires. Strictly speaking, these activi-

Trooper Eugene Goodrich took this photograph of Troop "K," Fourth U. S. Cavalry, at Camp A. E. Wood in 1896. Gabriel Sovulewski, who later spent thirty years as a civilian supervisor in Yosemite National Park, stands fifth from the right in the last row.

THE YOSEMITE GRANT: 1864–1906

ties were without legal sanction because the law providing for the use of troops limited their actions to "preventing trespassers or intruders from entering said reservations" and the removal of such trespassers.

One of the major problems with the army's administration of Yosemite was the constant reshuffling of commanding officers and troops, especially during the first decade that soldiers were in the park. During the twenty-four years between 1891 and July, 1914, sixteen different officers functioned as acting superintendent at various times.[6] On one occasion, three were in charge within a single year. The practice made for fluctuating and inconsistent policies because some commanders took a much more lenient approach and had a far different view about the park than others.

The most notable of the numerous army officers was Harry Coupland Benson (1857–1924), who first came to Yosemite as a lieutenant in 1895 and spent three summers in the field. In 1905, by that time a captain of the Fourth Cavalry (promoted to major in 1906), Benson returned to the park as acting superintendent, a position he held through 1909. Renowned for his map making, trail building, explorations, fish planting, and tenacity in ending the illegal incursions of sheep and cattle, Benson was a nemesis to all violators of the law. One contemporary report said that Benson was "such a terror to the wrongdoer, that the angry mother in the region reduces her obstreperous offspring to subjection by shouting, 'Be good, or Benson will catch you!'"[7]

Troop "F," Sixth U. S. Cavalry, was photographed in 1899 at the Fallen Monarch in the Mariposa Grove, even though the grove was still under state control at the time. Captain E. F. Willcox, acting park superintendent, is the officer standing without mount at the extreme right. The identity of the woman above him is unknown.

Harry Coupland Benson, resting here by his tent at Camp A. E. Wood, earned a deserved reputation as a strict administrator.

STATE MANAGEMENT OF THE YOSEMITE GRANT

Although the expansion of the reserved area by the federal government came in a different form from that contemplated by California officials, the commissioners took full credit for instigating the legislation. "We call attention to the response made to our request by the Federal Government for the preservation of the Yosemite watershed," the board said in its *Biennial Report* for 1893–94. The commissioners later added a none-too-subtle hint of their displeasure at being bypassed in the administration of the new preserve. After quoting Secretary John Noble's report of conditions in Yellowstone National Park ("squalid . . . in a repulsive condition"), the board noted that "Californians familiar with the Yosemite will see at once that the Federal Government may learn much from the experience of California in the management of such scenic reservations."[8]

The commissioners left no doubt of their continuing autonomy in the Yosemite Grant. Soldiers crossing the Valley en route to another area of the national park were not permitted to camp east of Bridalveil Meadow, and their presence anywhere in the grant—even when off duty—was not encouraged. At its annual meeting in June, 1890, the board adopted and published a comprehensive set of rules and regulations for Yosemite Valley and the Mariposa Grove. Some of the rules expanded on laws already in effect. Others set forth important new provisions such as the one giving law enforcement authority and direction to the guardian, including the right to hire patrolmen in the summer.[9]

Galen Clark's second term as guardian ended with his resignation, effective June 1, 1897, because of age (eighty-three). "I wish to retire in favor of a younger and I trust more effective man," Clark wrote in his notice to Governor James Budd. Clark was replaced at the June meeting by Miles Wallace, a member of the board of commissioners, who had to resign his position by law. Wallace,[10] a former Madera County district attorney, served two undistinguished years as guardian before resigning because of poor health. He was succeeded on October 1, 1899, by John F. Stevens, a former stage driver for the Washburn interests who was described as being "right out of the wild and woolly West."

Stevens crossed the plains from the Midwest in 1865 and settled in California in 1872. In the late 1870s he became a stage driver with the Yosemite Stage & Turnpike Company working out of Wawona. During his years in that capacity, he carried a number of famous visitors to Yosemite Valley. Stevens undoubtedly gained the guardian's position because of employer Henry Washburn's influence with the board of commissioners.[11] Despite his unpolished ways, Stevens lasted nearly five years as guardian, longer than any other except Galen Clark. He resigned on August 8, 1904, two years after Washburn's death, probably because of the many complaints received by the commissioners about his rough-and-ready management practices.

The last Yosemite guardian, George T. Harlow, served during the final two years of state administration of the Yosemite Grant. A San Francisco businessman, Harlow was engaged in mining and other enterprises in the San Francisco Bay Area. At the time of this appointment as guardian, he was superintendent of the Belt Railroad of the San Francisco Harbor. Harlow took office on September 1, 1904; the position was abolished by August 1, 1906.

LOSS OF THE STONEMAN HOUSE

Faulty construction inherent in the state-built Stoneman House finally led to disaster on the morning of August 24, 1896, when fire swept through the elegant frame hotel, burning it to the ground. Fortunately, few guests were on the premises at the time, and no serious injuries or loss of life resulted from the conflagration. Perhaps the biggest surprise, given its history of problems, was that the building lasted as long as it did. Seventeen months after the Stoneman House opened on April 1, 1888, engineer George D. Nagle inspected the structure and reported most prophetically to the commissioners: "It is only a question of time when the building will be destroyed by fire from defective chimneys."

In the spring of 1890, misgivings about the chimneys caused the commissioners to consider converting the Stoneman House to steam heat instead of wood, thereby reducing the fire danger. Faced with the expense of replacing the lower iron bridge, which fell into the Merced River on April 1, 1890, under the weight of accumulated ice and snow from the heavy winter, as well as repairing a number of damaged buildings and roads, the board pronounced the estimated price of twenty-nine hundred dollars for the hot-water heating apparatus "too costly." Proprietor J. J. Cook was instructed to close the hotel by September 15 before extensive use of the fireplaces would be required.

Only a year before the Stoneman House burned down, Guardian

Stoneman House

In the early 1890s, the commissioners added covered upstairs porches and repainted the Stoneman House. Taken from the northwest, this view shows the wing, sixty-eight and one-half feet long, that ran along the north side of the ill-fated hotel.

Galen Clark said in his annual report that "the roof over the hotel kitchen recently caught fire and it is a matter of great wonder that the house was saved from total destruction. This is the third time the roof of the house has caught fire from sparks from the chimneys."

The insurance adjuster who inspected the remains of the Stoneman House for J. J. Cook after the fire (Cook's furnishings were insured) attributed its loss to "the weight of snow of the previous winter settling the roof, thereby causing cracking of the concrete around the flues, as there were no brick chimneys in the building." Engineer Nagle's dire prediction seven years earlier turned out to be right on the mark.

The destruction of the Stoneman House created a serious shortage of tourist accommodations on the Valley floor because the commissioners lacked the funds with which to replace their premier hotel. "Under the laws of the State," the board said in a plea to Governor James H. Budd for help in the matter, "the Stoneman House could not be insured, and was not insured. The State insures its own property and, we are informed, has saved a great deal of money doing so. At the same time, under this policy, when any Commission loses a building or a portion of the State property under its care by fire, it seems only just and right that the State should take, from the amounts thus saved in insurance, a sum sufficient to compensate that particular branch of the State's service that is the loser. We are informed that the total cost of the Stoneman House was nearly $60,000, and we therefore submit the claim that the State still owes the Yosemite Valley Commission that sum of money."[12]

The legislature failed to act on the commissioners' request for indemnification. Subsequent petitions by the board for an appropriation to build a new hotel in the Valley—the last in 1904—also went unfulfilled.

THE SENTINEL HOTEL

The lengthy dispossession proceedings instituted by the state against John K. Barnard, proprietor of the Yosemite Falls Hotel, finally concluded on April 27, 1893, when the California Supreme Court awarded control of the premises to the commissioners. Barnard did not return to the Valley that spring to open his hotel as usual, most likely in anticipation of the adverse decision. In Barnard's absence, the county sheriff presented the writ of eviction to Guardian Galen Clark on May 11, 1893. Laurence Degnan described the aftermath: "Barnard's furniture and fittings—beds, mattresses, chairs, bureaus, matting, telegraph instruments, in fact all of Barnard's personal property—were dumped in a heap in the meadow [near the present chapel site]. That huge pile of stuff remained for most of the spring and summer . . . exposed to the elements and the high water that flooded the meadow and ebbed and flowed among the beds, chairs, and bureaus."[13] The few items that survived were gradually hauled away by local scavengers, and the residue burned.

On May 13, 1893, possession of the hotel was turned over to A. B. Glasscock, who had been awarded a lease on the property, effective January 1, 1892, undoubtedly at the behest of Henry Washburn (see note 11). Glasscock changed the name of the four-unit establishment to the Sentinel Hotel, moved in his furniture and fixtures from storage, and opened for business.

Albert Baldwin Glasscock (1843–1897), a native of Missouri, managed the Yosemite Stage & Turnpike Company's new hotel at the Raymond trailhead for Washburn in 1890–91. In the spring of 1892 he moved to Yosemite Valley expecting to take immediate charge of Barnard's hotel, but the changeover was delayed for a year by Barnard's continuing legal appeals (see note 6, Chapter VI). At their annual meeting, held June 8, 1893, the commissioners inspected Glasscock's facilities and decided to repair and refit the hotel in time for the 1894 season. Glasscock's rent was reduced to fifty dollars instead of the usual annual fee of eight hundred dollars because only the old Hutchings House (Cedar Cottage) was available for rent in 1893.

"Lessee Barnard permitted the hotel to fall into a state unfit for occupancy," the commissioners said. "The State was in danger of incurring criticism of the people for maintaining only one hotel in the valley. The remodeled place will be run on the European Plan, with rooms at $1.00 a day. Under this new arrangement, people will be able to live at the hotel for $2.00 a day. The Stoneman House is operated on the American Plan at $3.00 to $4.00 a day." The board then hired a large crew of carpenters and mechanics who worked nearly all summer renovating the main building, along with River and Rock Cottages.

In their *Biennial Report* for 1893–94, the commissioners reported: "The appearance of the Sentinel was changed considerably, particularly the roof. Diagonal members were added to the upper porch railings. The foundation was replaced and made permanently secure. New closets and baths [indoor toilets at last!] were constructed, and the sewerage and plumbing were put in first-class order. Lath and plaster were substituted for board or cloth partitions, securing the seclusion most desirable to occupants. The dining room and office were changed, porch and balconies rebuilt, and the work pushed as far to completion as the funds

*The Sentinel Hotel after it was remod-
eled and enlarged by the commissioners
in the mid-1890s. Note the new roof
line and diagonal porch-railing braces.*

available would allow. The Rock Cottage and the River were subjected to the same complete and attractive betterment. . . It is believed that the improvements put upon the Sentinel add a permanent asset to the property worth at least $20,000."

Guests had barely become accustomed to the Sentinel's refurbished facilities when the bothersome din of construction once again filled the Yosemite air. After the loss of the Stoneman House by fire in August, 1896, the commissioners again brought in a gang of workmen and began a hurried campaign to increase the accommodations at the Sentinel, then the only hotel remaining in the Valley. During 1897 the main building was extended west to fill in the area between it and River Cottage at a cost of four thousand dollars. "It is a sound, strong structure now, comfortable and convenient," the board said in its *Biennial Report* for 1897–98. The upstairs bedrooms in Cedar Cottage were enlarged by removing the four-foot hall running the length of the second floor and cutting outside doors to each room from a new upstairs porch. Eight more bedrooms were partitioned off on the first floor. New siding and a shake roof completed the sixteen-hundred-dollar-renovation of the Valley's oldest structure.

At the same time, the commissioners added the former Cosmopolitan saloon building to the Sentinel group by converting the interior into a fourteen-bedroom unit known as Locust Cottage. The guardian's office was removed to the old Sinning house across the road. A Madera contractor received $2,155 to construct a two-story, twenty-four-bedroom structure called Oak Cottage immediately west of Cedar Cottage. It was ready for guests in the spring of 1898. With the changes and additions, the Sentinel's maximum capacity increased to about two hundred guests, two to

This view from north of the Merced River shows how the Sentinel Hotel's main building and adjoining River Cottage hung over the river bank.

a room, as follows: main building, seventeen bedrooms; River Cottage (later called "The Annex"), fifteen bedrooms; Rock Cottage, ten bedrooms; Oak Cottage, twenty-four bedrooms; Cedar Cottage, twenty bedrooms; and Locust Cottage, fourteen bedrooms. The seven-room Ivy Cottage (originally known as the "New Saloon"), built in 1901 between Locust and River Cottages and used for a time as a bar, billiard hall, and barbershop, became the manager's residence in the fall of 1906.

Although the commissioners felt they had done as well as possible in replacing the lost accommodations of the Stoneman House, they continued to make the legislature aware of their dissatisfaction with the overall tourist facilities in the Valley. "The best that we can offer to the visitor today is a small room," the commissioners said in their *Biennial Report* for 1901–02. "The bathroom is removed probably fifty feet away. Everything connected with the hotel is cramped and utterly inadequate to supply the needs of the traveling public." They then reiterated their desire for a $300,000 appropriation to build a "splendid and substantial hotel of granite equipped with all modern conveniences."

On June 9, 1897, A. B. Glasscock suffered a sudden, fatal stroke while

The famous Big Tree Room can be seen here at the rear of Cedar Cottage about 1900. Newly built Oak Cottage stands just beyond. (Author's collection)

working in his hotel. He was buried in the Yosemite cemetery. The board then awarded the Sentinel lease to J. J. Cook, Henry Washburn's brother-in-law and the former proprietor of Cook's Hotel and the Stoneman House. Cook, who spent considerable time in San Francisco, named his son Jay Bruce Cook (1868–1910) resident manager. The elder Cook died in 1904, and J. B. Cook was given a four-year lease on the property in his own right at an annual rent of two thousand dollars. After the completion of the Yosemite Valley Railroad in 1907 made winter visitation possible, Cook installed a steam heating system in the Sentinel, and the hotel remained open year-round.

Later History: At five o'clock Christmas evening, 1910, after a seemingly cheerful holiday, Jay Bruce Cook retired to his little private office in the main hotel building and fatally shot himself in the chest. A news report in the *Mariposa Gazette* attributed Cook's actions to "temporary insanity" brought about by years of severe stomach problems, the recent loss of his position as Valley postmaster, and an impending investigation by the interior department into irregularities in his Yosemite business affairs.

Subsequent operators of the Sentinel were William Sell, Jr., 1911–14; the Desmond Park Service Company, 1915–18; the Yosemite National Park Company, 1919–24; and the Yosemite Park and Curry Co., 1925–38. After the opening of Yosemite Lodge in 1915 and The Ahwahnee in 1927, some of the Sentinel buildings were used for other purposes. Civilian Conservation Corps workers began razing the ramshackle structures in 1938. Consideration was given for a time to preserving historic Cedar Cottage, the oldest building in the Valley, but it finally suffered the same fate as the rest of the complex in 1941. Today, only an assortment of photographs and the marks on the trunk of the incense cedar enclosed by James Hutchings to form the Big Tree Room in 1867 are left to remind us of what was once Yosemite Valley's most important pioneer hotel.

THE GLACIER POINT MOUNTAIN HOUSE

In 1895 the state spent fifteen hundred dollars making "extensive repairs" to James McCauley's Mountain House at Glacier Point, which the commissioners deemed "almost uninhabitable." Cosie Hutchings said there was considerable criticism of McCauley's maintenance of the premises, "including bedbugs." On October 23, 1897, McCauley, who had a year-to-year lease at Glacier Point, closed his hotel and returned to his ranch west of present Foresta for the winter. Ten days later, the commissioners awarded the lease on the property to John Stevens (read Henry Washburn) on condition that Washburn "put in two bathtubs

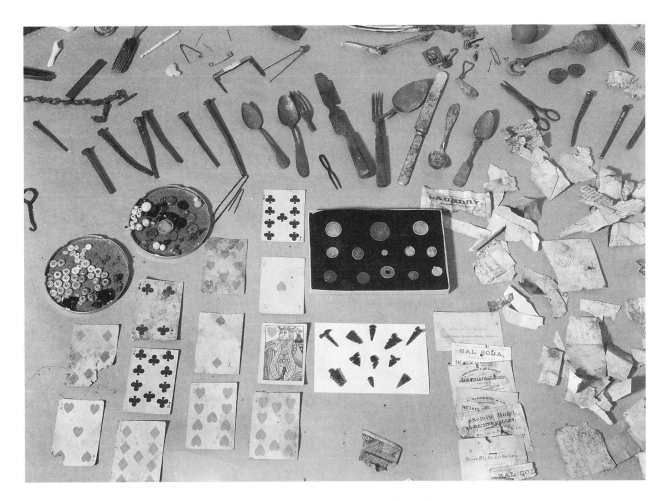

Among the artifacts found under Cedar Cottage after it was removed by Civilian Conservation Corps crews in 1941 were arrowheads, playing cards, coins, buttons, square nails, silverware, and miscellaneous other items.

and water closets at his own expense." Guardian Miles Wallace then sent a small group of state employees to break into the hotel and throw all of McCauley's things out, which they did. Laurence Degnan, whose father was a member of the eviction party, recalled that the "hotel supplies included a large quantity of choice wines and liquors, and you can imagine the condition of that gang when they arrived back in the Valley. . . My father was the only sober man in the crowd."[14] During the next few days, Washburn sent in wagons carrying beds, bedding, and other appurtenances to replace McCauley's household goods.

When McCauley heard the news, he and eldest son Jules immediately rode up the Four Mile Trail to Glacier Point. There they found his things strewn under the trees, Washburn's furnishings in the hotel, and the building secured with new locks. Furious, McCauley promptly broke into the hotel, threw Washburn's things out, and put his own back in. Lacking money for a long legal battle, McCauley moved his family to Glacier Point to wait until the first big snowstorm would prevent further action by the guardian that winter. According to son Fred, his father awoke one morning, took out his rifle, saddled up his horse, and declared that he was going to Wawona to murder Henry Washburn and his two brothers, John and Edward. Fortunately for everyone involved, McCauley's family was able to persuade the irate hotelkeeper to abandon his vendetta. Soon after, the Mariposa County sheriff arrived and took legal possession of the premises for the state. Friends said that McCauley left his beloved Glacier Point property a broken man and never fully recovered from the humiliating experience.

After John Stevens was named guardian in October, 1899, Jay Bruce

After Jay Bruce Cook took over the Mountain House in 1899, he added a dining porch, installed new partitions, and erected tents nearby to increase the accommodations.

The Glacier Point Hotel is shown at center; the updated Mountain House stands at the right in this photograph taken in the 1920s. (Author's collection)

Cook became the Mountain House proprietor of record. The commissioners granted Cook a four-year lease at an annual rent of two hundred dollars with the stipulation that he make "certain permanent improvements" to the facilities. Over the next several years, Cook enclosed the hotel's front porch to provide a larger dining area, replaced all the old cloth partitions and ceilings with solid material, and erected tents nearby to increase the overnight accommodations. Supplies for the Mountain House operation arrived at the Sentinel Hotel in the Valley by freight wagon and were carried on pack mules up the Four Mile Trail to Glacier Point.

Later History: After the army took over administration of Yosemite Valley in 1906, James McCauley obtained a contract to supply fresh meat to Valley outlets. On June 24, 1911, while he was traveling from his ranch down the steep section of the Coulterville Road between Big Meadow and the Merced River with two freshly killed cows, McCauley's team apparently bolted, upsetting his wagon, and throwing him hard to the ground. A few hours later, a passerby found McCauley lying dead in the road beside his upturned wagon.

In 1916–17, the Desmond Park Service Company built the three-story, eighty-room Glacier Point Hotel adjoining the old Mountain House on the south rim of Yosemite Valley. In later years, the Mountain House was used mainly for employee housing and a public cafeteria. Both buildings burned to the ground on August 9, 1969, in one of the worst structural fires in Yosemite history.

THE CURRY CAMPING COMPANY

On June 17, 1899, David and Jennie Curry,[15] two schoolteachers from Redwood City, California, arrived in Yosemite Valley to establish a tent camp offering inexpensive accommodations to tourists. The couple had first become acquainted with "God's great outdoors," as Jennie put it, through classes taught by David Starr Jordan at Indiana University in their home state. In 1892 they began leading camping tours to Yellowstone National Park during summer vacations from their teaching jobs in Ogden, Utah. Four years after settling in California in 1895, the Currys decided to forgo their Yellowstone outings in favor of a Yosemite Valley camp catering to tourists who did not wish to spend four dollars or more per night for a hotel room.

Beginning with seven sleeping tents and a larger one that served as a kitchen and dining room, the Currys originated a novel hotel/camp idea that was immediately successful. What started as a summer experiment employing one paid woman cook and several college students working for room and board soon turned into a full-time enterprise that continues to flourish in the same location to this day. At the end of the first season, Labor Day, 1899, twenty-five tents stood at Camp Curry, and even these had not always sufficed to handle the 292 registered guests, many of whom remained for a month or more. When all the beds were full, the Curry family gladly slept out in the adjoining woods.

Patronage at the camp continued to grow during the next few summers as word of the pleasant, two-dollars-a-night accommodations began to spread. By 1901, a large permanent dining room and rustic office had been built, along with forty or fifty more sleeping tents on wooden platforms. The next year, a sewer, restrooms, and bathhouse were added, and tennis nets and a croquet court set up. A nightly campfire, which concluded with the spectacular "Firefall" from the Glacier Point rim, provided the evening entertainment. By the time the federal government assumed control of the Yosemite Grant in 1906, Camp Curry was already an established commercial success.

Later History: On February 21, 1925, the Curry Camping Company merged with the Yosemite National Park Company to form the Yosemite Park and Curry Co. The move had been demanded by the National Park Service, which wanted a single concessionaire to handle all Valley guest accommodations. On October 1, 1993, the Yosemite Park and Curry Co. was purchased by the Delaware North Company, and its name was changed to Yosemite Concession Services Corporation.[16]

CAMP YOSEMITE (CAMP LOST ARROW)

The popularity of the Curry Camping Company's tent-hotel idea induced the Washburn interests to open a competing operation in 1901 called Camp Yosemite. Set up amid a grove of black oaks near the thundering roar of Lower Yosemite Fall in the area of Hutchings' old sawmill, the premises consisted of a group of canvas sleeping tents with wooden floors, an office-bathhouse, and screened outdoor dining room. The managing lessee, Jay Bruce Cook, had been awarded the privilege by the commissioners with the requirement that he spend two thousand dollars on the camp's facilities.

Camp Yosemite opened for business on May 15, 1901. Its host for the first six years was the venerated former guardian, Galen Clark, then eighty-seven years old. The arrangement proved to be mutually beneficial. Clark, who was far from wealthy, appreciated the income; Cook needed an attraction to lure customers to his new accommodations. Clark's duties were largely ceremonial: presiding at campfires, answering questions about the Valley, and generally making guests feel at home. A resident manager handled the more demanding tasks.

Camp Yosemite had a short season, usually from about mid-May until mid-August, or even earlier if Yosemite Falls prematurely dried up. The outlet creek served as the camp's sewer system. During its fifteen-year existence, the enterprise prospered, eventually containing electric lights, wood-frame office buildings, bathhouse with four bathrooms, warehouse, and a dining hall seating more than two hundred. The sleeping tents, which were similar to those in today's High Sierra Camps, had iron beds, washstands, mirrors, and chairs. In 1915, its peak year, Camp Yosemite accommodated 2,611 guests,

Later History: In May, 1907, the army designated its new Valley headquarters on the site of the present Yosemite Lodge as "Camp Yosemite." To prevent confusion, J. B. Cook changed the name of his operation to Camp Lost Arrow. The camp was discontinued after the season of 1915, following the opening of the original Yosemite Lodge nearby.

THE ARRIVAL OF THE HORSELESS CARRIAGE

On Saturday afternoon, June 23, 1900, the first automobile to conquer the Sierra grades entered Yosemite Valley to the astonishment of tourists and residents alike. The vehicle was a brand-new Locomobile, produced

by the Locomobile Company of Bridgeport, Connecticut, one of the first major manufacturers of automobiles in the United States. A standard production model, the car weighed 640 pounds empty, and 850 pounds when the gasoline and water tanks were full. A two-cylinder, ten-horsepower steam engine running at 150 pounds of pressure powered the vehicle; top speed was forty miles an hour.

The improbable owner of the Locomobile, a three-hundred-pound barrel of a man named Oliver Lippincott, operated the Art Photo Co. in Los Angeles. He was accompanied by Edward E. Russell, a thirty-six-year-old Los Angeles machine shop owner, who squeezed into the narrow space beside the corpulent Lippincott as the hired driver-mechanic. According to Russell, Lippincott hoped to generate interest in both Yosemite, where he set up a photographic sales tent the following summer, and the Locomobile Company, which used a picture of the Yosemite car in its advertising for the next several years.

Lippincott shipped his automobile from Los Angeles to Fresno by express freight over the Southern Pacific Railroad. At Fresno, the

Camp Curry opened in the summer of 1899 with seven sleeping tents and a kitchen-dining tent. This is one of the earliest photographs of David and Jennie Curry's innovative operation.

A stage at the Camp Lost Arrow office loads up outgoing passengers and luggage about 1908.

Locomobile was unloaded, and Lippincott and Russell drove on to Raymond, where they spent the night of June 22. Departing at 6:45 the following morning, the two pioneering motorists and their little machine covered the next leg of the unprecedented journey, Raymond to Wawona, in only five hours and eighteen minutes of actual running time. The stage took all day to cover the same stretch.

At Wawona, the hotel porch was crowded with people awaiting sight of the motor vehicle, for word of the adventure preceded the travelers. Upon arrival, Russell demonstrated the new method of transportation by taking some of the inquisitive guests for rides around the circular drive in front of the hotel. The twenty-seven-mile run from Wawona to Yosemite Village was accomplished in exactly three hours. "The records of speed made by our little box on wheels were quoted at many a campfire," Lippincott said. "The Yosemite stage drivers, however, looked askance at our method of traveling. One asked where I kept my hay, and another declared he wouldn't go steering that thing without a whip."

Lippincott and Russell spent several weeks in the Valley. During their visit they "kept the roads of the Valley warm" by treating tourists and locals alike to "propulsion amid the wilds of nature," according to Lippincott. The only serious mechanical failure of the trip occurred when a strut rod on the Locomobile gave way. Russell quickly repaired it by brazing the rod back together using brass from an opium box provided by a local Chinese man. Gasoline, which cost $1.50 a gallon delivered to the Valley, was brought in by stage from Madera as needed.

On July 26, 1900, only thirty-three days after Lippincott's arrival, Arthur Holmes, a San Jose hardware store owner, and his brother Frank H. Holmes, a Berryessa rancher, chugged into Yosemite Valley at 7:30 p.m. from Wawona in a modified Stanley Steamer, the second motor car to traverse the mountainous route. The brothers Holmes departed San Jose on Friday, July 20, at 3:30 p.m. heading south, and at 10 p.m. reached Los Banos, a distance of eighty-six miles. The following day, slowed by a bad water injector, they covered only the fifty-three miles to Madera. They then turned up the Yosemite road through Raymond, Ahwahnee, and Fish Camp, and arrived at the Wawona Hotel at 3 p.m. on Monday, July 23. After enjoying a two-day respite from their travels, the brothers left Wawona at 1 p.m., Thursday, July 26, and drove their steamer into Yosemite Valley that evening, having covered a distance of 235.6 miles in all.

"Had our rubber tires come from the East on time," driver Arthur Holmes told local residents, "we would have beaten Oliver Lippincott into the Valley." Holmes pointed out that he and his brother had driven all the way from home under their own power, whereas Lippincott and Russell had utilized the railroad for the greater part of their journey from Los Angeles.

"The two auto trips have fully demonstrated the fact that there is very little danger of frightening the stages or other horses," Foley's *The Yosemite Tourist* editorialized in August, 1900. "The animals pay little attention to it. In time an auto road book will be published showing where water can be had. Also, gasoline will be kept at convenient points. The auto will soon become a prominent factor in Yosemite travel."

Despite the *Tourist's* optimistic prediction, the impact of the motor car on Yosemite visitation was slow in coming. Although no official records were kept of early automobile travel to the Valley, news stories indicate that only a dozen or so adventurers managed to complete the demanding journey between 1900 and 1906.

Later History: In June, 1907, Major Harry Benson, who took active charge of the Yosemite Grant on August 1, 1906, following the state's recession of the preserve to the federal government, suddenly banned all motor vehicles from the park. Benson said the Yosemite roads were "too steep and narrow" to permit the combined operation of horse teams and automobiles. The ruling remained in effect until April 30, 1913, when Secretary of the Interior Franklin K. Lane announced that he was rescinding the six-year-old order barring automobiles from Yosemite. Lane added that because of the inadequacy of most park roads, he

Portly Oliver Lippincott, shown here in his Locomobile on the Valley floor, drove the first automobile into Yosemite Valley on June 23, 1900. (Author's collection)

An early touring car rattles along the Big Oak Flat Road near Crane Flat en route to Yosemite soon after automobiles were readmitted to the Valley in 1913. (Tuolumne County Historical Society collection)

Arthur Holmes, at the tiller, posed with his brother Frank in their modified Stanley Steamer in July, 1901, for photographer Julius Boysen near Yosemite Falls. The Holmes brothers' vehicle was the second car to enter the Valley.

would soon issue comprehensive regulations governing the use of motor vehicles in Yosemite.

On August 5, 1913, the rules became public. Cars were permitted entry only on the Coulterville Road—a route in such poor repair that even horse-drawn vehicles avoided it—and then only if they observed sixty-five restrictive rules. For example, cars reaching the Merced Grove entrance station after 3:30 p.m. were not permitted in the park until the following day. Drivers could stop in front of hotels or camps to unload passengers and luggage, but only for five minutes, and only if the driver remained in the car. Maximum speed on straight stretches was ten miles an hour, with a six-mile-per-hour limit at all other points. Teams and horses had the right of way, even to the extent that motorists were required to pull over and stop the engine if the "approaching animals manifest signs of fear." Campers were compelled to proceed directly to the segregated automobile campground, and camp by their cars. All other motorists had to leave their cars in a tent garage opposite army headquarters until ready for departure.

On August 23, 1913, the first automobiles since June, 1907, were allowed to enter Yosemite. Despite the lateness of the season, 127 cars snaked their way down the Coulterville Road and into the Valley during the remainder of the year. Automobile visitation increased to 739 cars in 1914, 2,270 in 1915, and 4,043 in 1916. On August 8, 1914, after the federal government spent $2,500 to improve the steep descent into Yosemite Valley from Inspiration Point, the Washburn-controlled Wawona Road opened to automobile travel. The toll was $1.25 per car, in addition to the government entry fee of $5.00—a considerable sum at the time. Another $2.50 fee was exacted should the motorist also wish to visit the Mariposa Grove. On September 16, 1914, the Big Oak Flat

This map of the Yosemite road system accompanied the commissioners' Biennial Report for 1887–88. (Author's collection)

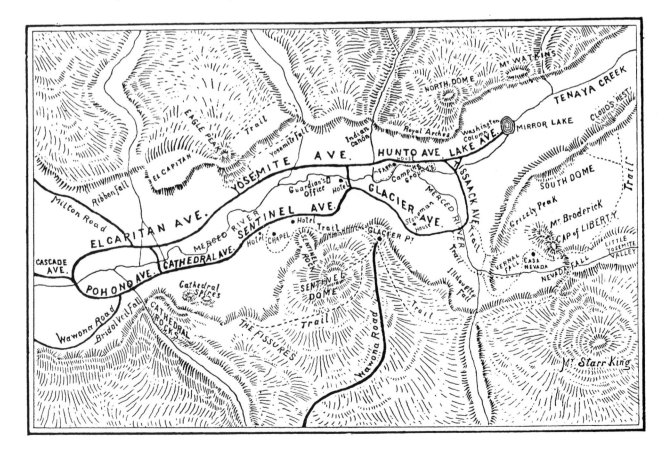

Photographer Julius T. Boysen (at left) took this self-portrait standing with aged Galen Clark at the Mariposa Grove in the early 1900s.

Photographer George Fiske photographed Daniel Foley and wife Josie at the foot of the Four Mile Trail in 1897, the year the Foleys were married. Their printing and photography shop endured in Yosemite Valley for half a century.

Road was approved for motor vehicles, which improved access to the Valley from the north.

On November 19, 1913, the first automobile stage, an open-air, eighteen-passenger White, made the fourteen-mile run from the Yosemite Valley Railroad terminal at El Portal to the Sentinel Hotel in the Valley "speedily and successfully" in one hour and thirty-five minutes. The horse stage took four hours for the same trip. On June 2, 1915, the Yosemite Stage & Turnpike Company replaced its horse-drawn stages with an automobile service that carried tourists between the Mariposa Grove and the Valley. Before the opening of the 1916 season, the company retired its remaining horses, thus ending the forty-year era of stage travel in Yosemite. The restrictions on motor vehicles were then dramatically eased.[17]

DEVELOPMENT OF YOSEMITE VILLAGE

After the removal of its three main buildings in the summer of 1888, the Lower Village contained only a few private residences, Fiske's Studio, and the Yosemite Chapel. From then on, the Upper Village—soon called Yosemite Village (after 1925, Old Village)—became the focal point of settlement in the Valley. By the early 1900s, the village area consisted of some two dozen structures of varying quality and size situated along both sides of the south river road just west of the present Sentinel Bridge. From west to east on the north stood Nelson Salter's two-story general store, Boysen's Studio, Foley's Studio, the guardian's office and residence, Best's Studio, a dance and lecture pavilion, Locust Cottage, the New Saloon (later Ivy Cottage), River Cottage, and the main Sentinel Hotel building.

On the south side were the Yosemite Chapel (moved there in 1901), Julius Starke's woodworking shop (taken over by Roland B. Dexter in 1903), the Studio of the Three Arrows, Degnan's residence and bakery, a state barn, the Sierra Club headquarters in the front of Sinning's old cottage (which became George Fiske's Studio in 1904), Rock Cottage, Oak Cottage, and Cedar Cottage. Scattered among the larger structures was an assortment of residences, outbuildings, and tents.

Julius T. Boysen (1868–1939) asked the commissioners for a permit to operate Snow's abandoned hotel near the base of Nevada Fall in 1895, but was turned down. On May 8, 1897, Boysen applied to the board for "a curio and souvenir shop and photo privileges of groups with a 4 by 5 camera." The permit was approved in 1898, whereupon Boysen opened a tent studio on the site of Gustavus Fagersteen's former shop. In 1900, after the commissioners ruled there would be no more tents fronting the main road, Boysen erected a rustic one-story building made of undressed boards and battens in the same location just east of the new general store. Boysen, who specialized in photographing the Big Trees of the Mariposa Grove and the local Indians, operated his studio (moved to

The guardian's office, shown here in the Upper Village. This was Fiske's original studio building in the Lower Village. The state moved it to this location in 1899 and gave Fiske permission to occupy a different structure nearer the road.

The main south side road in Yosemite Valley passed directly through the Upper Village. The four buildings pictured here in the early 1900s are, left to right: the Yosemite Store, Boysen's studio, Foley's studio, and the guardian's office and residence (Fiske's original studio building, moved here in 1899).

the present village in 1926) until his death in 1939. His wife Mabel kept the business until she died in 1943.

Daniel Joseph Foley (1857–1934), a native of Dubuque, Iowa, came to Yosemite in the spring of 1891 from Pleasanton, California, where he had previously published a newspaper. Awarded the right to open a "printing and job office and photography shop" by the commissioners on February 24, 1891, Foley put up a long, narrow shake structure called the Tourist Printing Office (later known as the Yosemite Falls Studio) in which he installed a job case containing a number of fonts of hand-set type, and a small printing press. That same year he began publication of a souvenir newspaper called *The Yosemite Tourist*. Usually consisting of four pages, the paper provided stock information about Yosemite and its sights, local news items, and long lists of tourist parties complete with names and anecdotes. It also carried a variety of advertisements for Valley hotels and businesses, including, of course, Foley's own photographic studio. *The Yosemite Tourist* was issued during the summer months ("as often as the travel will justify its appearance, sometimes daily, at other times only three times a week") until July, 1934.

In 1892 and 1894, Foley put out a fifty-six-page *Yosemite Valley Guidebook*, with a table of distances and a map. In 1901 he printed the first of fifteen annual (and some seasonal) editions of the *Yosemite Souvenir and Guide*, loosely patterned after his earlier guides, but considerably expanded with photographs, maps, and historical information. Foley, who moved his shop to the present village in 1926, died in Lewis Memorial Hospital in Yosemite Valley in September, 1934, at the age of seventy-seven. His widow Josie continued the business until the early 1940s.

The guardian's office and residence were situated in a building constructed by photographer George Fiske as a studio in 1883. It first stood in front of his house near the Merced River just west of the Lower Village complex. After the removal of Cook's and Leidig's Hotels, Folsom's hall, and the stables from the area in 1888, Fiske's photographic sales suffered from lack of tourist traffic. In 1898 Fiske was given the use of a "building near the Chapel" and relocated his studio. Whether it was an existing structure or one erected for the purpose is not clear from the commissioners' lease records.

In the spring of 1899, the board ordered Fiske's former studio moved to the Upper Village and relocated on a site next to Foley's print shop. The building was enlarged by an addition at the rear. From 1899 until August 1, 1906, it served as office and residence for the last two Yosemite guardians, John Stevens and George Harlow. After the army assumed control of the Yosemite Grant in 1906, the structure became the acting superintendent's headquarters and residence.

Harry Cassie Best (1863–1936), a thirty-seven-year-old landscape painter, arrived in Yosemite Valley in the spring of 1901 on a sketching trip with a fellow artist. There he met and on July 28 married Sarah Anne Rippey, a charming young woman fifteen years his junior who was employed at Oliver Lippincott's photographic sales tent for the summer. Anne had previously worked for Lippincott at his shop in the Hotel Del Coronado in San Diego. Before returning to San Francisco in the fall, the newlyweds successfully applied to the commissioners for a permit to sell photographs and paintings in the Valley the following year.

In the spring of 1902, the Bests pitched a tent just west of the old Cosmopolitan building (then known as Locust Cottage) and began an art and photography business that is still operating nearly a century later. That first summer, Harry Best erected a small wooden structure made of undressed lumber covered with roofing paper that he painted to simulate stone. Like most of the other commercial structures in the village, the studio was gradually enlarged over the years. The Bests sold photographic prints and cards to tourists, as well as Harry's own hand-framed landscape paintings.

Anne Best died in 1920. Harry and the couple's only child, Virginia, born in 1904, carried on the business, which moved to a location in the present village in 1926. In 1932, Virginia Best married Ansel Adams (1902–1984), who subsequently achieved fame as one of the world's foremost landscape photographers. After Harry Best died in 1936, Virginia and Ansel took over the studio. Today, still under the family's direction, the art and photography store is known as the Ansel Adams Gallery.

The Pavilion, an open-air dance floor and lecture place (later also used to show motion pictures), was constructed at a cost of $250 by the commissioners in 1901 on the riverbank back of Best's Studio and Locust Cottage. The structure was damaged during the great Valley floods of 1950 and 1955 and subsequently repaired. After being partly destroyed by fire in June, 1963, the Pavilion was razed by the Yosemite Park and Curry Co.

The Studio of the Three Arrows was formed by Harold A. Taylor (1878–1960), who arrived in the Valley in April, 1902, as an assistant to

Julius T. Boysen, and Eugene Hallett, an agent for the Santa Fe, when they bought the photography business of Oliver Lippincott in the winter of 1902–03. Lippincott, the noted Locomobile driver, had moved from his tent studio to a structure on the site of Cavagnaro's former store in the spring of 1902 and operated there for that season. Hallett and Taylor called their enterprise the "Studio of the Three Arrows" because Taylor's family crest contained three arrows, and the name reflected the Indian history in the Valley. Soon after the army took over administration of Yosemite Valley in August, 1906, Hallett had a series of conflicts with Acting Superintendent Major Harry Benson. This may have led to the partners selling their studio to Arthur Pillsbury (1870-1946), an Oakland photographer, in 1907. Pillsbury continued the business in two locations before selling out to the Yosemite Park and Curry Co. in 1928.

John (1863–1943) and Bridget Degnan emigrated to the United States from their native Ireland in 1884 and settled briefly with relatives near Coulterville. Later that year they moved to Yosemite Valley where John, a man of great physical strength, obtained seasonal employment working on roads and trails for the state. During slack times, he took on odd repair and construction jobs for the hotels and stage companies. The Degnans, who eventually had eight children, lived first in one end of an abandoned barn built by William Howard, the one-time proprietor of the Mirror Lake House, on a flat where Yosemite Lodge now stands. There, using a wood-fired Dutch oven, Bridget baked soda bread, which she sold to residents and campers. In the fall of 1888, the family moved

Harry Cassie Best, a talented painter, first came to Yosemite in 1901.

Best's Studio was a one-story structure, fifteen feet by forty-eight feet, made of rough boards covered with roofing paper painted to simulate stone. It stood about twenty feet east of the guardian's office. Destroyed by heavy snows in 1921, it was rebuilt the next year. The building was torn down after Best moved the operation to the present village in 1926.

to Kenneyville where John served two winters as caretaker for the stable complex. Abnormally heavy snows during the second winter frequently kept Degnan shoveling off the roofs of the various buildings almost around the clock to prevent their collapse under the accumulated weight.

In 1890 Degnan received permission from the commissioners to move into George Kenney's former residence at the west end of Yosemite Village. Bridget soon acquired a larger Dutch oven that would bake fifty loaves of bread at a time, which she sold through Cavagnaro's Store. John, who continued his work with the state, began a small dairy herd to supply the demand for fresh milk.

As the Degnan family increased in both size and income, the need for larger accommodations became obvious. With the commissioners' approval in 1898, Degnan built a spacious two-story house on the same location with four bedrooms and two baths. A bake room attached to the rear housed a huge brick-and-masonry oven capable of baking a hundred loaves of bread simultaneously. During the ensuing years, the Degnans expanded their house and opened a prosperous delicatessen and bake shop in a separate building nearby.

Later History: Following the deaths of Bridget and John Degnan in 1940 and 1943, daughter Mary Ellen Degnan continued the business, later joined by her brother Dr. John Degnan and his son-in-law Frank Donohoe. In March, 1973, Degnan, Donohoe, Inc., which had moved to a modern A-frame structure erected at the east end of the present village in 1958, was purchased by the Yosemite Park and Curry Co., whose successor continues the operation today.

The Sinning cottage was taken over by the state upon Sinning's death in 1889. Mrs. Elizabeth Glynn occupied it for two winters because her own house nearby was almost impossible to heat. In 1892 the commissioners leased the rooms in the rear of the building to Charles Atkinson, a state employee, who lived there with his family until he left the Valley in 1905. In 1897 the front rooms of Sinning's former shop served briefly as the guardian's headquarters. The following year the commissioners agreed to allow the recently formed Sierra Club[18] to use that part of the building as a public reading room and information center for tourists. The club furnished the rooms with appropriate books, maps, and other material and hired a summer attendant paid for equally by the club and the state. In 1903 the Sierra Club completed an imposing rough-granite structure named LeConte Memorial Lodge behind Camp Curry and transferred its Valley headquarters to that location.[19]

In the early summer of 1904, the commissioners leased the space vacated by the Sierra Club in Sinning's building to George Fiske, the long-time Yosemite photographer, soon after his second studio in the old Lower Village burned to the ground in May. The fire destroyed two cameras worth six hundred dollars, three-quarters of his negatives, and most of his prints. The *Mariposa Gazette* reported in June, 1904, that the board had reduced Fiske's rent to a token one dollar a year "because of his age [sixty-nine] and almost total loss of his property in the fire."

Fiske's first wife, Elmira "Mira" F. Morrill of San Jose, whom he married in that city on April 16, 1873, died of cancer in 1896. (The couple's

The Pavilion, erected on the riverbank back of Best's Studio by the commissioners in 1901, was a popular site for dances and parties. Damaged in two floods and subsequently repaired, the structure was razed in 1963 after being partially destroyed by fire. This photograph shows the building after the flood of 1955.

two sons died of cholera in childhood.) The next summer Fiske met a handsome, Ohio-born woman named Caroline Paull, who bought photographs at his studio while visiting the Valley with a church group from Massachusetts. When she later wrote to order more pictures, a correspondence began that culminated in their marriage a year or two later at San Francisco's Occidental Hotel.[20] The newlyweds took up housekeeping in Fiske's residence along the Merced River. Their only near neighbor was Galen Clark, Fiske's closest friend. As time went on, Fiske became very dependent on his second wife, who was nineteen years younger than he.

"I think Fiske got the better of the deal," Laurence Degnan said some years afterward. "Carrie was a wonderful woman and worked hard and faithfully to help with his photograph business." Virginia Best Adams remembers seeing the Fiskes walking together between their house and studio, a mile apart, almost every morning and evening during this period.

Caroline Fiske died on December 30, 1917, at the age of sixty-three. Less than a year later, on the morning of October 20, 1918, Fiske, despondent and suffering greatly from "a severe pain in the head," fired a bullet through his heart while alone in his Valley house. His suicide note said in part: "What is the use of trying to live when you have so much pain and life is a burden. . . I am worn out and want a rest." Fiske's remains were interred beside his second wife in the Yosemite cemetery.

Christian Jorgensen (1860–1935), a native of Norway and an accomplished painter, came to Yosemite Valley in 1898 and camped two summers before obtaining a permit from the commissioners to build a permanent building. In 1900 he erected a combination studio-residence on the north side of the Merced River across from the Sentinel Hotel. Later, he added a barn, storehouse, and a separate one-story log residence with a wood-shingle roof.[21] Jorgensen and his family spent the next

John Degnan, a man of great physical strength and endurance, propelled himself around Yosemite Valley during the winter months by means of long wooden skis and a sturdy pole. He is pictured in 1894. (George Fiske)

The Degnan family shown in front of their residence in Yosemite Village. Laurence, the oldest of the eight children, is at right.

227

twenty summers, and a few winters, as respected members of the Yosemite community. In 1936 the Yosemite Museum acquired 198 oil and watercolor paintings from Jorgensen's heirs.

IMPROVEMENTS IN THE YOSEMITE GRANT

In the early years of state management of the Yosemite Grant, news of the outside world was hand-carried by visitors arriving on foot or horseback from the nearest populated areas. The first telegraph line reached the Valley from Sonora in 1872.[22] James Hutchings said that after the completion of stage roads in 1874–75, the line was not sufficiently patronized to pay for its maintenance and soon fell into disuse. "In 1882, however," Hutchings wrote, "a new line was constructed by the Western Union Company . . . via Berenda, Grant's Sulphur Springs, and Wawona to Yo Semite, so that now telegrams can be sent thence to every nook and corner of civilization."[23]

On August 26, 1882, the *Mariposa Gazette* reported that a telephone line had been constructed to the Valley from the booming mining town of Bodie, eighty miles east across the Sierra. "Mr. Childs, Supt. of the Telegraph and Telephone Line is now camped in the valley at Mirror Lake," the Gazette said, "and will complete the telephone line from Barnard's to Lundy and Bodie this evening [August 24]."[24]

According to Laurence Degnan, the line did not operate very long. "I think it had gone out of business by the time our family came to the Valley [1884]," Degnan said. "When I was a youngster, maybe ten or eleven years old, Jack Leidig used to tell me about the Yosemite people listening to the band music in Bodie on the telephone."[25]

In their *Biennial Report* for 1891–92, the commissioners noted "that the first telephones used in the valley were put in during the year, con-

necting Glacier Point, the Stoneman House, the stables, and the Guardian's Office, and thereby greatly adding to the convenience and comfort of visitors." The rudimentary internal line served until 1907 when an extensive telephone system was installed linking all of the developed areas of the park with the outside world.

In that same 1891–92 report, the commissioners announced that they were considering the introduction of electric lights into the Valley. "Electric lights on the Yosemite trails and summits would enable effects unrivaled in their awe-inspiring beauty," the board reported, "and will serve to carry the fame of the valley farther than ever."

The preliminary plan, estimated to cost $12,700, proposed piping water under pressure from the stream at the foot of Vernal Fall approximately one mile to a Pelton waterwheel coupled to an alternating generator. The system would be capable of delivering a current of two thousand volts to the Valley floor—sufficient to operate 150 sixteen-candlepower incandescent lamps, and four arc lights for outside illumination. In addition, "a motor-driven searchlight at Glacier Point, which would be novel and exceedingly attractive, could be made to illuminate in various colors the Yosemite Falls, Vernal and Nevada Falls, Mount Starr King, Cloud's Rest, and the various domes and cliffs, and could be used to illuminate a fountain at night with its various rainbow colors, and to produce most novel night effects in Mirror Lake."

In 1896 Professor Clarence L. Cory of the Electrical Engineering Laboratory at the University of California at Berkeley, submitted a proposal to the board to accomplish the project. "The powerhouse should be built of granite," Cory said, "to contain the generators and other expensive machinery incident to the electric light and power system. . . I would not advise the location of a searchlight on Glacier Point. Any ordinary searchlight would be insignificant in its effect when placed at such an altitude. The cost of conducting the current to the top of such a cliff would practically be prohibitive." Cory estimated that the expense of the "model water-powered system" would be about fifteen thousand dollars.

In 1902 the legislature finally answered the commissioners' repeated requests to allocate sufficient funds for the installation of an electric plant by appropriating twenty-five thousand dollars for the undertaking.

"Competitive bids were thoroughly advertised for," the commissioners said in their *Biennial Report* for 1901–02, "and the contract was finally awarded to Henshaw, Bulkley & Co. of San Francisco, they being the lowest and best bidder." The bid was for $20,322. The added expense of incidental labor, a fifty-thousand-gallon water tank, and additional steel piping eventually used up all but $34 of the $25,000 appropriation. The project was completed in 1902.

George Fiske moved his photography business to this studio along the road in the Lower Village about 1898. The structure burned in May, 1904, destroying many of Fiske's negatives and prints. (Albert Gordon collection)

The powerhouse was situated at the head of the Valley near Happy Isles. Water to run the operation was diverted into a pipeline from the Merced River at the Illilouette Creek junction, giving a 150-foot head. The machinery was housed in a permanent frame building containing a concrete floor with imbedded wooden beams to which the frames holding the Pelton wheels and generators were bolted. "The road from the power-house to the hotel," the commissioners said, "a distance of about two miles, is lighted with incandescent lamps, distributed at reasonable distances apart. The hotel [Sentinel] and all of the buildings around the hotel have been well supplied with light, so that coal-oil lamps and candles around the hotel are now a thing of the past. The plant has been all paid for."

Later History: The powerhouse remained in use until a new hydro-electric facility was erected on the Merced River west of the Valley in 1917–18. This second powerhouse functioned until the park converted to commercial power in 1985. Today, minus the 1918 machinery, the building is used as a sub-station in the power distribution system and as a workshop for the high-voltage crew.

THE DEATH OF JAMES HUTCHINGS

Early in the summer of 1899, Hutchings took over management of the Calaveras Big Tree Grove Hotel above Murphy's Camp. He described the hotel, situated northwest of Yosemite, in his book *In the Heart of the Sierras:* "Here will be found a good table, cleanly accommodations, polite service, and reasonable charges."

At the close of the 1902 season, Hutchings and his third wife, Emily Ann Edmunds Hutchings, were traveling over the old Big Oak Flat Road en route from the Calaveras Grove to Yosemite where they

FISKE'S STUDIO

planned to camp for a week before going on to San Francisco. As they neared the Valley floor about 3:30 in the afternoon of October 31, their team suddenly became frightened at a sound or a smell and bolted, pitching them from the careening buggy. Emily was thrown clear and not seriously injured, but Hutchings landed headfirst on a pile of rocks. "I am very much hurt," were the only words he uttered when his wife reached him moments later. Within five minutes he was dead.

Emily Hutchings stayed with her husband until dark in the hope that help would come along. When no one arrived, she started for the Valley on foot. Two hours later, cold and bewildered, she walked into the Sentinel Hotel and told her sorrowful story.

Hutchings' funeral, like elder daughter Floy's and second wife Augusta's twenty-one years earlier, was held in the famous Big Tree Room of his former hotel. On Sunday morning, November 2, 1902, Hutchings was buried in the Yosemite cemetery next to Floy and Augusta. The graves are marked by a large piece of rough granite and a trim stone cross. A plaque attached to the granite also honors Gertrude (Cosie) Hutchings, younger daughter of James and first wife Elvira, although Cosie is not buried here. Widow Emily Ann Hutchings died in her native England in 1928 at the age of eighty-nine.

ROOSEVELT AND MUIR

Early in March, 1903, President Theodore Roosevelt began making plans for an extensive exploratory train trip through a portion of the western United States. Included in his itinerary was a two-week tour of California extending from the Mojave Desert to the Oregon border. One of Roosevelt's particular desires was to spend several days camping

In June, 1904, the commissioners gave Fiske the use of the old Sinning cottage in the Upper Village after the Sierra Club vacated the premises in 1903. Fiske called the wheelbarrow that he used to transport his camera equipment his "cloud-chasing chariot." He operated his business from this location until his death by suicide in 1918, but continued to reside in his Lower Village home. (Author's collection)

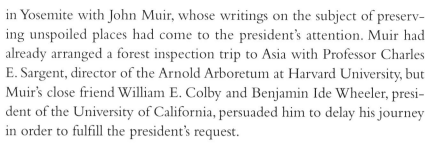

in Yosemite with John Muir, whose writings on the subject of preserving unspoiled places had come to the president's attention. Muir had already arranged a forest inspection trip to Asia with Professor Charles E. Sargent, director of the Arnold Arboretum at Harvard University, but Muir's close friend William E. Colby and Benjamin Ide Wheeler, president of the University of California, persuaded him to delay his journey in order to fulfill the president's request.

"An influential man from Washington wants to make a trip into the Sierra with me," Muir apologetically wrote Sargent. "I might be able to do some forest good in freely talking around the campfire."[26]

The necessary arrangements followed, and at 7:30 on the morning of May 15, having traveled overnight from Oakland, the presidential special train pulled into Raymond station, the nearest mainline rail connection to Yosemite, with Muir and Roosevelt on board. According to witnesses, a band was playing, bunting and flags waved from every building, and more than a thousand cheering spectators were assembled in eager anticipation of the president's arrival. Somewhat discomfited by the unexpected attention, Roosevelt, dressed informally in Norfolk coat, baggy breeches, leather puttees, neckerchief, and nondescript sombrero, briefly addressed the crowd from the veranda of the Bowen Hotel before entering the first of two eleven-passenger stages that were waiting to transport him and his entourage to the Mariposa Grove of Big Trees.

The president sat in the front seat of the lead vehicle beside veteran Yosemite Stage & Turnpike Company driver Bright Gillespie. Muir sat directly behind Roosevelt so he could point out places of interest. They were joined by the remaining members of the official party: Secretary of the Navy William H. Moody; California Governor George C. Pardee; Dr. Presley N. Rixie, surgeon general; Nicholas Murray Butler, president of Columbia University; Roosevelt's private secretary William Loeb, Jr.; and Benjamin Ide Wheeler. The second stage, which followed a short distance behind, carried four Secret Service agents and various other attendants. Accompanying the stages was a crack detachment of thirty U. S. cavalrymen, mounted on matching dapple-gray horses, commanded by a Lieutenant Mays.

After the customary lunch stop at the

Christian Jorgensen spent twenty summers, and a few winters, in Yosemite Valley as a resident artist. In this unusual photograph, Jorgensen is pictured making a painting of the Wawona Tunnel Tree at the Mariposa Grove.

James and Emily Hutchings were photographed departing Crocker's Station on the Big Oak Flat Road only hours before he was thrown from his buggy and killed. (Celia Crocker Thompson)

Ahwahnee Tavern, eighteen miles above Raymond, the party proceeded directly to the Mariposa Grove of Big Trees. Following some preliminaries such as picture-taking at the Grizzly Giant and the Wawona Tunnel Tree, the president dismissed the troops, thanking them for their services and calling out as they departed, "God bless you." He also sent away the press and photographers, who fully expected Roosevelt to rejoin them later at the bedecked Wawona Hotel where a lavish banquet was scheduled for 6:00 p.m. The president then bade a temporary good-bye to the members of his party who, except for Muir, reboarded the stage and headed for the sanctuary of the hotel six miles away.

This left Roosevelt, Muir, park rangers Charles Leidig and Archie Leonard, and an Army packer named Jackie Alder alone in the grove. Camp was soon set up near a cool spring not far from the Sunset Tree. Leidig, a first-rate camp cook, prepared fried chicken and beefsteak for dinner served on tin plates by the campfire. After drinking several cups of strong black coffee, the president bedded down early among forty thin army blankets, which had been piled under a shelter-half to provide both mattress and covering. "He got just as deep into these as he wanted," Leidig said.

At 6:30 the following morning (May 16), the group was already in the saddle, heading for Glacier Point. The *San Francisco Chronicle* described their journey: "Avoiding the main road, and long before most of his associates were out of bed at Wawona, the President, filled with his usual enthusiasm for adventure, passed rapidly down the narrow defile known as the 'Lightning Trail' and struck off for Yosemite Valley. An hour later the main road was reached, and the steep ascent to the top of

Chilnualna Fall was begun. The party reached the summit before noon, and then the difficult portion of the trip began. Here the party not only had the steep ascents but the deep snow as well."

Floundering in drifts sometimes five feet deep, and further slowed by a blinding snowstorm that continued all afternoon, the weary travelers took turns breaking trail until they reached the meadow back of Glacier Point where they gladly pitched camp for the night. Early the next morning (May 17), after shaking five inches of new snow from his blankets, Roosevelt shaved by the light of a great campfire, then joined Muir for a prearranged photographic session with a cameraman from the firm of Underwood and Underwood who was waiting to take the official pictures at Glacier Point. Four photographs were made on the Overhanging Rock: two of the president standing alone, and two with Muir at his side. After a hurried breakfast, the party started on the fourteen-mile ride to the Valley via Nevada Fall.

About 2:30 that afternoon, a dust-covered Roosevelt and his equally begrimed companions rode into Yosemite Village to find a large gathering of residents, tourists, and the curious from as far away as Coulterville and Merced expectantly awaiting the distinguished visitors. Unbeknown to the president, Guardian John Stevens and the Yosemite commissioners had made elaborate arrangements to receive him. A huge green "Welcome" sign hung across the upper iron bridge; four hundred dollars worth of fireworks were ready to be shot off; a sumptuous banquet catered by a chef imported from the Bohemian Club of San Francisco was in preparation at the Sentinel Hotel; and Stevens, some of the commissioners, and the other members of the presidential party were there to greet him.[27]

Annoyed at seeing the crowd, Roosevelt headed straight for artist Chris Jorgensen's studio across the Merced River, which had been provided for his use while in the Valley. Dismounting, he joined the collected dignitaries in a glass of cold champagne served by Jorgensen, after which Guardian Stevens presented him with the "key" to the Valley (made of manzanita by local woodworker Julius Starke). When Governor Pardee began to talk of the banquet, fireworks, and other festivities planned for that evening, the president's booming voice broke in: "We will pitch camp at Bridalveil!" Muir had previously suggested that site for their last night in Yosemite.

Roosevelt thanked the Jorgensens for their courtesy, remounted his horse, and headed back across the bridge. He paused long enough to briefly recall the stormy days of his famous charge up the hills near Santiago with a Mr. McPherson, a former member of the Seventh Infantry, who had been closely associated with the Roughriders in Cuba. When the President saw Ellen Boysen, two-year-old daughter of Yosemite photographer Julius T. Boysen, standing alongside her mother holding a flag, he reached down, picked her up under the pits of her arms, and kissing her, said, "God bless you, you little angel," and put her down.

As the five original riders turned west toward Bridalveil Meadow, a youngster called out, "Hi, Teddy." The president reined in his horse and gave the disrespectful lad a severe reprimand. (Laurence Degnan, who was away at school at the time, said his mother always suspected his younger brother Chris, thirteen, of being the culprit, a charge Chris stoutly denied.) Roosevelt then waved his companions on, and while the assemblage of disappointed spectators, including the chagrined com-

President Roosevelt's party paused for the obligatory photograph at the Wawona Tunnel Tree on May 15, 1903. Roosevelt stands just under the top of the tunnel opening. Muir is second from the left (partially obscured).

missioners, stood watching, the presidential party slowly disappeared in the distance, trailed by a long string of people on horseback, in surreys and buggies, and on foot.

Camp was set up in a choice spot at the edge of Bridalveil Meadow just west of Bridalveil Fall (a marker identifies the approximate site today). Across the Merced River, El Capitan bulked impressively, and Ribbon Fall, the highest single drop in the Valley, thundered down in full view. Privacy was finally achieved after rangers Leidig and Leonard succeeded in chasing the congregating spectators away. "They went quietly," Leidig said, "some of them even on tiptoe, so as not to annoy their president."

Muir and Roosevelt talked long into the night around the campfire. "I stuffed him pretty well," Muir said in a letter to Dr. C. Hart Merriam, "regarding the timber thieves, the destructive work of the lumberman, and other spoilers of the forest." That dialogue may have played a part in the president's subsequent pro-conservation actions. During the remainder of his term in office, Roosevelt assisted in adding 147 million acres to the country's forest reserves, created eighteen national monuments, and used his influence in the establishment of five national parks.[28]

On the morning of May 18, Muir and the president joined the other members of the official party aboard the Cannonball stage to return to the waiting special train at Raymond. The trip was important in itself because driver Tom Gordon set a record for speed that was never equalled in the forty years of horse-drawn vehicles. In just ten hours of actual driving time, the party covered the sixty-seven miles from Yosemite Valley to Raymond. The total elapsed time was just short of twelve hours.

At Wawona, the president and his companions were treated to a champagne lunch by hosts Edward and John Washburn. Roosevelt toured Thomas Hill's studio (the artist gave him a painting of Bridalveil Fall he admired), signed the guest register, and said a few words to the assembled crowd before departing. When he arrived at Raymond, reporters asked him about the Yosemite adventure with Muir. The president told them he had thoroughly enjoyed it. "It was bully," he said. "I had the time of my life!"[29]

EVENTS LEADING TO THE RE-CESSION OF THE YOSEMITE GRANT BY CALIFORNIA

The commissioners' ongoing struggle to obtain sufficient funds from the legislature to manage and improve the Yosemite Grant has been noted several times in the text. During the first twenty-eight years of state administration, 1864 through 1891, appropriations for the grant totaled only $275,022. Of this amount, more than half was allocated for three specific purposes: fifty-five thousand dollars to indemnify the Valley claimants in 1874—a payment the commissioners considered unnecessarily generous; forty-five thousand dollars to build the Stoneman House and water system—a sum far less that the board had requested and one not reimbursed after the hotel burned down; and fifty thousand dollars for the purchase of roads and trails within the grant, which obligated the state for additional maintenance expense without any compensating allotments. Over the same period, less than seventy-five thousand

The official presidential party at the Grizzly Giant in the Mariposa Grove on May 15, 1903. From left: two Secret Service men; Secretary of the Navy William H. Moody; California Governor George C. Pardee; President Roosevelt; Dr. Presley N. Rixie, surgeon general; John Muir; Nicholas Murray Butler, president of Columbia University; Roosevelt's private secretary William Loeb, Jr.; and Benjamin Ide Wheeler, president of the University of California.

President Roosevelt rides across the upper iron bridge after visiting Chris Jorgensen's house in Yosemite Valley.

The Muir-Roosevelt party approaches
its Valley camping site near Bridalveil
Meadow on May 17, 1903. Rangers
Archie Leonard (left, behind Muir) and
Charles Leidig (behind Roosevelt) kept
onlookers away. Packer Jackie Alder and
his four pack mules have proceeded
ahead to set up camp.

dollars was appropriated for "general preservation and improvement" of
the Valley and Big Tree Grove, an average of only twenty-six hundred
dollars annually.

During the last fifteen years of state ownership of the grant, 1892 to
1906, the legislature's tight-fisted policy did not appreciably change, and
the constant, crippling shortage of money prevented any sort of long-
range planning or consistent management by the commissioners, who
did the best they could with the limited funds available.

"The meager appropriations for the care of the valley and grove were
reduced to nearly one half from appropriations of former years," the
commissioners said in their *Biennial Report* for 1895–96. "In the meantime, buildings may be burned, bridges destroyed, the wonderful Big
Trees endangered, and the winter's ravages so disfigure trails and roads as
to involve a large expenditure of money to repair them. . . The
Commissioners respectfully recommend and earnestly request that a
much larger appropriation of money be placed at their disposal, as the

money for the present fiscal year will scarcely pay the absolutely necessary expenses of caring for the valley."

In their 1901–02 *Biennial Report*, the commissioners reiterated their plea for additional funds, saying "that the amounts appropriated are grossly inadequate to supply even the pressing needs of the valley. [This] must surely be admitted by everyone who has given any thought whatever to the conditions in the valley requiring the expenditure of money. For this reason the Commission earnestly requests much larger appropriations if good work is expected to be done in the preservation of the valley. Inasmuch as the State of California has accepted from the United States Government the trust of taking care of and maintaining the Yosemite Valley, to which full justice cannot be done by the use of any adjectives, however extravagant, the State of California should undertake to fulfill her trust properly and well and with credit to herself."

Two years later, the commissioners again complained about the legislature's lack of concern for California's spectacular scenic preserve. One

Roosevelt and Muir on the overhanging rock at Glacier Point, May 17, 1903.

of the biggest problems was the condition of the Valley roads, which were usually a sea of mud in the spring, and a dusty calamity by late summer. "We desire to protest most strongly against the insufficient appropriations for general care and maintenance of the valley," the board wrote in its *Biennial Report* for 1903–04. "It is impossible to set aside from the small sums of money at the disposal of the Commission anything for the construction of new roads. To construct a good road in Yosemite Valley will cost perhaps $5,000 a mile, and as there are about twenty-five miles of roadway in Yosemite Valley, to put the entire system in first-class condition would cost over $100,000. We therefore submit, that if the valley is to be properly taken care of by the State of California, $100,000 should be set aside for general work during the next two years, and $20,000 for the same period to cover the expense of general work in the Mariposa Grove of Big Trees. With these amounts something can be done and a showing made. The improvement in the conditions in the valley and of the grove, if such a sum is set aside, would be so marked and the showing so good that all will feel the State has received full value for every dollar spent."

The commissioners' repeated requests failed to move the legislature to action, and the resultant deterioration of the Valley led to increasing criticism of the state's management of the Yosemite Grant. Foremost among the faultfinders was the Sierra Club, whose leading spokesman was its president, John Muir. Muir, who was strongly in favor of the fed-

Driver Tommy Gordon and the president as they departed the Wawona Hotel after lunch on May 18, 1903, en route to the Raymond station. Abner Mann, San Francisco agent for the Yosemite Stage & Turnpike Company, stands at right with hat. Edward and John Washburn appear just behind Roosevelt and Mann.

THE YOSEMITE GRANT: 1864–1906

eral government's reacquisition of Yosemite Valley, praised the army's efforts in keeping sheep and cattle out of the high country. "Blessings on Uncle Sam's soldiers," he said in 1895. "They have done their job well, and every pine tree is waving its arms for joy."[30] At the same time, he characterized the Yosemite commissioners as "blustering, blundering, moneymaking vote-sellers who receive their places from boss politicians as purchased goods."

In a letter written in 1895 to Robert Underwood Johnson, editor of the *Century Magazine,* Muir said: "Only the Yosemite itself in the middle of the grand park is downtrodden, frowsy, and like an abandoned backwoods pasture. It looks ten times worse than when you saw it seven years ago. Most of the level meadow floor of the Valley is fenced with

Muir complained about fencing in the Valley. In this photograph, taken about 1900, Degnan's dairy herd grazes behind the fence along the road leading to the upper iron bridge. Hutchings' old cabin is the building near the foot of Yosemite Falls.

The first bear trap used in Yosemite was made by woodworker Roland B. Dexter in 1903, just before Roosevelt's visit. A group of local residents posed with the new curiosity in front of the Yosemite store. Bears were trapped for their fur in the Yosemite Grant until the federal government took over in 1906.

Although handicapped by lack of funds, the commissioners managed to enlarge the cabin at the Mariposa Grove in 1902. Galen Clark is the man sitting on the porch.

barbed and unbarbed wire and about three hundred head of horses are turned loose every night to feed and trample the flora out of existence.[31] I have little hope for the Yosemite. As long as the management is in the hands of eight politicians appointed by the ever-changing Governor of California, there is but little hope."

Muir may have been unfairly harsh in his criticism of the commissioners. The shortsighted attitude of the state legislature seems to have been far more to blame for the Valley's seedy appearance than the commission's management practices. In 1972 Theodore Goppert, who made a detailed study of the situation for his master's thesis, concluded that "the legislature's failure to provide funds was the chief reason for the eventual failure of the state administration in Yosemite. The commissioners' policies were developed to meet the park's needs and in fact were very similar to later National Park Service policies, but the state administration usually lacked the funds to implement them. . ."[32]

Soon after the turn of the century, a movement to return the Yosemite Grant to the federal government to be part of the national park began to gain widespread support. A number of prominent individuals and groups[33] in various parts of the state spoke out in favor of ending divided control of the park and the Valley. Many of California's major newspapers such as the *San Francisco Chronicle, San Francisco Call, Oakland Tribune, Sacramento Union, San Francisco Bulletin, Santa Barbara Press, Fresno Republican,* and *Los Angeles Times* published editorials endorsing the re-cession proposal. Their essential argument was that the state could not afford to provide the financial backing that Yosemite required, and that a unified park management under the federal government would be better for everyone. Backing this viewpoint were economy-minded members of the legislature who felt that Yosemite was costing the state too much money.

Surprisingly, the most prominent opponent of re-cession was the same *San Francisco Examiner* that had vilified the commissioners' administration of the grant fifteen years earlier in conjunction with Charles Dorman Robinson's charges of state mismanagement in the Valley. In late 1904 and early 1905, the *Examiner* published a series of articles about Yosemite, mostly quoting persons objecting to re-cession. Calling the Valley "California's greatest pride," the *Examiner* argued that re-cession would "disgrace California and advertise that the State lacked the necessary money to support the park."

On January 11, 1905, the battle moved from the newspapers to the legislature when bills calling for re-cession of the Yosemite Grant to the federal government were introduced simultaneously in the California senate and assembly.[34] The bills were sent on to the appropriate committees for recommendations, and on January 18, the assembly committee voted six to one in favor of the legislation. The senate committee gave its approval the following day.

SIGN THIS

To the Honorable, the Legislature of the State of California:

We respectfully petition your honorable body to oppose any movement for the purpose of receding the Yosemite Valley to the Federal Government.

The Yosemite Valley is California's greatest pride. It should be cared for by California in a manner reflecting glory upon the State.

There is no legitimate reason for placing the management of this marvel of natural scenic beauty in the hands of the Federal Government,

NAME ....

ADDRESS ....

Sign this, cut it out and mail it to the Yosemite Editor, Examiner Office, San Francisco

EL CAPITAN.

The San Francisco Examiner *first printed this coupon urging the public to express opposition to re-cession of the Valley on December 18, 1904. Later, the newspaper presented a petition containing several thousand names to the California legislature during its debates about re-cession.* (Author's collection)

The re-cession bill faced little opposition in the state assembly, and on February 2 passed easily by a vote of forty-six to nineteen. The decision now rested with the senate. Here the most vocal opponent was Senator John B. Curtin of Tuolumne County, who owned several hundred acres of patented land within the park in the general area of Crane Flat. Curtin was engaged in an ongoing quarrel with the army over his right to drive cattle through public property to his ranch. In an eloquent two-hour speech, Curtin recounted his exasperating experiences with the "czar-like" federal authorities so effectively that re-cession appeared to be headed for defeat. Proponents of the bill then managed to table the measure rather than risk an immediate vote.

Author Holway Jones, in his book *John Muir and the Sierra Club,* provides considerable evidence that the Southern Pacific played the decisive role in getting re-cession passed, although the railroad never took a public stand on the matter. In 1899 John Muir accompanied Edward Harriman, who became president of the Southern Pacific the next year, on an expedition to Alaska. According to Jones, Muir then called on his powerful friend for help with the Yosemite legislation. Harriman obliged by using his influence with certain senators who, for good or evil, were well-known to be controlled by the railroad company. When the senate vote was finally taken on February 23, it passed by a margin of twenty-one to thirteen. Jones states that at least nine senators who at first had openly opposed re-cession ultimately cast their ballots in the affirmative.[35] On March 3, 1905, Governor George Pardee signed the Re-cession Act into law.

Because the California act contained the requirement that it would be made "operative upon the acceptance by the United States," congressional approval was needed before the federal government could take legal possession of the grant. Delays brought about by a poorly worded congressional resolution and a battle over a reduction in the park boundaries prevented formal acceptance until June 11, 1906, when President Roosevelt signed the bill just as he had promised Muir he would three years earlier in Yosemite.

On June 15, 1906, Major Harry Benson, the acting superintendent of Yosemite National Park, was directed to move his headquarters to Yosemite Valley and take charge of the Valley and Big Tree Grove. The commissioners temporarily prevented Benson's occupation by refusing to surrender the power plant or any other state property pending its evaluation and purchase by the federal government. On July 23, 1906, the California attorney general ruled that the electric plant was a permanent fixture of the Valley, and that title transferred to the United States under the terms of the Re-cession Act. The remainder of the state's equipment was appraised at $1,750 and placed in storage. On or about August 1, 1906, Major Benson moved Troops "K" and "M" of the Fourteenth Cavalry to the Valley, leaving only an outpost at Wawona, and established a headquarters camp on the site of present Yosemite Lodge. After forty-two pioneering years, the Yosemite Grant had passed into history.[36]

NOTES AND REFERENCES

1. The Sequoia Act signed by President Benjamin Harrison on September 25, 1890, provided that two townships in Tulare County, plus four adjacent sections (74,560 acres in all), be "reserved as a public park, or pleasure ground, for the benefit and enjoyment of the people." The Big Trees of Giant Forest were not included, apparently because of claims in that region by the Kaweah Co-operative Colony, a socialistic experiment carried on by some forty or fifty families from about 1885 to the early 1890s. When the Yosemite Act was passed six days later, it was amended by consent, tacking on two areas unrelated to Yosemite. One of these areas more than doubled the size of the reservation stated in the Sequoia Act of September 25, this time including Giant Forest and a large region surrounding it. The other area set aside four square miles (not contiguous to the first) encompassing the General Grant Grove.

2. Secretary Noble's designation of "Yosemite National Park" remained unofficial until Congress legally changed the name of the Yosemite Forest Reserve to Yosemite National Park as part of the act of February 7, 1905, which redrew the boundaries of the original reservation. The Boundary Act (33 U.S. Stat. 702) eliminated some 542 square miles from the park, including a number of mining and timber claims in the southwestern section, and added 113 square miles, mostly on the north to conform to natural terrain.

3. The Sundry Civil Act of March 3, 1883, authorized the secretary of the interior to ask the secretary of war for troops to protect and preserve Yellowstone National Park if needed (soldiers first arrived in August, 1886). When Yosemite and Sequoia came into being in 1890, Secretary Noble advised the president that the use of soldiers would be the best arrangement for guarding the new reserved areas as well. President Harrison approved the plan, although the Act of 1883 technically did not apply to Sequoia, General Grant, or Yosemite. After the Spanish-American War of 1898, opposition to the use of troops in the Sierra parks arose in the War Department, and the secretary threatened to halt the practice. The secretary of the interior then appealed to Congress for legislation. The Sundry Civil Act, approved June 6, 1900, authorized the War Department to make troops available in all the reserved areas, and the presence of the cavalry in the California parks finally became legal.

4. Captain Wood, a genial, well-liked officer, graduated from West Point in 1872 and was assigned to duty in the West. During his three-year command in Yosemite, he suffered greatly from an incurable cancer of the tongue. At times he may have tried to ease his pain by drinking too much. Cosie Hutchings remembered that "Captain Wood used to occasionally go on a binge and drive a horse and buggy around the loop in front of the Wawona Hotel in a very unmilitary manner." Wood died on April 14, 1894, after undergoing two unsuccessful operations on his tongue.

The army's Yosemite administration post was originally designated "Camp Near Wawona" under Special Orders No. 38 to the First Garrison. When Captain George H. G. Gale, Wood's successor, arrived for summer duty with Troop "C" of the Fourth Cavalry on May 24, 1894, he changed the name to "Camp A. E. Wood" in honor of his recently deceased comrade. The title became official in 1901.

5. After months of isolated duty in the backcountry of the Sierra, the troopers sometimes celebrated their return to civilization by getting drunk. The *Mariposa Gazette* described such a situation on November 28, 1896: "Prior to leaving the camp at Wawona, the boys in blue received their pay [thirteen dollars

a month], and a number of them had a jollification, two at best being sentenced to walk to San Francisco as punishment for their misdeeds. At Madera the two companies from Wawona were joined by the two companies that had been doing similar duty at Sequoia Park during the past summer and were on their way to the Presidio. The four companies spent several days in camp near Madera and during the time they had a general review drill, sham battles, etc. Here again the temptation was too strong, and the opportunity offering, a number of the troops imbibed too freely of Madera firewater, and when the troops moved towards San Francisco there were just twenty horses without riders. The riders were not slain in battle. Insubordination had caused them to be court-martialed, and the sentence was that they walk to San Francisco in the wake of the troops. Hence, when the troops marched homeward, twenty soldiers appropriately guarded, followed on foot. Nor will this be the only punishment inflicted, for part of the twenty will have to do service in the guard-house for some time to come."

6. Of the sixteen military officers who served as acting superintendent during the army's twenty-four-year administration of Yosemite National Park, eleven were West Point graduates. During the Spanish-American War of 1898, no troops were sent to the reserved areas. Instead, J. W. Zevely, a special investigator for the Department of Interior, headed a group of civilian agents who patrolled the several parks. They were succeeded in Yosemite on September 1 by the First Utah Volunteer Cavalry. Regular army troops returned in 1899. On January 1 of that year, Archie Leonard (1846–1921) and Charles Leidig, the first white boy born in Yosemite Valley, were appointed forest rangers to cover the winter months when the soldiers were absent.

Leidig was stationed at Crocker's Station, a stopping place (1880–1920) on the Big Oak Flat Road about six miles northwest of the Tuolumne Grove; Leonard worked out of Wawona. On August 25, 1907, Leonard was fired by Major Harry Benson, the acting superintendent, who accused him of incompetence and malfeasance. In 1914 he was hired as a park ranger after civilian administrators replaced the army in Yosemite. He worked in that capacity through the summer of 1917 when he was furloughed because of age (seventy-one). Leidig left government service in 1907 and became a teamster with the Yosemite Stage & Turnpike Company. From 1916 until retirement he was employed by the Hayward City Park Department.

7. Captain John A. Lockwood, U.S.A., "Uncle Sam's Troopers in the National Parks of California," *Overland Monthly*, 2d Series, 33 (1899): 361.

8. *Biennial Report of the Commissioners to Manage the Yosemite Valley and the Mariposa Big Tree Grove*, 1893–94 (Sacramento: State Printer, 1894), 9.

9. The rules and regulations originally contained twenty-eight articles. They were amended and increased in 1895–96 to thirty-six articles. The final revised set of twenty-nine articles, adopted in 1898, is reprinted as Appendix E.

10. Miles Wallace (1861–1917), a native of Tennessee, graduated from Bethel College in Kentucky in 1880; received a law degree from Cumberland University, Tennessee, in 1882; practiced law in Arkansas and Tennessee for seven years; moved to California and became Madera County district attorney in 1891. Wallace was married, with two daughters, and a member of the Fresno Bar for twenty years. After his guardianship, he practiced law in Fresno until his death from a heart attack at age fifty-six. He had been in poor health ever since receiving a severe leg injury when he was nineteen.

11. Before the turn of the century, Washburn gradually gained control of the major hotel concessions in the Yosemite Grant by using relatives or employees as the purported leaseholders. "Whatever Henry wanted, Henry got," said Laurence Degnan (1884–1963), who spent his boyhood and youth in Yosemite Valley. "This I know to be a fact: there was no pretense that the nominal holders of those concessions owed allegiance to, or took orders from, anybody but Henry Washburn." Conversation with Laurence Degnan, quoted in Shirley Sargent, *Yosemite's Historic Wawona* (Yosemite: Flying Spur Press, 1979), 50. Before being named guardian, Stevens functioned for two years as Washburn's "front man" in the acquisition of the lease to the Glacier Point Mountain House (described later in this chapter).

12. *Biennial Report of the Commissioners,* 1897–98, 9–10.

13. Letter from Laurence Degnan to Ralph Anderson, July 1, 1952, copy in the Yosemite Research Library.

14. Whether the commissioners ousted McCauley because of complaints about his maintenance practices, or acceded to political pressure from the Washburn interests, is not really clear. Laurence Degnan said that McCauley was "hornswoggled" out of his hotel, but other factors may have contributed to the board's decision. Degnan's remarks are quoted in Shirley Sargent, *Historic Wawona,* 50.

15. David Alexander Curry (1860–1917) was born in rural Indiana; graduated from Indiana University in 1883; married fellow Hoosier Jennie Etta Foster (1861–1948) in 1886; came to California in 1895 as a high school principal at Redwood City; died of blood poisoning on April 30, 1917. Jennie Curry, also a teacher, continued with their Yosemite concession until her death in 1948.

16. For a readable summary of the Curry Camping Company, see Shirley Sargent, *Yosemite and Its Innkeepers* (Yosemite: Flying Spur Press, 1975).

17. An extensive account of early automobile visitation to Yosemite is given in Hank Johnston, *Yosemite's Yesterdays* (Yosemite: Flying Spur Press, 1989), 6–19.

18. On June 4, 1892, twenty-seven residents of the San Francisco Bay area signed articles of incorporation bringing the Sierra Club into existence. John Muir was elected president (he was not, however, the "founder," as is often mistakenly stated). By the end of that summer there were 182 charter members, including James Hutchings, Galen Clark, D. J. Foley, Dr. John T. McLean, and Charles D. Robinson—all important figures in the Yosemite Grant. For information on the early Sierra Club, read Holway Jones, *John Muir and the Sierra Club: The Battle for Yosemite* (San Francisco: Sierra Club, 1965).

19. Joseph LeConte (1823–1901), a noted professor of geology, botany, and natural history at the University of California, made his first visit to Yosemite in 1870. It resulted in a classic book called *A Journal of Ramblings through the High Sierras of California by the University Excursion Party* (1875; reprint, Yosemite: Yosemite Association, 1994). At age seventy-eight, LeConte was on his eleventh visit to Yosemite Valley when he had a heart attack on July 5, 1901, and died in his tent at Camp Curry the following morning.

The Sierra Club raised five thousand dollars to erect the LeConte Memorial Lodge, which was dedicated on July 3, 1904. In 1919, the lodge stood in the way of expansion at Camp Curry. Jennie Curry paid a contractor thirty-five hundred dollars to move the building to a new site a half mile west. The stone walls proved impossible to remove intact, but the roof and some of the stones were utilized in a replica, which is still in use by the Sierra Club.

20. Because of the shortness of Fiske's acquaintance with Paull, according to Laurence Degnan, "there was some doubt about whether they could be sure of recognizing each other when they met, and so they wore identifying marks or labels to take care of the problem when Carolyn arrived at the railroad station in Oakland." Letter from Laurence V. Degnan to Douglass Hubbard, October 13, 1958, in "Yosemite Cemetery" file at the Yosemite Association.

21. Jorgensen's log residence was moved to the Pioneer Yosemite History Center at Wawona by the National Park Service in 1962. The other buildings were razed at that time.

22. *Bodie Daily Free Press,* January 29, 1881.

23. James Hutchings, *In the Heart of the Sierras* (Oakland and Yosemite: Pacific Press Publishing House, 1886), 358.

24. Harry L. Childs married Abbie Crippen, hotel proprietor John Barnard's eldest stepdaughter, on October 24, 1884. This was the first wedding held in the Yosemite Chapel.

25. Letter from Laurence Degnan to Douglass Hubbard, October 9, 1958, in "Yosemite Cemetery" file at the Yosemite Association.

26. Linnie Marsh Wolfe, *Son of the Wilderness, the Life of John Muir* (New York: Alfred A. Knopf, 1945), 290.

27. In their *Biennial Report* for 1903–04, the Yosemite commissioners listed an expense of $794.70 "for the entertainment of President Roosevelt."

28. The forest reserve acreage is listed in Bernard Frank, *Our National Forests* (Norman: University of Oklahoma Press, 1955), 9; the national monument and park figures are from Paul Russell Cutright, *Theodore Roosevelt, the Making of a Conservationist* (Urbana and Chicago: University of Illinois Press, 1985), 225.

29. Information about the Roosevelt-Muir journey is taken in part from "Charles Leidig's Report of President Roosevelt's Visit in May, 1903," n.d., typewritten manuscript in the Yosemite Research Library; and William F. Kimes, "With Theodore Roosevelt and John Muir in Yosemite," in *The Westerners Brand Book,* Doyce Nunis, ed., no. 14 (Los Angeles: The Westerners Los Angeles Corral, 1974), 189–204.

30. Yosemite Park Historian Jim Snyder, who has done considerable research on the cavalry's occupation of Yosemite including extensive field work, is of the opinion that both the number of sheep involved over the years and the permanent disfiguration they supposedly caused were greatly exaggerated for political and other reasons. "At least one army officer actually advocated allowing grazing to reduce the fire danger," Snyder says. "And Muir himself [in *John of the Mountains, The Unpublished Journals of John Muir* (Boston: Houghton Mifflin Company, 1938), 352] reported that the mountains were 'healthy again' only two years after the soldiers arrived. How much destruction was there from more than thirty years of grazing if the land could recover so quickly? It seems quite possible to me that the cavalry's overall administration of the park was responsible for more lasting change in Yosemite's backcountry than the sheepherding." James Snyder, interview with author, April, 1994.

31. At that time, sixteen public camping areas were in use in Yosemite Valley, all situated near a meadow for pasturing horses and mules, and many without sanitation facilities of any kind. Grazing continued to be a serious problem in Yosemite Valley until motor vehicles replaced horses in 1915. See Gabriel Sovulewski, "The Story of Campgrounds in Yosemite Valley," *Yosemite Nature Notes* 16, no. 11 (November 1937): 81–84.

32. Theodore A. Goppert, "The Yosemite Valley Commission, the Development of Park Management Policies, 1864–1905" (master's thesis, California State College, Hayward, 1972), 90.

33. Besides the Sierra Club, these included the California Forest and Water Association, the Native Sons of the Golden West, and the California State Board of Trade.

34. Assembly Bill No. 248 was introduced by Assemblyman Miguel Estudillo from Riverside; Senate Bill No. 170 by Senator C. M. Belshaw from Antioch.

35. Jones, *John Muir and the Sierra Club*, 71–72.

36. The army administration of Yosemite National Park ended on July 14, 1914, when Major William Littebrant was relieved by civilian agents Gabriel Sovulewski and Mark Daniels, working for the Department of Interior, with a force of fifteen rangers. The *Mariposa Gazette* reported on December 12, 1914, that "Sergeants Larner and Lynch left Yosemite Friday after a stay of many months engaged in duties relating to interests of the Department of War. Such property that was not turned over to the Department of the Interior was shipped to Army quarters elsewhere, the last going out a few days ago. This probably marks the close of military life in Yosemite." On August 25, 1916, President Woodrow Wilson signed into law an act creating the National Park Service, authorized to promote and regulate the federal government's reservations, national parks, and monuments.

Appendices

Appendix A

The following is one of the eighteen unratified treaties of 1851-52 between the California Indians and the federal government (see note 11, Chapter I).

TREATY MADE AND CONCLUDED AT CAMP FREMONT, STATE OF CALIFORNIA, MARCH 19, 1851, BETWEEN REDICK McKEE AND OTHERS, COMMISSIONERS ON THE PART OF THE UNITED STATES, AND THE CHIEFS, CAPTAINS, AND HEAD MEN OF THE SI-YAN-TE, ETC., ETC., TRIBES OF INDIANS.

A treaty made and concluded on the nineteenth day of March, in the year eighteen hundred and fifty-one, at Camp Fremont, near the little Mariposa river, in the State of California, between Redick McKee, George W. Barbour, and Oliver M. Wozencraft, commissioners appointed by the President of the United States to treat with the various tribes of Indians in the State of California, of the one part, and the chiefs, captains, and head men of the Si-yan-te, Pó-to-yun-te, Co-co-noon, Apang-as-se, Aplache, and A-wal-a-che tribes of Indians, of the other part.

ARTICLE 1. The said tribes of Indians severally acknowledge themselves to be under the jurisdiction, control and authority of the government of the United States, and as such, that they severally agree and pledge themselves to refrain in future from the commission of any act of hostility or aggression towards the government of the United States, or any of the citizens thereof, and to live on terms of peace and friendship, not only with the citizens of the United States, but with all Indian tribes.

ART. 2. The said tribes hereby severally relinquish, and forever quit claim to the government of the United States, all the right, title, claim, or interest, of whatsoever character, that they, or either of them may have had, or now hold, in and to any lands in the limits of the State of California, or the United States.

ART. 3. It is agreed between the contracting parties, that the district of land lying between the Mercede and Touolumne rivers, to wit: commencing at a point on the Mercede river, opposite the mouth of a small stream emptying into said river, on the south side of said river, about one mile above what was formerly known as Ford's ferry, now known as Stone and Company's ferry; running thence a direct line to the Touolumne river, striking or intersecting said river at the mouth of a gulch emptying into said river at a bend about two miles above Spark's old ferry, being at or near the foot of the first fall or rapids of said river, above said Spark's ferry; thence down the middle of said stream to a point one-half of one mile above Harr's ferry; thence a straight line across, so as to intersect the Mercede river at a point about one-quarter of one mile above the present residence of Dr. Lewis, on said stream; thence up the middle of said Mercede river to place of beginning; the said district, supposed to contain about four full townships of land, is hereby and shall be forever set apart and held for the occupancy of said tribes of Indians; and it is further stipulated, that said tribes shall have free access to all the country between the Mercede and Touolumne rivers, extending above said described district to the Sierra Nevada mountains, for the purpose of hunting and collecting fruits, nuts, &c.; but in no event shall they remove their women and children from the lands hereby set apart for their occupancy. The government of the United States reserving the right to establish a military post, and to erect the necessary buildings for an agent or other officers, within the limits of said land.

ART. 4. In further consideration of the aforesaid premises, and for the purpose of aiding in the subsistence of said tribes of Indians during the years eighteen hundred and fifty-one and two, it is agreed by the party of the first part to supply said tribes jointly with one hundred head of good beef steers, and one hundred sacks or barrels of flour each year.

ART. 5. It is further agreed, that as soon after the ratification of this treaty by the President and Senate of the United States as may be practicable and convenient, the said tribes shall be furnished jointly and free of charge by the government of the United States, the following articles of property, to be divided among said Indian tribes, according to their respective numbers, to wit: ten brood mares and one jack or stallion, twenty-five cows and one bull, five large and five small ploughs, ten sets of gear or harness complete, one hundred axes, one hundred hatchets, one hundred hoes, ten mattocks or picks, all necessary seeds for sowing and planting for one year, eight hundred pounds of iron, two hundred pounds of steel, two hundred pairs of two and a half point blankets, two flannel shirts and two pairs of coarse pants for each man and boy, one linsey gown for each woman and girl, two thousand yards of brown sheeting, two thousand yards of calico, twenty-five dollars worth of thread, needles, buttons, scissors, &c.

ART. 6. The United States agree further to furnish a man skilled in the art of farming, to live among and instruct said tribes, and such others as may be placed under his supervision, in the business of farming, one blacksmith, one man skilled in working in wood, (wagon maker or rough carpenter,) one superintendent, and such assistant school teachers as may be necessary, all to live among and work for, and teach said tribes and such other tribes as they may be required to work for and teach; said farmer, blacksmith, worker in wood and teachers to be supplied to said tribes as aforesaid, for the period of five years, and as long thereafter as the President of the United States shall deem advisable: a school-house and other necessary buildings for the accommodation of the persons named in this article to be erected at the cost of the government of the United States.

ART. 7. It is further agreed between the parties, that for any violence done by individuals to the person or property of any citizen of the United States, by an Indian or Indians, of either of said tribes, or if done by a citizen or citizens of the United States, to the person or property of any of said tribes, or any of the members thereof, no personal retaliation shall be attempted, but the party aggrieved shall apply to the civil authorities of the country for a proper redress of their aggrievances; each party pledging themselves to bring, if possible, all guilty offenders to justice, by delivering them up to the officers of the law when in their power.

ART. 8. These articles of agreement to be binding on the contracting parties when ratified and confirmed by the President and Senate of the United States of America.

In testimony whereof, the said parties have hereunto signed their names and affixed their seals upon the day and date above written.

    REDICK McKEE [SEAL.]

    G. W. BARBOUR [SEAL.]

    O. M. WOZENCRAFT [SEAL.]

For and in behalf of the Si-yan-te tribe.
 TRAI-PAX-E, chief, his x mark.
 HABITO, his x mark.
 CO-TOS, his x mark.
 E-LI-UM, his x mark.
 AN-GOT, his x mark.
 HO-MO-LUCK, his x mark.
 PE-TE-LA, his x mark.
 MA-LA-TIA, his x mark.
 A-WAS-SA, his x mark.

For and in behalf of the Po-to-yun-te.
 BAU-TIS-TA, chief, his x mark.
 IA-WACK-NO, his x mark.
 LE-KEN-A, his x mark.
 US-SA, his x mark.
 FELIZ, his x mark.
 MAN-TU-PA, his x mark.
 WA-LIL, his x mark.
 HE-WO-WEE, his x mark.
 CHUCUS, his x mark.

For and in behalf of the Co-co-noon.
 NEN-O-LO, chief, his x mark.
 MAN-LIN-O, his x mark.
 JO-SE, his x mark.
 WAS-SAL-IS-CO, his x mark.
 JOSE VEN-TU-RA, his x mark.

For and in behalf of the A-wal-a-che.
 CY-PRI-ANO, chief, his x mark.
 WOO-MA-ACK, his x mark.
 AT-CA-NA, his x mark.
 AC-TON, his x mark.
 IO-TO-CO-NO, his x mark.
 HA-MA-CHA, his x mark.

For and in behalf of the A-pang-as-se, or Appang-assa, tribe.
 NU-MAS-E-CA-NO, chief, his x mark.
 CO-NO-TO, his x mark.
 PON-SIL-LO, his x mark.
 LO-PE-AC, his x mark.

For and in behalf of the Aplache tribe.
 HAW-HAW, chief, his x mark.
 OU-TU-PI-TU, his x mark.
 IN-TE-A-TA, his x mark.
 TAS-SE-O, his x mark.
 OU-MA, his x mark.
 WA-PA-TA, his x mark.

Signed, sealed and delivered, after being fully explained, in presence of—
John McKee, *Secretary.*
Adam Johnston, *Agent.*
H. S. Burton, *Interpreter.*
E. D. Keyes, *Captain third artillery, commanding escort.*
I. H. Lendrum, *First lieutenant 3d artillery.*
J. Hamilton, *Lieutenant 3d artillery.*
T. Moore, *Lieutenant 2d infantry.*
H. G. J. Gibson, *Second lieutenant 3d artillery.*
N. H. McLean, *Second lieutenant 2d infantry.*
John E. Durivage.
Thos. J. Roach.

Appendix B

AN ACT AUTHORIZING A GRANT TO THE STATE OF CALIFORNIA OF THE "YOSEMITE VALLEY," AND THE LAND EMBRACING THE "MARIPOSA BIG TREE GROVE." – Approved, June 30, 1864.

Be it enacted by the Senate and House of Representatives of the United States of America, in Congress assembled:

SECTION 1. That there shall be, and is hereby, granted to the State of California, the "Cleft," or "Gorge" in the Granite Peak of the Sierra Nevada Mountains, situated in the County of Mariposa, in the State aforesaid, and the head waters of the Merced River, and known as the Yosemite Valley, with its branches and spurs, in estimated length fifteen miles, and in average width, one mile back from the main edge of the precipice, on each side of the Valley, with the stipulation, nevertheless, that the said State shall accept this grant upon the express conditions that the premises shall be held for public use, resort, and recreation; and shall be inalienable for all time; but leases not exceeding ten years may be granted for portions of said premises. All incomes derived from leases of privileges to be expended in the preservation and improvement of the property, or the roads leading thereto; the boundaries to be established at the cost of said State by the United States Surveyor-General of California, whose official plat, when affirmed by the Commissioner of the General Land Office, shall constitute the evidence of the locus, extent, and limits of said Cleft or Gorge; the premises to he managed by the Governor of the State, with eight other Commissioners, to be appointed by the Executive of California, and who shall receive no compensation for their services.

SEC. 2. *And be it further enacted,* That there shall likewise be, and there is hereby, granted to the State of California, the tracts embracing what is known as the "Mariposa Big Tree Grove," not to exceed the area of four sections, and to be taken in legal subdivisions of one quarter section each, with the like stipulation as expressed in the first section of this Act as to the State's acceptance, with like conditions as in the first section of this Act as to inalienability, yet with the same lease privilege; the income to be expended in preservation, improvement, and protection of the property; the premises to be managed by Commissioners, as stipulated in the first section of this Act, and to be taken in legal subdivisions as aforesaid; and the official plat of the United States Surveyor-General, when affirmed by the Commissioners of the General Land Office, to be the evidence of the locus of the said Mariposa Big Tree Grove. *(Chap. CLXXXIV of the Statutes at Large, passed at the 38th Congress, Session I.)*

Appendix C

AN ACT TO ACCEPT THE GRANT BY THE UNITED STATES GOVERNMENT TO THE STATE OF CALIFORNIA OF THE YOSEMITE VALLEY, AND OF THE LAND EMBRACING THE MARIPOSA BIG TREE GROVE, AND TO ORGANIZE THE BOARD OF COMMISSIONERS, AND TO FULLY EMPOWER THEM TO CARRY OUT THE OBJECTS OF THE GRANT AND FULFIL THE PURPOSES OF THE TRUST.

[Approved April 2, 1866.]

Preamble

WHEREAS, By an Act of Congress, entitled an Act authorizing a grant to the State of California of the Yosemite Valley, and of the land embracing the Mariposa Big Tree Grove, approved June thirtieth, A.D. eighteen hundred and sixty-four, there was granted to the State of California in the terms of said Act, said valley and the lands embracing said grove, upon certain conditions and stipulations therein expressed; now, therefore,

The People of the State of California, represented in Senate and Assembly, do enact as follows:

Acceptance of grant.

SECTION 1. The State of California does hereby accept said grant upon the conditions, reservations, and stipulations contained in said Act of Congress.

Commissioners

SEC. 2. The Governor, and the eight other Commissioners, Frederick Law Olmstead [*sic*], Prof. J. D. Whitney, William Ashburner, J. [*sic*] W. Raymond, E. S. Holden, Alexander Deering, Geo. W. Coulter, and Galen Clark, appointed by him on the twenty-eighth day of September, eighteen hundred and sixty-four, in accordance with the terms of said Act, are hereby constituted a Board to manage said premises, and any vacancy occurring therein from death, removal, or any cause, shall be filled by the appointment of the Governor.

Powers and duties.

They shall be known in law as "Commissioners to manage the Yosemite Valley and the Mariposa Big Tree Grove," and by such name they and their successors may sue and be sued, and shall have full power to manage and administer the grant made and the trust created by said Act of Congress, and shall have full power to make and adopt all rules, regulations, and by-laws for their own government, and the government, improvement, and preservation of said premises, not inconsistent with the Constitution of the United States or of this State, or of said Act making the grant, or of any law of Congress or of the Legislature. They shall hold their first meeting at the time and place to be specified by the Governor, and thereafter as their own rules shall prescribe, and a majority shall constitute a quorum for the transaction of business. They shall elect a President and a Secretary, and any other officers from their number, as their rules may prescribe.

No compensation.
Guardian

SEC. 3. None of said Commissioners shall receive any compensation for their services as such. They shall have power to appoint a Guardian, either of their number or not, of said premises, removable at their pleasure, to perform

Compensation

such duties as they may prescribe, and to receive such compensation as they may fix, not to exceed five hundred dollars per annum.

Report.

SEC. 4. The Commissioners shall make a full report of the condition of said premises and of their acts under this law, and of their expenditures, through the Governor, to the Legislature, at every regular session thereof.

State Geologist.

SEC. 5. The State Geologist is hereby authorized to make such further explorations on the said tracts and in the adjoining region of the Sierra Nevada Mountains as may be necessary to enable him to prepare a full description and accurate statistical report of the same, and the same shall be published in connection with the reports of the Geological Survey.

Report.

Trespass, and willful injury of natural objects, etc.

SEC. 6. It shall be unlawful for any person wilfully to commit any trespass whatever upon said premises, cut down or carry off any wood, underwood, tree, or timber, or girdle or otherwise injure any tree or timber, or deface or injure any natural object, or set fire to any wood or grass upon said premises, or destroy or injure any bridge or structure of any kind, or other improvement that is or may be placed thereon. Any person committing either or any of said acts without the express permission of said Commissioners through said Guardian shall be guilty of a misdemeanor, and on conviction thereof shall be punished by fine not exceeding five hundred dollars, or by imprisonment in the County Jail not exceeding six months, or by both such fine and imprisonment.

Penalty.

Appropriation.

SEC. 7. The sum of two thousand dollars is hereby appropriated for the eighteenth and nineteenth fiscal years out of any moneys in the Treasury not otherwise appropriated to pay said Guardian and the incidental expenses of the Commissioners and to be expended under the supervision of said Commissioners; *provided,* that not more than one half of said sum shall be expended during the eighteenth fiscal year.

SEC. 8. This Act shall take effect immediately.

[Chapter DXXXVI of the Statutes of California, passed at the Sixteenth Session of the Legislature, 1865-6.]

Appendix D

BY-LAWS OF BOARD OF COMMISSIONERS TO MANAGE THE YOSEMITE VALLEY AND MARIPOSA BIG TREE GROVE.

[Adopted 1866; revised 1882]

ARTICLE I.

The principal place of business of the Board shall be in Yosemite Valley, but the Executive Committee shall have an office in the city of San Francisco.

ARTICLE II.

The President of the Board is the Governor of the State.

ARTICLE III.

The other officers of the Commission shall be a Vice-President, and a Secretary, who shall also be the Treasurer, and an Executive Committee of three Commissioners, all of whom shall be elected by ballot at the annual meeting of the Board, and shall hold office for one year.

ARTICLE IV.

It shall be the duty of the President to preside at the meetings of the Board, and to perform such other duties as properly appertain, by usage, to the office of President.

ARTICLE V.

In case of the absence of the President, or of his inability to serve, the Vice-President shall perform his duties.

ARTICLE VI.

SECTION 1. The Secretary shall keep a record of the proceedings of the Commission in proper books, to be provided for that purpose; shall conduct the correspondence of the Commission, making letter-press copies of all official letters written by him, and preserving and properly filing all communications which he may receive as Secretary of the Commission, or which may appertain to its business, and shall exhibit the same, and give an account of his correspondence whenever required so to do either by the Board of Commissioners or by the Executive Committee; and during business hours the same shall be open to examination by any individual Commissioner. He shall, also, keep a record in the minute book, of all votes obtained by correspondence, and votes given by Commissioners in that way shall have the same effect as though cast in general meeting. He shall, also, officially attend all meetings of the Executive Committee, performing such clerical duties as may be required of him.

SEC. 2. As Secretary and Treasurer, it shall be his duty to keep a record of the financial transactions of the Board, covering a circumstantial account of all sources of revenue, including appropriations made by the State of California, and of disbursements from the same.

It shall be his duty to receive all moneys on behalf of the Commission, making proper record of each several items, and to transmit all moneys received for account of rents, privileges, or any other source, to the State Treasury, in accordance with law.

He shall make up vouchers, from the monthly reports of the Guardian, of his liabilities for wages of laborers employed in Yosemite Valley and in the Mariposa Big Tree Grove, and, also, for supplies and material purchased by him from month to month; and upon said vouchers being approved by the Executive Committee, to transmit the same to the State Controller for payment. Said vouchers shall be made payable to the Secretary and Treasurer of the Board of Commissioners, the better to enable him to keep a correct account of all disbursements; and he shall, upon receipt of the Controller's warrant, immediately apply the proceeds of said warrant to the payment of the various sums to the several claimants covered by such warrant.

His account moneys received and disbursed shall be explicit and full; and, whenever legally called upon to do so, shall deliver up all moneys, books, papers, and other property of the Commission in his hands, to his successor in office, or to such other person as may be designated by the Board to receive the same.

He shall obey the orders of the Board, rendering such services as may be required of him relating to the treasury, and shall at all times during business hours, open his books and exhibit his papers to any individual Commissioner upon request.

ARTICLE VII.

SECTION 1. The Executive Committee shall, in addition to the discharge of the usual duties of such a body, also act as a Committee on Finance, having the oversight and control, subordinate to any special orders of the Board of Commissioners, of all sources of revenue and of expenditures of money. It shall approve all bills before they are paid; and no payments shall be made by the Treasurer, except on vouchers countersigned by at least two members of the Executive Committee.

SEC. 2. The Executive Committee, as nearly as possible carrying out the wishes of the Board, shall issue all instructions to the Guardian; and it shall receive applications for leases, and for rights and privileges, with power to act on the same, subject to review by the Board at its first meeting.

SEC. 3. Whenever, in the judgment of the Executive Committee, any question of special gravity arises, it may, through the Secretary, submit such question to the members of the Board for their votes severally thereon; and the result of action so had shall have the force of a vote taken at a general meeting. And such action is compulsory upon the Executive Committee, when request therefor in writing is made by any member of the Board of Commissioners.

SEC. 4. The Executive Committee, when unanimously agreed as to the necessity or propriety of such action, may call a special meeting of the Commissioners, to be held in the Yosemite Valley, or in Sacramento or San Francisco; and it shall be its duty to make such call, upon written request of three members of the Board not of the Executive Committee.

SEC. 5. It shall be the duty of the Executive Committee to make a full report at each annual meeting of the Board, of all business transacted by it during the past year; and biennially, during the month of November, to prepare a report, which, when approved by the Board of Commissioners, shall be transmitted to the Legislature through the Governor; said report to cover an account of the administration of its trust by the Board, for a period of two years, showing in detail the manner in which the revenues of the Valley and Grove, and the appropriations of the State, have been expended, together with the present conditions of the trust and its needs.

SEC. 6. The Executive Committee is empowered to issue residence and business permits that shall entitle the holder thereof to reside and transact business in the Valley and Grove. The committee may adopt the form of such permits. Permits shall not be issued for a longer term than one year, and may be issued from year to year or from month to month. They shall recite the name and business of the holder, and shall specify the tenement or locality assigned for occupancy.

Permits shall be revoked upon a violation of any of the rules of the Commission, or at any time, in the discretion of the Executive Committee.

Permits shall be issued only to persons of good moral character, upon the unanimous consent of the Executive Committee, and signed by both the Chairman and the Secretary of the same.

SEC. 7. The Executive Committee shall establish the rates to be charged by hotels; the rates for carriage and horse hire; the rates for the sale of provender; and, generally, shall regulate the prices to be charged by all persons transacting business in the Valley and Grove.

SEC. 8. A wise discretion is reposed in the Executive Committee, unanimously expressed, as to the rigid enforcement of any or all rules and regulations governing the Valley and Grove.

ARTICLE VIII.

In case of a vacancy by death, resignation, removal from the State, or by any other inability to serve, on the part of the Vice-President, Secretary and Treasurer, or any member of the Executive Committee, the President shall appoint some one to the place.

ARTICLE IX.

It shall be the duty of the Executive Committee to prepare and present an order of business for guidance of the Board at each meeting.

Appendix E

[Adopted 1889-90; revised 1895-96; revised 1897-98]

Be it resolved, That the rules and regulations for the government of the Yosemite Valley and Mariposa Big Tree Grove be amended to read as follows:

I.

No person shall reside or transact business within the Yosemite Valley and Mariposa Big Tree Grant without permission from the Commissioners.

II.

No application for residence or privilege to transact business within the Valley or Grove shall be considered if the applicant be in arrears to the Commission. Applicants must be in good standing.

III.

Any person having permission to reside or transact business within the Valley or Grove, who shall transfer or sublet the whole or any part of the premises or business in said permit, without the written consent of the Commission, shall ipso facto forfeit the same.

IV.

The Guardian shall report to the Board all persons residing or transacting business within the grant without permission, and shall cause the immediate discontinuance of such residence or business.

V.

No person residing or transacting business within the grant shall retain in his or her employ any person who is detrimental to good order or morals.

VI.

Upon complaint made to the Commission by the Guardian against any person specified in Rule V, the employer of such objectionable person shall be notified of the facts, and the employé must be dismissed.

VII.

Any employer neglecting or refusing to dismiss such objectionable employé, shall thereby forfeit his or her permission to reside or transact business within the Grant.

VIII.

No person shall be employed as a guide who has not a good moral character, and approved by the Guardian.

IX.

The Guardian shall, upon the complaint of any tourist or other visitor of the conduct or behavior of the Guide, inquire into the cause, and advise the complainant of the result, enforcing Rule V, if necessary, and report same to Secretary.

X.

The Guardian has the power to suspend the Guide from his privilege during the investigation of the charges preferred against said Guide. If the Guide be found in fault, he shall be dismissed in accordance with Rule V.

XI.

The Guardian shall inspect all horses, trappings, and vehicles used for hire, and if any such horses, trappings, or vehicles may be deemed unsuitable or unsafe by him, he shall cause the same to be removed at once from the Valley or Grove.

XII.

Any person offering for hire or otherwise any horse, mule, trapping, or vehicle, or refuses or neglects to remove the same from the Grant, after the Guardian shall have condemned the same, shall forfeit his privilege to reside or transact business within the Grant.

XIII.

The Guardian shall direct campers to the grounds set apart for their use within the Grant, and shall establish such rules as will contribute to their comfort.

XIV.

Campers upon entering the Valley must go to the office of the Guardian and enter their names and residence upon the register there provided. This rule shall be printed and placed in some conspicuous position so that campers will not fail to see same upon entering Grant.

XV.

No campfires shall be permitted within the Grant, or either Valley or Grove, without the express permission of the Guardian.

XVI.

No trees shall be cut or injured, or any natural object defaced.

XVII.

The discharge of firearms within the Grove or Valley is strictly prohibited.

XVIII.

No horses, cattle, or stock of any kind shall be allowed to run at large within the Grant, except on permission given in writing to the owner or owners thereof. Campers and all others, save those holding a license from the Commission, are prohibited from hiring their horses, trappings, or vehicles to tourists or visitors within the Grant.

XIX.

No person shall drive or ride faster than a walk over any of the bridges.

XX.

The Guardian shall promptly cause the arrest of any person violating Rules XV, XVI, XVII, XVIII, and XIX, and prosecute the offender or offenders to the full extent of the law, under section six of the Act of April 2, 1866, as found in the last division of this book.

XXI.

Rates of charges at hotels, and also for horses, trappings and vehicles, or for provender, as published by the Commission from time to time, must not be exceeded, under pain of forfeiture of privilege to keep a hotel, or conduct a livery business, or to sell provender.

XXII.

The Guardian shall notify the lessees of hotels of any action of the Commission, forbidding any objectionable persons from residing or transacting business in the valley or grove.

XXIII.

The Guardian shall, from time to time, enter all tenements for the purpose of inspecting the sanitary condition and examining all property in pursuance of his official duties.

XXIV.

No building or improvement of any kind shall be erected or made upon the ground without the written authority from the Commission.

XXV.

All buildings and improvements of every kind erected or made upon the grant, belong to the grant, and shall be so recognized and treated.

XXVI.

The Guardian shall exercise general police supervision in the valley and grove, and shall forbid and prevent all acts that tend to a breach of the peace, for the discomfiture of visitors, or injury or destruction to property.

XXVII.

There shall be no pooling of the hotels, stage lines, or other concessions granted by the Commission; and, it being ascertained by the Commission that such rule has been broken, the said concession shall be forfeited.

XXVIII.

The Guardian shall make no changes, nor shall he incur any liability without specific authority, and he must refer all questions of policy, touching the management of the trust, to the Board, for its discussion. He must promptly remit all collections to the Secretary and Treasurer, and is especially forbidden to disburse any funds of the Commission, unless directed so to do by the Board. His vouchers must be full and self-explanatory, and must be taken by him in triplicate; one must be retained in his office in the valley, and the other two be transferred to the Secretary and Treasurer. His accounts covering the last month past shall be made out by him and forwarded to the Secretary on the first of each month. He shall also transmit to the Secretary his estimate of labor and materials, and await the approval of the same before purchasing or ordering the same. No standing timber shall be cut without special authority in writing from the Board. He must, at the close of the season, and during the month of March of each year, if possible, report the condition of the State property and what repairs and changes he deems necessary, together with the estimated costs thereof. He may, in case of emergency, use his discretion in incurring indebtedness without the order of the Board, the same to be subject to the approval thereof, however, not exceeding the sum of one hundred (100) dollars.

XXIX.

No dogs shall be allowed to run at large within the grant, except on permission, given in writing, to the owner or owners thereof, by the Guardian.

Appendix F

MEMBERS OF THE COMMISSIONERS TO MANAGE THE
YOSEMITE VALLEY AND MARIPOSA BIG TREE GROVE

1864-1906

PRESIDENTS

Governor Frederick F. Low	1866-1867
Governor Henry H. Haight	1867-1871
Governor Newton Booth	1871-1875
Governor Romualdo Pacheco	1875
Governor William Irwin	1875-1880
Governor George C. Perkins	1880-1883
Governor George Stoneman	1883-1887
Governor Washington Bartlett	1887
Governor Robert W. Waterman	1887-1891
Governor Henry H. Markham	1891-1895
Governor James H. Budd	1895-1899
Governor Henry T. Gage	1899-1903
Governor George C. Pardee	1903-1906

COMMISSIONERS

Frederick Law Olmsted	1864-1866
Josiah Dwight Whitney	1864-1878
Israel Ward Raymond	1864-1888
Erastus Saurin Holden	1864-1880
Alexander Deering	1864-1873
George W. Coulter	1864-1875
William Ashburner	1864-1880
Galen Clark	1864-1880
Henry W. Cleaveland	1866-1880
Edgar Mills	1873-1880
Peter D. Wigginton	1875-1875
William C. Priest	1878-1884
Thomas P. Madden	1875-1880
and	1886-1890
John Putnam Jackson	1880-1884
William Harrison Mills	1880-1889
George Solon Ladd	1880-1884
James L. Sperry	1880-1884
A. J. Meany	1880-1884
Martin C. Briggs	1880-1886
Emery W. Chapman	1884-1892

Charles L. Weller	1884-1885
Jonathan Mentzer	1884-1888
J. H. O'Brien	1884-1896
J. M. Griffith	1884-1888
William B. May	1886-1889
George G. Goucher	1888-1890
Benjamin C. Truman	1888-1890
Israel West Taber	1888-1892
Marcus H. Hecht	1890-1892
Joseph G. Eastland	1890-1892
Frank M. Pixley	1890-1892
John P. Irish	1889-1894
John F. Kidder	1892-1894
T.S.C. Lowe	1892-1894
Charles S. Givins	1896-1905
Max Goldberg	1894-1898
H. J. Ostrander	1894-1898
Charles G. Clinch	1892-1901
George B. Sperry	1892-1896
Henry K. Field	1892-1897
John Boggs	1894-1897
William G. Henshaw	1898-1905

William H. Metson	1898-1906
W. W. Foote	1897-1904
Franklin Hamilton Short	1898-1905
Abbott Kinney	1897-1901
William G. Kerckhoff	1898-1906
Thomas A. Hender	1902-1906
J. C. Wilson	1900-1906
Miles Wallace	1896-1900
J. J. Lerman	1898-1906
John F. Sheehan	1894-1898
E. P. Johnson	1894-1898

GUARDIANS

Galen Clark	1866-1880
James M. Hutchings	1880-1884
Walter E. Dennison	1884-1887
Mark L. McCord	1887-1889
Galen Clark	1889-1897
Miles Wallace	1897-1899
John Stevens	1899-1904
George T. Harlow	1904-1906

Appendix G

Year	Count	Year	Count
1855	42	1879	1,385
1856–63	650	1880	1,897
1864	147	1881	2,173
1865	369	1882	2,525
1866	650	1883	2,831
1867	450	1884	2,408
1868	623	1885	2,590
1869 (a)	1,122	1886–87 (d)	
1870	1,735	1888	4,000
1871	2,137	1889–98 (d)	
1872	2,354	1899	4,500
1873	2,530	1900–01 (d)	
1874 (b)	2,711	1902	8,023
1875 (c)	2,423	1903	8,376
1876	1,917	1904	9,500
1877	1,392	1905	10,103
1878	1,183	1906 (e)	5,414

(a) Overland railroad completed
(b) Coulterville and Big Oak Flat Roads completed
(c) Wawona Road completed
(d) No travel record available
(e) San Francisco earthquake and fire

These figures were compiled from James Hutchings' books, the commissioners' records, newspaper accounts, and other sources. They should be used as approximations rather than exact numbers.

Index